Pelican Book A802
The Violent Gang

Lewis Yablonsky is Professor of Sociology and Chairman of the
Department of Sociology at San Fernando Valley (California)
State College. He has taught sociology at the University of California at Los Angeles and criminology at Columbia and Harvard
Universities. Educated at Rutgers and New York University,
where he earned his Ph.D. in 1958, he is well known for his out-
standing work with youth. He is the author of numerous articles
on crime prevention and juvenile delinquency, as well as various
papers on sociology and psychotherapy. His most recent book
is *Synanon: The Tunnel Back* (to be published in Pelicans).

THE VIOLENT GANG

Lewis Yablonsky

Penguin Books

Penguin Books Ltd, Harmondsworth, Middlesex, England
Penguin Books Australia Ltd, Ringwood, Victoria, Australia

First published in the U.S.A. by The Macmillan Company 1962
Published in Great Britain by Collier–Macmillan Ltd 1962
Published in Pelican Books 1967
Copyright © Lewis Yablonsky, 1962

Made and printed in Great Britain by
Richard Clay (The Chaucer Press) Ltd,
Bungay, Suffolk
Set in Monotype Scotch Roman

Contents

Preface

Gang boys do not respond uniformly to questions about themselves and their activities. Some are purposely evasive – and try to throw inquiries off the track. Others tell you what they think you want to hear about gangs. A large number want to let you in on their feelings and motives for violent action – but simply do not have clear answers about themselves. There are several ways to interpret:

GANG BOY: Momentarily I started to thinking about it inside; I have my mind made up I'm not going to be in no gang. Then I go on inside. Something comes up, then here come all my friends coming to me. Like I said before, I'm intelligent and so forth. They be coming to me – then they talk to me about what they gonna do. Like, 'Man, we'll go out here and kill this cat.' I say, 'Yeah.' They kept on talkin'. I said, 'Man, I just gotta go with you.' Myself, I don't want to go, but when they start talkin' about what they gonna do, I say, 'No, he isn't gonna take over my rep. I ain't gonna let him be known more than me.' And I go ahead just for selfishness.

Another block to firsthand research into the violent gang is the nature of the subject. Gang boys are by definition lawbreakers. Their characteristic response to question-naires investigating the gang's organization or personal activities is one of suspicion and distrust. The response is a reasonable one. To the gang boy every researcher could be a 'cop'.

Despite the enormous difficulties of reaching the gang in the open community, research is required if knowledge about gangs is to go beyond popular speculation. Professor Albert K. Cohen cogently summarizes the problem in his theoretical analysis of gangs:

. . . it would be desirable to continue and expand research on delinquent groups as social systems, that is, research whose object is the structure, the processes, the history and the sub-culture of the group as such rather than the delinquent indi-

vidual. . . . Needless to say, this type of research is fraught
with great difficulty. Our techniques for the study of small
groups in action are crude and the problems of 'getting close'
to live delinquent groups and observing them at first hand are
enormous. On the other hand, no type of research is of potentially greater value for throwing new light on delinquency and
the challenge is worth all the ingenuity we can muster.[1]

In 1953 I found myself in a fortunate position to carry
out such 'live research' with gangs. I was appointed by a
community organization to develop and direct a crime-
prevention programme on the upper West Side of
Manhattan. The organization was sponsored by thirteen
educational, religious, and medical institutions, including
Columbia University, Union Theological Seminary, and
Barnard College. During the four-year period I directed
this programme, I had excellent co-operation from many
private and government agencies in New York.

More important than this support was a strategic position vis-à-vis the boys. Youths in the area had a basis for
understanding our work. To them we were not simply pok-
ing around in their lives for some vague research reason.
Our agency was attempting to do something concrete to
prevent and control the difficult crime and delinquency
condition of the area. Residents in this area of almost a
half-million people from every possible ethnic, racial, religious, class, and economic background also had some
awareness of our efforts.

The overall crime picture included robbery, burglary,
homicide, drug addiction, and assault. However, the violent
gang was considered a basic problem. The attempt at prevention work with about seventy-five gangs in the neighbourhood spotlighted a lack of substantial knowledge about
them necessary to develop effective methods of gang control. This limitation and an apparent lack of effective
methods available to other professional and social agencies
in New York engaged in gang work spurred this study.

Our many interviews, questionnaires, gang discussions,

1. Albert K. Cohen, *Delinquent Boys – The Culture of the Gang* (Glencoe,
Illinois: The Free Press, 1955), pp. 173–4.

agency conferences, talks with the Police Youth Squad, police commanders, and other officials were not designed for research purposes alone; they were part of the prevention programme's day-to-day activity. Information about gangs was secured from this position in an ongoing programme.

My relationship to the boys and the neighbourhood was similar to that of an anthropologist engaged in field work. During the four-year period I directed the project, I lived and worked in the area. It was natural for gang boys to 'hang out' in my office and under certain conditions to visit my home. Phone calls at all hours from gang boys with special problems, youths in jail, citizen volunteers with emergency gang-war problems, or the police were daily routine. The research was carried on under circumstances where my daily operation involved a continuing relationship with the people and conditions I was studying.

This kind of relationship is a two-way street. Not only was I concerned with the motives and activities of the gang boys – they were concerned with mine. Many long, 'philosophical' afternoons and evenings were spent with varieties of gang boys in my office or on the corner discussing 'life'. Much was learned on both sides about the world and our relation to it. More specifically, the essence and meaning of gang behaviour and its violence were often more clearly revealed in these discussions than on designed questionnaires.

Another important source of data consisted of about twenty 'emergency gang conferences'. Local gangs were free to use our offices and meeting rooms to discuss their problems. A continuing and persistent problem for gangs is a real and imaginary threat of attack by other gangs. The 'threat' of attack is often used by violent-gang leaders in a way somewhat similar to Fidel Castro's use of the 'threat' of a Yankee invasion of Cuba. It serves the purpose of mobilizing the group, takes their mind off internal gang problems, personal problems, and provides the boys with a common enemy towards whom they can express their hostility.

The gang-war meetings consist of harangues about other gangs, plans for attack, elaborate means of defence, and a counting of real and imaginary members and brother gangs. Emotional heat is always high, and many deep fears and feelings are freely expressed.

In exchange for the use of the meeting room I was allowed to tape-record these sessions. The boys' further condition was that no information would be divulged to the police. One reason for their permitting tape-recordings was the desire to hear themselves on a playback. Their egos seemed to be nourished by the official nature of a taped conference. Increasingly I was permitted a voice in their emergency meetings, and in some cases I succeeded in intervening to control their post-meeting violent behaviour. These records were a source of invaluable information, since the boys tended to become spontaneous and open in these discussions. In the gang-war-discussion situation they appeared to be freer than they were when other, more formal, research devices were employed.

The more standard approaches used in collecting gang information included: (1) depth interviews with gang members, individually and in groups, both in the project's office and on the street; (2) tape-recordings of field notes; (3) prepared, printed questionnaires; (4) employment of two ' former' gang leaders as paid research interviewers; (5) data from an unusual diary kept by a gang leader; and a number of other innovations necessary to 'get at' these difficult youths.

Research information was compiled on over one hundred gangs and gang-warfare incidents. Essential material was intensively collected on two particular gangs: the Egyptian Kings and the Balkans. The Kings committed a homicide that received nationwide attention. Its members stabbed and beat to death a polio-crippled youth, Michael Farmer, in an upper Manhattan park.[1]

---

1. More than ten hours of tape-recorded interviews with the Egyptian Kings and the Dragons provide essential material for this book. A portion of these taped interviews with the Kings and the Dragons became the basis for a Columbia Broadcasting System radio documentary. The programme,

The other gang studied intensively, the Balkans, was closely observed and worked with over a one-year period. Their organization was analysed in detail during a number of gang-war incidents. One of these gang wars was characterized by the Press as the largest 'rumble' in the history of New York City.

The violent gangs studied in general, and the Kings and the Balkans in particular, are representative of a recent trend in youth violence – a type of violence of concern not only to people in large urban areas and communities in America but also to countries throughout the world.[1] The current form of the violent gang may hopefully become a social fossil. However, the fact of its special pattern of homicidal destructiveness and violence highlights it as a phenomenon deserving detailed description, analysis, and a place in the historical chronicle of social structures and events.

ACKNOWLEDGEMENTS

This analysis could not have been presented without the co-operation, however involuntary, of hundreds of youths and gangs. Some gang youths were willing informants for 'the guy writing a book on gangs and bopping'. Others became subjects as part of the Morningside Heights, Inc., programme for controlling crime on the upper West Side of Manhattan.

Most gang youths are unable to communicate to the larger society. This is one of their significant problems. In gratitude for their co-operation I have attempted to tell their story as close to reality as possible. Wherever relevant

narrated by Edward R. Murrow and produced by Jay McMullen, was called 'Who Killed Michael Farmer?' I served as a special consultant in the preparation of this broadcast, which told the story of the gang homicide through the voices of the boys who committed the act.

1. Violent gangs as a 'New Form of Delinquency' was a subject of major concern at the U.N. Congress on the Prevention of Crime and the Treatment of Offenders held in London in 1960. At the Congress, attended by more than 900 delegates from over ninety countries, recent gang violence was considered a major issue for discussion.

their original statements, however raw they may appear, are presented intact. Because the average gang youth's ability to conceptualize his own condition is limited, I assumed this task. Whenever possible I attempted to validate my observations with the boys. In the interchange, various theories and concepts presented here were sharpened and clarified.

The names of gang members have been changed to protect them from identification. For their invaluable help in producing this volume I am most grateful to these 'gang men' from the upper West Side (even those who wanted to throw me in the Hudson River, blow up my office, or 'burn me' for being a 'stoolie' to the 'nabs').

Three men have been most responsible for my sociological and criminological training: Professor Wellman Warner, Professor Paul Tappan, and Dr J. L. Moreno. Each has provided me with ideas that have been woven into the body of this volume. No number of specific credits or footnotes would be sufficient to acknowledge their contribution to my sociological thought.

My gang research on the upper West Side could not have been carried out without the support of the excellent institutions and my professional colleagues and friends associated with the Morningside Heights, Inc., project. I am especially grateful to Mr David Rockefeller, then President, and Dr Henry Van Dusen, then Chairman, of the Crime Prevention Committee of Morningside Heights, Inc. On the executive level Lawrence Orton, Margaret Bartlett, and Robert Harron (of Columbia University) helped immeasurably in supporting my research activities. Without the daily 'sociological' interaction and support of Larry Sherwood and Barney Weinberg either the Kings, Villains, or Balkans would certainly have blown up our office. Two local citizen 'gang workers', Charlie Klein and Sam Hendrix, were of enormous help in both our work with gangs and the collection of data.

My good friend Richard Korn read the manuscript with a keen eye for its many defects and possibilities. Wherever possible the final product was strengthened by his sharp theoretical imagination. This aid was almost as helpful toward the development of the manuscript as our close and productive friendship.

The possibility of ending this analysis of gang violence on a positive note was not foreseen when I began the volume. Chapter 2 is a grim description of a brutal killing committed by the infamous Egyptian Kings. Ralph, one of the youths involved in this gang killing, is found in this chapter. At that time, in 1957, his older brother Frank, also an upper West Side gang leader, was in prison.

In 1961, while completing the final draft of this volume in California, I encountered a unique self-help rehabilitation project for drug addicts operating in a converted beach club at Santa Monica. The operation, called Synanon, founded by a masterful social planner, Charles Dederich, was in an almost miraculous fashion maintaining about eighty ex-addicts and criminals free from drugs, crime, and violence. Living in this anti-criminal society I found Ralph's older brother Frankie. He has been functioning effectively in this 'therapeutic community', and leading a constructive life for over two years. The Synanon approach provided the idea for sketching a hopeful plan for treating gang leaders that comprises the foundation of my closing chapter. For providing this encouraging possibility I am deeply grateful to my good buddies Chuck, Reid, Frankie, and the rest of the Synanon gang.

Los Angeles, California   LEWIS YABLONSKY
June 1962

Introduction
to the Pelican Edition

The use of violence for acquiring things that man desires is generally deplored, but nevertheless has a frame of logic. However, violence flowing from uncontrollable compulsions, committed upon previously unknown victims with no logical or apparent goals, has always created a mood of terror.

American society has had its share of so-called 'senseless' violence. Notable in recent history were the rampage in 1949 of Howard Unruh in Camden, New Jersey, that accounted for thirteen deaths, and the homicidal trail in 1958 of Charles Starkweather in the mid-west that resulted in ten brutal killings. In 1966 two incidents involving the killing of eight student nurses in Chicago and thirteen people on the University of Texas campus stand out grotesquely in the archives of so-called senseless and apparently unpremeditated violence.

What are the factors that delineate 'logical' from 'senseless' violence? One context for analysis is society's viewpoint of the crime. Following are four categories that would encompass almost all brands of violence.

Legal Violence. Many violent acts are supported in law. The violent soldier is aggrandized as a hero (or not) based upon the intensity of his violent behaviour in the 'line of duty'. He is accordingly well trained for violent action. In fact, a non-violent soldier may, under certain conditions, be court-martialled and executed. Police officers enact another role that is supported by legal violence. Other legally justified violence is found in certain aggressive sports (e.g. football, boxing, etc.) and certain acts of self-defence.

Socially Sanctioned Violence. A significant factor in examining violence is its degree of social sanction or support. No one would argue that an assault committed by a deceived husband on an adulterer was legal, but many would sanction this violence. (In many cases, even where homicide is the result, the 'unwritten law' is supported.) Other examples of violence which are illegal yet sanctioned and considered rational would include a violent response to insults or an attack upon one's honour, or assaulting a Negro in some sections of the South. Violence, even when it is illegal, thus has varying degrees of acceptance within different segments of American society.

'*Rational*' *Violence*. Some violent acts which are illegal and non-sanctioned are still considered rational in the context of deviant behaviour. Our most prevalent form of crime, violence for financial gain, would generally fit into this category. Robbery and assault upon the person, or the commission of a homicide within the framework of 'organized crime', may be non-sanctioned and illegal, yet considered rational behaviour. The norms thus tend to support the rationality of certain criminal acts of violence, if it is acted out within a particular socio-cultural framework.

Illegal, Non-sanctioned, Irrational Violence. This category, popularly referred to as 'senseless' violence, includes such crimes as the methodical murder of eight student nurses in sequence, the shooting to death of thirteen people (and the wounding of thirty-one) from a university tower, three youths who committed a 'kill-for-kicks' assault on an elderly man who was whistling a tune they didn't like, and the stabbing and bludgeoning to death of a fifteen-year-old polio victim by a teenage gang. This kind of 'senseless' violence outrageously defies the law, social sanction, and rationality, yet under a sociological microscope certain facets of this social virus can be isolated, analysed, and understood.

This book, in total, is an effort to chronicle my personal and professional investigation of this pattern of violence. Hopefully my 'trip' into this destructive dimension of human action provides some cues for controlling a pathology that seems to be contagious and on the rise in American society.

Table 1   **Patterns of Violence**

Type	1	2	3	4
	Legal sanctioned, rational	Illegal, sanctioned, rational	Illegal, non-sanctioned, rational	Illegal, non-sanctioned, irrational. Focus of *The Violent Gang*
Examples	Soldier violence in war; police violence in law enforcement; boxer in prize fight.	Husband's violence against adulterer; assault in response to insult; racial assault.	Robbery-assault for financial gain; assault or homicide for 'crime syndicate'.	Unpremeditated, spontaneous, assault on stranger(s); violent gang homicide, 'kill-for-kicks' violence.

Los Angeles, California
1967

LEWIS YABLONSKY

The Violent Gang

1. The Modern Gang

The violent gang is not a new phenomenon. Yet its contemporary form reflects a brand and intensity of violence that differentiate it from earlier gang patterns. The 'kill for kicks' homicide is today a source of concern not only in the large city (eleven gang homicides in New York City in the summer of 1958) but also in the suburbs and the small towns.

The more developed violence of rumbles, of 'gang presidents', 'war lords', 'territory', and other gang trappings is generally a big-city operation. Yet a parallel can be found in less populated areas. 'Senseless' and spontaneous violence is the thread that ties Iowa's Charley Starkweather and his eleven killings in two days to New York City's gang leader Leroy 'Magician' Birch and the Egyptian King homicide.

Today's violent delinquent is a displaced person – suspicious, fearful, and not willing or able to establish a concrete human relationship. The formation of the violent gang, with its impermanence, its possibilities for hollow glory, its limited expectations of any responsibility on the part of its members, is all-inviting to youths who have difficulty fitting into a more integrated and clearly defined world.

Among gang members little is expected and little is given. Membership definition is vague. A youth can join one day and quit the next by merely stating 'I no longer belong.' Violent-gang organization is ideally suited to the defective personality and limited social ability of these disturbed youths.

A prime function of the modern gang is to provide a channel to act out hostility and aggression to satisfy the continuing and momentary emotional needs of its members. The gang is a convenient and malleable structure quickly adaptable to the needs of emotionally disturbed youths who are unable to fulfil the demands required for participation in more normal groups. They join gangs because they lack the social ability to relate to others, not because the gang gives them a 'feeling of belonging'.

Since the gang is both flexibly organized and amenable to wild distortions of fantasy, it is an ideal vehicle for acting out the desire for status so characteristic of adult society. In the gang a youth can be president and control vast gang domains. The members reinforce one another's fantasies of power – 'Don't call my bluff and I won't call yours' is their motto. In the gang it is necessary only to talk big, support the talk with violent action, and one achieves 'success'.

To raise his low estimate of himself, the gang boy has carved out his own world and a system of values that entails demands he can easily meet. He inverts society's norms to suit himself and the limits of his partly imagined and partly real potential. He makes lying, assault, thievery, and unprovoked violence – especially violence – the major activity or dream of his life.

The very fact that it is 'senseless' rather than pre-meditated violence that is most highly prized by the gang boy tells us a great deal about the meaning of violence to him. He looks for an easy, quick, almost magical way of achieving power and prestige. In a single act of un-premeditated intensity he establishes a sense of his own existence and impresses this existence on others. No special ability is required to commit violence – not even a plan – and the guilt connected with executing the act of violence is minimized by the gang code of approval – especially if the violence fulfils the gang's idealized standards of a swift, sudden, and senseless outbreak. This is the gang's classic form.

The gang trades in violence. Brutality is basic to its system. Talk of assault is a constant theme. 'Getting even' is characteristic – even when there is nothing to 'get even' about. 'Sounding', a technique of 'picking on' others through constant harassment, is standard practice. Illegal behaviour is viewed as a badge of merit. Society, adults, outsiders are all enemies. Knife- and gun-carrying are part of getting dressed to go out.

These modern groupings are not the 'nostalgic' social-athletic street-corner clubs of the past. Today's gangs are, in action, hysterical, mob-like cliques that kill and maim for no logical purpose (at least not logical to most people). They are groups whose members, when later describing their killing of a youth in a gang fight, comment:

I was watching him. I din't wanna hit him. Then I kicked him twice. He was laying on the ground looking up at us. I kicked him on the jaw or someplace; then I kicked him in the stomach. *That was the least I could do, was kick 'im.*

Or another boy describing a stabbing:

I just went like that, and I stabbed him with the bread knife. You know, I was drunk, so I just stabbed him. [*Laughs.*] He was screamin' like a dog.

They may terrorize an entire community. A report to the Mayor of New York City on the effects of a gang killing in one neighbourhood revealed:

. . . About forty per cent of children between the ages of three and sixteen reacted immediately with a variety of physical and emotional symptoms. For the first time some children began to carry knives for their own protection. . . .[1]

Current gangs are not in the same context as the gang image of 'the good old days'; today there is a different problem. It is difficult to detect a 'feeling of belonging' in a youth group where a boy comments on a 'brother' gang member:

Magician grabbed him; he turned [him] around and stabbed him in the back. I was . . . I was stunned. And then Magician . . . said to me, 'You're gonna hit him with the bat or I'll stab you.'

Although 'senseless' violent acts of the past were often as extreme in their results, they seemed to have more

1. This is taken from the Greenhill Report. This was a study carried out by a team of social scientists into the Washington Heights, New York City, neighbourhood following the Egyptian King homicide. The study was commissioned by Mayor Robert F. Wagner for the City of New York.

understandable and rational motives. Youth gangs of the twenties and thirties were basically friendship organizations in which boys helped one another. In addition to illegal or occasional violent activity, these groups carried on comparatively harmless gang behaviour – including sports and social activities. They were not organized essentially around violence – the core spirit of the modern gang.

Thrasher's famous analysis of Chicago youth gangs in the mid twenties describes groups that bear a limited similarity to the violence-dominated gangs of today.[1] Thrasher's gangs

. . . broke into box cars and 'robbed' bacon and other merchandise. They cut wire cables to sell as junk. They broke open telephone boxes. They took autos for joyriding. They purloined several quarts of whiskey from a brewery to drink in their shack. . . .

The gangs of the thirties and early forties described by Whyte in *Street Corner Society*[2] also bear little resemblance to the violent gang of today. The difference becomes strikingly evident when we compare the following comments by two Egyptian Kings with those of Doc, the leader of Whyte's so-called Norton Street Gang:

THE KINGS: I saw this face; I never seen it before, so I stabbed it.
   The guy that stabbed him in the back with the bread knife, he told me that when he took the knife out of his back, he said, 'Thank you.'

Doc, leader of the Norton Street Gang, describes one of his assaults this way:

Nutsy was a cocky kid before I beat him up. . . . After that, he seemed to lose his pride; I would talk to him and try to get him to buck up. . . . I wasn't such a tough kid, Bill. I was always sorry after I walloped him.

1. Frederic M. Thrasher, *The Gang* (University of Chicago Press, 1927).
2. William F. Whyte, *Street Corner Society* (University of Chicago Press, 1943).

Doc's expressed regrets about beating up Nutsy – 'I would talk to him and try to get him to buck up' – 'I was always sorry after I walloped him' – are sharp contrasts to the post-assault comments of the Egyptian Kings. Here is one of the Kings' reply to my questions about his part in the homicide (the interview took place in a reformatory):

KING: I stab him with the butcher – I mean the bread knife and then I took it out.

QUESTION: What were you thinking about at the time – right then?

KING: What was I thinking? [*Laughs.*] I was thinking whether to do it again.

QUESTION: Are you sorry about what happened?

KING: Am I sorry? Are you nuts? Of course I'm sorry. You think I like being locked up?

The element of friendship and camaraderie – one might almost call it co-operativeness – that was central to the Norton Street Gang and others like it during the past is almost entirely absent from the violent gang of today.

To be sure, candy-store or corner hangout groups similar to those described by Whyte still exist, but it is not these groups that are responsible for the killings and assaults that have caused so much recent concern – nor are they our subject here.

Today's violent gang is characterized by flux. It lacks features of an organized group, having neither a definite number of members, specific membership roles, a consensus of expected norms, nor a leader who supplies logical directions for action. It is a mob-like collectivity that forms around violence in a spontaneous fashion, moving into action – often on the spur of an evening's boredom – in search of kicks.

As indicated, violence ranks extremely high in the loose scheme of values on which such gangs are based. To some boys it acts as a kind of existential validation,[1] proving (since they are not sure) that they are alive. Boys clinging to membership in this amorphous organization also

1. This theme will be amplified later in a chapter on the functions of violence.

employ violence to demonstrate they are 'somebody'. Gang members use violence for upward mobility to acquire prestige or raise their 'rep':

I didn't want to be like . . . you know, different from the other guys. Like they hit him, I hit him. In other words, I didn't want to show myself as a punk. You know, ya always talkin', 'Oh, man, when I catch a guy, I'll beat him up', and all of that, you know. And after you go out and catch a guy, and you don't do nothin' they say, 'Oh, man, he can't belong to no gang, because he ain't gonna do nothin'.'

Another King states:

If I would of got the knife, I would have stabbed him. That would have gave me more of a build-up. People would have respected me for what I've done and things like that. They would say, 'There goes a cold killer.'

The gang as a vehicle of rep for 'cold killers' is well represented by the Egyptian King gang killing. It is an excellent prototype. In the following chronicle I attempt to let the boys tell their own story – intruding only where I feel my personal experience or some sociological view adds to this portrayal of a modern violent gang in action.

2. The Gang in Action

On the night of 30 July 1957 a fifteen-year-old boy partially crippled by polio was beaten and stabbed to death in a New York City park. His best friend was critically injured by stab wounds inflicted with a bread knife in the same attack.

The motives for this crime fit no simple category. No money was taken. No direct revenge was involved. According to all reports the victims did not personally know their assailants, nor did the youths who committed the homicide know their victims.

It was a hot summer night. A casual observer of the boys huddled in discussion in a tenement hallway near the corner of 135th Street and Broadway would detect nothing unusual about this gathering. In New York City youths often congregate like this when there is no place to go, but this group had a destination.

They talked excitedly, calling each other by nicknames. Magician, Little King, Louie, Big Man were familiar names. One youth clutched a long brown paper bag in his hand. It contained a machete. Another had a razor-point five-inch-long knife tucked away in his clothes. Still another held a harmless-appearing chain – used normally to hold a dog on a leash; the chain had a heavy metal sinker on the end.

Part of the discussion revolved around the previous evening. 'I think we scared the shit out of them – they'll show up.' 'They better or I'll get the bastards myself,' claimed another. 'Anybody who doesn't swing out will have to tangle with me when we get back.' They were not talking about enemy gang members; they were referring to their 'own boys':

See, because we say before, if anybody don't beat up somebody, when we get back, he's gonna get beat up. So I say 'OK'. They got special guys, you know, to keep their eyes on the boys. Anyone who don't swing out is gonna get it when we come back.

They got to pass through a line; they got about fifteen boys over here, and fifteen boys over there, and you know, in a straight line, like that. They got to pass through there and they all got belts in their hand.[1]

On the previous night, 29 July, two boys had been subjected to this 'kangaroo court'. They were found 'guilty', had to pass through the line, and were lacerated with garrison belts. The boys did not really take this 'court-room procedure' seriously. In some ways they were producing what was to them a caricature of adult justice. One of the 'judges' later commented, 'Oh, man, we just jive around with that stuff – but they better show anyway.'

Discussion about 'who would show' was important, but a side issue to the central theme of the violent discussion. 'They think they can get away with chasing us out of the pool – they're crazy.' Another boy described how they had called him a 'Spick':

They kept on callin' me a Spick. They kept on saying, 'You dirty Spick, get out of this block.' Every time I go in the pool, they said the same thing to me. I don't bother them, 'cause, you know, I don't want to get into no trouble with them, but one day they beat me up. You know, there was about five of them, and they wouldn't leave me alone. They beat me up, and I had to take a chance to get the boys so we could beat them up.

This boy was Puerto Rican. The Kings, however, had a mixed background. Although dominantly Puerto Rican and Negro, a number of gang members came from Italian and Irish origins. One boy was from the Dominican Republic. They were generally representative of the neighbourhood population. Some boys used racial or ethnic discrimination as a reason for 'calling on the rumble' with the Jesters. However, the main overt complaint of the group in the scarred-up tenement hallway of 602 West

1. This statement and those to follow in this section are verbatim comments taken from some ten hours of taped interviews with gang members.

135th Street was that the Jesters had barred them from swimming in the pool at Highbridge Park.

Egyptian King version:

They came behind the pool. One guy, the president, he's a Negro, he said, 'I'm gonna burn you.' So he pulled out a gun; it looked like a .45, but we weren't too sure. So he put it behind my back; and the rest of the guys' backs, and one pulled out a sawed-off rifle, and pointed it at us. Everyone said, 'Run to the water,' you know, so I ran. I dived into the water, they were waiting outside, you know around the pool, we seen them, so we told some little kids to go down and get some of the fellas, so we could get out of the pool. So they went down, and three of them came to the pool, in front of the gate, and told us it was all right to come out now, 'cause we had the fellas around.

Jester version:

There was about fifteen of them in the pool, and a few of us walked behind there, and we looked in, and we seen them, and they started hollerin' things out, like, you know, names and you're gonna be blasted, and all this, so we told them they weren't going home then, and we went back around the block, and we thought they were gonna come around the block for a fight. And this boy was walkin' in the park, and he isn't on a team, or anything like that, just walkin' through the park lookin' at the pool, and about thirty-five guys from the Kings come out and they smacked him on the head with a bat. And he got eight stitches. . . .

Both versions distort an incident that occurred two weeks before the gang killing. There were many versions, and in a sense they are all true – at least to each gang observer. Whatever the variations, the overt theme was conflict over the use of a public pool. So-called 'turf' (gang territory) rights were at stake.

The Jesters were the uptown gang with whom the Egyptian Kings were feuding. According to one spokesman for the Jesters, they were a 'defensive fighting team':

We're mostly defensive fighting team, you know, but they're offensive. You know, they . . . they start the trouble. Then we just . . . you know, we're just protectin' ourselves. Now, like they . . . they come up here on raidin' parties then we'll fight, you know, but if they don't come up we don't fight. There's never been a time when we've invaded them when they haven't come up here first.

The Egyptian Kings and Dragons in the hallway were the core of an offensive or fighting gang. Their origins went back several years to two gangs then known as the Scorpions and the Villains. They joined forces to become the West Side Dragons. The Dragons about a month prior to this evening had developed a brother-gang association with the Egyptian Kings. The Kings and Dragons 'controlled' gang turf from 125th Street to 155th Street. The Dragons came from the southern part of this territory, primarily from 135th Street and below. The Kings came from the northern section; their main hangout was a candy store at 152nd Street and Broadway.

The hallway discussion became more intense and violent. It had some characteristics of the violent rituals engaged in by the Hollywood version of warlike Indian tribes about to go on the warpath. This core part of the gang moved out of the 602 hallway at about 7.00 p.m., bound north for the candy store at the corner of 152nd Street and Broadway.

This was the rendezvous point for the now consolidated Dragons and Egyptian Kings. The administrator of this consolidation was a 'man', or at least he was twenty-six years old. Frankie Cruz was better known to the gang boys in this area of the upper West Side as Frankie Loco. Loco was a standard 'professional' teenage gangster. He was always giving advice on gang organization, telling gang boys when and with whom to fight. Most of the time he was discussing non-existent enemies conjured up in his wild fantasy world:

GANG BOY: Oh, Frankie Loco, he's from the East Side Dragons. Like he would tell us what to do. He got us [the Dragons] together with the Kings. Yeah, sometimes he acts crazy – always talkin', talkin', talkin'. . . .

Loco travelled up and down the West Side 'talkin', talkin', talkin'' and stirring up gang trouble. Loco at one time was under psychiatric observation at Bellevue. Short in stature, he had a scar across the top of his head – the result of a childhood battle. Loco's favourite topic was blood. He had a job cleaning up the blood in an operating room at a city hospital. He liked his work. In one taped interview he mentioned the world *blood* over thirty times.

Loco had provoked the gang action. At the Egyptian King court trial he was mentioned by almost all the defendants, on trial for first-degree murder, as their adviser; yet the night of this homicide he was nowhere around. He was primarily a 'consultant', and was not with the group swaggering up Broadway from 135th Street to 152nd Street.

The walk up this part of Broadway passes pool halls, a kosher delicatessen, and *bodegas* – Spanish grocery stores. It is a neighbourhood in transition.

One pool hall is a hangout for 'junkies' (drug addicts). Some former gang boys may have smiled as they detected this entourage – obviously going to fight a gang war. They smiled because, as they put it, 'We don't fool with this punk gang stuff any more.' They had found another way out of this world. For many gang youths drug addiction is a next step – when gang kicks become for them 'kid stuff'.

On the way up Broadway the gang leader with the machete under his arm met an 'old friend' on his way to a movie:

GANG BOY: I was walkin' uptown with a couple of friends, and we run into Magician and them there. They asked us if we wanted to go to a fight, and we said, 'Yes.' When they asked me if I wanted to go to a fight, I couldn't say, 'No.' I mean I could say, 'No', but for old-time's sake, I said, 'Yes.'

This boy later took an active role in striking down Michael Farmer. 'He got up and I knocked him down again.'

The candy store at 152nd Street and Broadway is a standard part of New York's scenery. It stands cluttered with forceful advertising: 'Be sociable', 'They said it couldn't be done', 'The pause that refreshes'. Steps lead down into the candy store, which was heavily congested that evening.

When the group arrived at the store they were greeted by a number of other gang youths who had heard about the evening's expedition through the rumour mill. There was a shifting group of seventy or eighty boys present around the candy store that night, all ready for action.

'Some of the gang drank sodas, played the jukebox, and joked around.' About 8.30 p.m. one King leader, Louis Alvarez, phoned a candy-store hangout on Jackson Avenue in the Bronx. He spoke to a then famous gang leader called Michael 'Pee Wee' Ramos. Pee Wee was supposed to command a brother-gang Dragon division. He was another Loco-type gang leader. At the Egyptian King trial he gave the following testimony describing his end of the phone conversation:

I answered the phone and then he told me he was Louis from the Dragons, from the West Side. So he told me that Frankie Loco says when he gets in trouble, give me a ring, to call me up. So I told him Frankie Loco was my boy, he was with me in the old Dragons. I told him, what the trouble was? Then he told me he got some trouble with the Irish boys up on the West Side.

Did he ask you for anything?

He told me – you know, the rifle.

What else did he say, if anything?

Make it, up there with my boys, up to the West Side. Yes, I told him I make it up there, ten o'clock I make it up there. Told him I'd come down with some weapons, you know, some guns in a car, some rifles and a car.

Did you tell him you would come down right away, or that there would be a delay?

I told him I had some trouble of my own. After I finished that I may get down there.

Later that night there had been another telephone conversation. It was the same voice on the telephone, Pee Wee said:

I said – he said, what happens, why can't I make it up there?

I told him I still got my own troubles up here and that I can't make it up there. He said, then he told me, 'You got experience', you know. So I said, 'Yes, that is where I got it from.' That is where, you know, I got it from, you know, experience from. So I told him like this, in the old Dragons, you know, we used to bop, we used to hit, you know, and talk later. So go right up there and whip it on them.

Now, have you ever met Louis Alvarez in your life?
Never.

(On 27 April 1959 Pee Wee's gang-leader activities were curtailed. A boy named Raymond Serra, another gang leader, confronted Ramos in a candy store. According to Serra, Ramos gave him a 'bad look'. Serra, who was holding a shotgun, blew away most of Pee Wee's head.)

At 9.00 p.m. several core members of the gang left the candy store and walked down to the park along Riverside Drive. They carried with them, in addition to their weapons, a few bottles of cheap liquor. They 'talked about plans and joked around'. They were accompanied by some girl friends, who were also around the candy store that night:

We went down to the park and we sat around for a while. Then we started drinking and we drank whisky and wine and we was drunk. Then we started talkin' about girls. We started sayin' to the girls that if they get us to bring us some roses an' all that – that if we get caught to write to us and all this.

After bolstering their courage they walked back up the block to the candy store. The collection of some eighty boys inside, in front of the candy store, and on the concrete 'island' in the centre of Broadway was a mixed group. Some had no intention of participating in gang action. Some were worried and had doubts:

I didn't wanna go at first, but they said come on. So then all the big guys forced me to go. I was scared. I was worried. I realized like I was doing I'd probably get in trouble.

Central leaders of the gang did not know what the excursion north to Highbridge Park would bring, but they had no doubts about making the trip. They were ready to go in any direction.

Judge Irwin Davidson, the trial judge, summarized his reflections on the gang's mood that night prior to the homicide, based on court testimony:

There had been up to seventy-five boys gathered around the island at one time or another during the evening, all ready to take off and go up to battle the Jesters. They had been assured by Alvarez that reinforcements were arriving from other parts of the city, riding in cars, bringing guns. During the long – and, as it turned out, fruitless – wait [at the candy store] for the allies, the boys had begun to drift away. Some had to go home because they had been adjured by their mothers and fathers to return at certain times. Others simply had lost interest in the rumble and wandered off, indicating that they originally had been more interested in the prospect of excitement and violence than in coming to terms with the Jesters; they probably would have been just willing to go along, in order to pass the time, if Alvarez, Lago and the rest of the leaders had proposed an expedition down to fight one of the Italian kid gangs in Greenwich Village. . . .

The seventy-five-odd boys on the island had dwindled to eighteen. I wondered again where the police had been. Surely there had been patrol cars in the neighbourhood. The boys had sticks, knives, and a machete wrapped in paper. Any passer-by could have seen that they were there for no good reason.[1]

A police station was one block away. Citizens in cars and on foot passed this gang build-up for almost two hours. Gang activity blends well into some New York City neighbourhoods. At about 10.00 p.m. eighteen members of the gang collected and headed north towards Highbridge Park. In one hour Michael Farmer would be dead.

The walk from 152nd Street and Broadway to Highbridge Park is about twenty New York City blocks. The route passes slum tenements, modern apartment buildings, and old residential homes abandoned to deterioration. A police station is on the way. More than half-way

1. Judge Irwin D. Davidson, *The Jury Is Still Out* (New York: Harper & Brothers, 1959), pp. 56–7. This volume gives an analysis of the Egyptian King trial as seen by the judge.

to the Park, on Edgecomb Avenue in the Bronx, a dusty view encompasses the East Side Highway, the soon-to-be obsolete Polo Grounds, and thriving Yankee Stadium. That night thousands of fans were engrossed in watching the Yanks beat the Red Sox eight to five. The Bronx County Courthouse looms in the background.

What were the thoughts of the boys making this journey? We can only speculate from later comments: 'Nobody's gonna steal my rep.' 'I felt kinda cold inside.' 'They'll get me later if I don't swing out at somebody.' 'I'm going to kill some mother fucker.'

Of more than seventy boys, eighteen made the final trip, travelling in twos and threes to avoid detection. They reconvened at 10.15 p.m. in Stitt Park, a small park that faces Stitt School about seven blocks from Highbridge Pool. The boys discussed a plan of action, then sent out scouts to patrol the neighbourhood 'to see how many Jesters were around'. There is some evidence of other boys hanging around in the park; however, they were not necessarily Jesters. To the 'scouts' all youths looked like Jesters by this time:

EGYPTIAN KING: We walked around the block to see how strong the club was we was gonna fight. To see if they had lots of guys and whatnot. What we saw, they had lots of big guys. I'd say about nineteen, twenty, or eighteen, like that. And we figured it out so we kept on walking around the block.

Gang boys under these extreme emotional conditions often perceive all youths in a neighbourhood as potential enemies. By this time they were ready to 'swing out' at anyone.

Highbridge Pool is rather large, roughly half a city block in size. An American flag waves high over the pool; near by is the tall old water tower. In a city like New York, with its few available recreation opportunities, it is a treasured spot for cooling off in the hot summer. On a hill overlooking the East River, it provides a welcome breeze for people sitting on benches around the pool.

The Kings and Dragons entered the bushy area surrounding the pool in twos and threes to avoid attention.

Staked out around the pool, at this time they were, in their own words, 'ready to jump anyone who came along'.

Michael Farmer and a friend, Roger McShane, were at this time in the Farmer apartment about a block from the park, listening to rock 'n' roll records.

MRS FARMER: They stayed in his room playin' these new records that they had bought and Michael came out to the kitchen, just as I asked my husband what time it was, to set the clock. It was then five after ten. He asked for a glass of milk and as he walked from the kitchen, he asked, 'I'm going to walk Roger home.' [*Sighs.*] That was the last time I saw him.

Youngsters in the area were warned to stay out of the park at night when the pool was closed but not drained. However, it was usual for some of the local boys to slip through a break in the gate entrance and sneak an evening swim.

The slightly curved footpath that enters the park at Amsterdam Avenue and 174th Street is about a one-minute walk to the high concrete stairway entrance to Highbridge Pool. It was Michael Farmer's last walk:

MCSHANE: It was 10.30 when we entered the park; we saw couples on the benches, in the back of the pool, and they all stared at us, and I guess they must 'ave saw the gang there – I don't think they were fifty or sixty feet away. When we reached the front of the stairs, we looked up and there was two of their gang members on top of the stairs. They were two smaller ones, and they had garrison belts wrapped around their hands. They didn't say nothin' to us, they looked kind of scared.

FIRST EGYPTIAN KING: I was scared. I knew they were gonna jump them, 'an everythin' and I was scared. When they were comin' up, they all were separatin' and everything like that.

MCSHANE: I saw the main body of the gang slowly walk out of the bushes, on my right. I turned around fast, to see what Michael was going to do, and this kid came runnin' at me with the belts. Then I ran, myself, and told Michael to run.

SECOND E. KING: He couldn't run anyway, cause we were all around him. So then I said, 'You're a Jester', and he said, 'Yeah', and I punched him in the face. And then somebody hit him with a bat over the head. And then I kept punchin' him. Some of them were too scared to do anything. They were just standin' there, lookin'.

THIRD E. KING: I was watchin' him. I didn't wanna hit him, at first. Then I kicked him twice. He was layin' on the ground lookin' up at us. I kicked him on the jaw, or some place; then I kicked him in the stomach. That was the least I could do, was kick 'im.

FOURTH E. KING: I was aimin' to hit him, but didn't get a chance to hit him. There were so many guys on him – I got scared when I saw the knife go into the guy, and I ran right there. After everybody ran, this guy stayed, and started hittin' him with a machete.

FIRST E. KING: Somebody yelled out, 'Grab him. He's a Jester.' So then they grabbed him. Magician grabbed him, he turned around and stabbed him in the back. I was . . . I was stunned. I couldn't do nothin'. And then Magician – he went like that and he pulled . . . he had a switch blade and he said, 'You're gonna hit him with that bat or I'll stab you.' So I just hit him lightly with the bat.

SECOND E. KING: Magician stabbed him and the guy he . . . like hunched over. He's standin' up and I knock him down. Then he was down on the ground, everybody was kickin' him, stompin' him, punchin' him, stabbin' him so he tried to get back up and I knock him down again. Then the guy stabbed him in the back with a bread knife.

THIRD E. KING: I just went like that, and I stabbed him with the bread knife. You know, I was drunk, so I just stabbed him. [*Laughs.*] He was screamin' like a dog. He was screamin' there. And then I took the knife out and I told the other guys to run. So I ran and the rest of the guys ran with me. They wanted to stay there and keep on doin' it.

FOURTH E. KING: The guy that stabbed him in the back with the bread knife, he told me that when he took the knife out o' his back, he said, 'Thank you.'

MCSHANE: They got up fast right after they stabbed me. And I just lay there on my stomach and there was five of them as they walked away. And as they walked away they . . . this other big kid came down with a machete or some large knife of some sort, and he wanted to stab me too with it. And they told him, 'No, come on. We got him. We messed him up already. Come on.' And they took off up the hill and they all walked up the hill and right after that they all of 'em turned their heads and looked back at me. I got up and staggered into the street to get a cab. And I got in a taxi and I asked him to take me to the Medical Centre and get my friend and I blacked out.

The coroner's report reveals the intensity of the violence:

'I found a fifteen-year-old white boy, five feet and a half inches in length, scale weight 138 pounds, the face showing an ecchymosis ... [a] hemorrhage beneath the skin ... you would compare it to a black-and-blue mark.

'There was an ecchymosis of the outer aspect of the right eye, with a superimposed superficial abrasion. ... There was an incised wound ... one made with a very sharp implement ... situated over the bridge of the nose and [extending] ... over the right eyebrow.'

He had found wounds and abrasions on the knuckles and hands of the body, the doctor said, which seemed to indicate that Michael Farmer had raised his hands to defend himself against the torrential blows being inflicted upon him. He had also found an incised wound beneath the left armpit, but that one had not penetrated deeper than the epidermis. A wound on the right thigh had been deeper: 'It measured one and a half inches in length with a gap that was slightly less than three-quarters of an inch ... a gaping wound with sharp edges. ...'

On the left side was another penetrating stab wound, lower and more deadly. This one 'went through the entire back into the pleural cavity', and 'severed a vein and a nerve'. This wound, four inches deep, had caused Farmer's death.

Aftermath

Roger McShane was on the critical list at the Presbyterian Medical Centre. Michael Farmer's parents were notified the same evening of his death.

MR FARMER: The sergeant from the 34th Precinct called us, and asked who I was, and was I the father of Michael Farmer. I said I was, and he said, 'Well, your boy is in Mother Cabrini

Hospital, in serious condition.' I identified myself further, as a fireman in this area, and he said, 'Oh, I'll come right down and give you a lift down to the hospital.' So this sergeant drove us down to the hospital; as we walked in, the officer who was on duty there called the sergeant, and he said the boy had died fifteen minutes earlier.

MRS FARMER: And the sister there in the hospital took us downstairs to identify the body. He had an expression as though he was just calling for help.

After the stabbing the gang scattered and fled. The gang members reported their post-killing reactions in various ways. One boy went home, had a glass of milk, went to bed, but couldn't sleep.

GANG MEMBER: I couldn't sleep that night or nothin' 'cause I used to fall asleep for about half an hour. Wake up again during the middle of the night. My mother said, 'What was the matter with you? Looks like something was wrong.' I said, 'Nothin'.'

ANOTHER GANG MEMBER: First I went to the river to throw my knife away and then I went home. An' then I couldn't sleep. I was in bed. My mother kept on askin' me where was I and I . . . I told her, you know, that I was in the movies. I was worried about them two boys. If they would die . . . I knew I was gonna get caught.

This boy was more concerned with getting caught and locked up than remorseful over his violent act. In a later interview with him in a reformatory I asked him:

QUESTION: Well, how do you feel about this all now? Are you sorry about the killing?
ANSWER: Of course I'm sorry. I'm locked up, ain't I?

The banner headlines of the homicide shocked many residents of New York City on their way to work the following morning. A large number of detectives worked through the night to piece the crime together. By dawn they began to round up the gang.

At 6.30 a.m. one gang member heard a knock on the door of his apartment in a housing project on 125th Street:

I hear this knockin' on the door. I didn't think it was the police, you know. 'Cause, you know, I thought I wasn't gonna get caught, so I was layin' in bed and told my mother, 'Mommie, I think that's the milkman knockin' on the door or somebody.' She said, 'Why don't you answer it?' and I said, 'No, I'm in my underwear.' So she says, 'OK, I'll go.' She opened the door and my mother comes over, 'You get in any trouble last night?' And I says, 'No Mommie, I didn't get in no trouble last night.' And then she says, 'Well, there's a policeman over here, wants to see you.' And I says, 'What for?' and he says, 'Somethin' that happened last night,' and I says, 'OK,' then I started thinkin' of my clothes and acted innocent, you know. He said to me, 'You know what happened last night?' I say, 'No, no. I don't know a thing that happened last night. I was in the car from ten on.' He says, 'Oh, if that's the truth, you have nothin' to worry about. You like to come down to the police station with us?' And I said, 'OK'.

Another gang member spent the following morning in Children's Court, pleading innocent to a robbery committed two weeks earlier. He was released, pending a hearing. When he returned home, police were waiting to question him about the murder of Michael Farmer. This was the boy who used a bread knife in the assault at Highbridge Park. During my later hour-long interview with him, he was quite calm in relating the killing and his role in it. He became excited only once:

Well, when we was goin' to the . . . to the paddy wagon, the detective, he kept wipin' his feet on my suit. So I told him to cut it out, and he still won't cut it out. So then, then the sergeant says, 'Cut it out,' so then he said, 'Why don't you mind your business?' and he kept on doin' it. He kept on wipin' his feet on my suit, and I just got the suit out of the cleaners', that's all. I told him, 'I just got the suit out of the cleaners',' and he says to me, 'That just too bad. That suit belongs in the garbage can.' So he kept on wipin' his feet on my suit, and he kept on sayin', 'You murderer' and all this. They kept on sayin', 'You're gonna get the electric chair, you're gonna get the electric chair, you murderer, you murderer, you're gonna get the electric chair.' He kept on sayin' that to me; he made me mad. If I had a gun, I would have shot them all.

This same boy later told a police officer, 'I always wanted to see how it would feel to stick a knife through human bone.'

Another youth felt 'all right with the fellas' after he was arrested:

I was crackin' up 'cause I wanted them to hurry up and come and get me and get it over with, so when I got picked up, I felt safe then. We went in the car and then they threatened me. I mean, not exactly a threat, but they told me what was goin' to happen: I'd get beat up if I didn't talk. So I told them, 'Tell me, who was the guy that squealed?' They told me, 'Who do you think you are, Dillinger or somebody – ya gonna get even with the guy?' I said, 'No, I just wanted to know.' They said, 'No.' So they took me to the precinct; it made me laugh to see all the guys sitting there in the ... in the ... when I walked in, everybody said, 'Ha, ha,' and started laughin' so I felt all right with the fellas.

In court Mr Farmer made an observation about the Kings as he watched them arraigned:

They are monsters – in my mind I classify them as savage animals. That's all. I don't think that they have any civilization in them. I think they're just two-legged animals. They haven't any concept of living with other people, outside of to show that they can do something worse than the other or to claim any sort of notoriety. These boys didn't even hang their heads, most of them, when they came to court. They stood erect and looked around the court for their relatives. And so forth. One of them had a small smirk when they looked in our direction. They should be put away, and kept away. Or if the penalty is death, to be executed. Certainly they set themselves up in the form of a judge, jury and execution squad in the case of my son. All in the matter of minutes. This is pure jungle activity.

A killing of this kind also has a profound impact on many people not directly related either to the offenders or to the victims. A typical reaction of the general public to this act was shock, at its seeming sens lessness and ir-rationality. One might expect that people close to these youths could have foreseen or expected this behaviour.

The gang boys' parents also reacted with shock and disbelief:

MOTHER: I had absolutely no problems with him. Everyone in the neighbourhood can vouch for that. When I walked out there this morning, all my storekeepers and everythin' just can't believe that my son is mixed up in anything like this. I have no idea what I can do for him right now. I doubt if there is anything we can do for him right now. I can't let him down now. Even though he was wrong, I still can't just turn my back on him.

Shame was another characteristic response:

GANG BOY: My mother said she was ashamed of me, and everything, and I told her that it wasn't my fault and I couldn't help it. My father wanted to kill me at first, and after I explained to him what happened he was still . . . he was still like . . . felt bad about it, ashamed to walk the streets.

Shock was expressed in several forms:

GANG BOY: My father understood. He didn't actually understand, but you know, he didn't take it as hard as my mother. My mother . . . it came out in the newspapers, she had a heart attack. It's a lucky thing she's alive today.

One mother described her guilt:

He has lived with my mother all his life from birth. I lived there up to two, three years ago. It seems like since I left my child everything has happened. Not that I just walked out on him, but when I planned to get married I spoke to him. He said, 'Well, go ahead, you have to have some happiness; you can't just stay with me all the time.' So I said, 'Will you be willing to come with me?' He said, 'No, I don't want to leave my grandparents.'

Do you think that it would have been important if he had stayed with you?

I think it would have been important had I stayed with him and not left him at the age of fifteen.

One mother gave covert approval to the act. This even shocked the tough gang members who related the incident:

The Gang in Action   43

When she sees him she says to him, 'How did it feel when you
did that to Farmer? It was good, eh?' You know, jokin' around
with the kid. So we told her, 'You know what your son did?'
I says, 'He stabbed him in the back.' She says, she just went
like that, shrugged her, you know, shoulders. Then we didn't
pay any attention to her, because ya know, you don't like to
see a mother actin' like that with a kid.

The legal forces of society moved swiftly in this case.
Within twenty-four hours the eighteen youths involved in
the crime were apprehended and arraigned. The eleven
younger members of the gang, age fifteen or under, were
quickly tried in Children's Court and committed to various
state reformatories for indeterminate sentences.

The older group of seven, ranging in age from fifteen to
eighteen, were indicted and tried for first-degree murder in
an unprecedented trial lasting ninety-three days and involving twenty-seven trial lawyers for the defence. An all-
male, blue-ribbon jury rendered the following verdict:

CHIEF JUROR: Louis Alvarez and Charles Horton guilty of
    murder in the second degree. Lencio de Leon and Leroy
    Birch guilty of manslaughter in the second degree. Richard
    Hills and George Melendez not guilty because we believe
    these boys were forced to go along with the gang the night
    of the murder. John McCarthy not guilty because we were
    convinced, beyond a reasonable doubt, that this boy was
    mentally sick and didn't know what was going on at any
    time.

Three of these boys were released immediately. Two
were sentenced to twenty years to life imprisonment. One
was sentenced to seven and one-half to fifteen years and
the other was sentenced to five to fifteen years.

The Natural History of a Gang

3. The Rise of the Balkans

The Egyptian Kings and the Balkans

The Egyptian Kings homicide reveals the dynamics of the gang in action. The killing was the major event in the Kings' brief, but intense life history, which was restricted to a few weeks of organizational manipulation leading up to the Farmer incident. Soon after the Kings had fulfilled their homicidal destiny, they were dismantled by arrest, judicial process, and incarceration.

Most violent gangs skirt the border of murder. Their careers most generally entail some organizational manipulation, a series of assaults, then a break-up, either through outside intervention or by self-destruction. The organizational rearrangements of the Egyptian Kings are typical of urban violent gangs. Although they were short-lived as an entity, the Egyptian Kings had a longer history under other names. One King described this gang process: 'Man, in bopping gangs the gang names change, but most of the same faces stay on the scene.'

The organizational roots of the Egyptian Kings go back about two years to two upper West Side groups, known as the Villains and Scorpions. These two gangs later merged themselves into a gang called the West Side Dragons. They later affiliated with the widely known East Side Dragons of East Harlem. The new gang later merged with another newly formed group from farther uptown (152nd Street and Broadway) called the Egyptian Kings. This final product was the gang that killed Michael Farmer in Highbridge Park.

My view of the earlier forms of the Egyptian Kings was taken from the vantage point of the Balkans, a gang enemy to the south with whom our agency was working. The 1955 version of the Kings (known first as the Scorpions-Villains and then as Dragons) did battle with the Balkans in a series of rumbles and violent skirmishes.

The Balkans were representative of the shifting, violent gang. Because of our agency's proximity to them, I was able to observe and study them closely over the eight-month period of their existence. The Balkans' organizational 'rise and fall', their rationales for violence, their paranoia about real and imagined attacking enemies, their resistance to control and treatment, and their daily assaultive life pattern were closely studied over their brief lifetime. A look inside the Balkans provides a further representative view of the origins, development, and demise of violent gangs.

The Balkans Protect their Turf

On the upper West Side of Manhattan stands a monumental cluster of large institutions that have been appropriately referred to as the 'modern Acropolis'. Here Columbia University, Teachers College, Union Seminary, and other world-renowned institutions of learning and religion make their home. A historian of the area has described Morningside Heights:

By the second half of the Twentieth Century, almost 60,000 people had come to live near the institutions: to teach and to learn, to heal and to be restored, to give guidance and to pray. No less than 48 countries of national origin were represented by those who lived in the more than one-half square mile of land.

To the intercultural strengths of the community was added a permanent note of intelligence and youth. Nearly 4,000 students live in Morningside Heights and add buoyancy and vision to its spirit.

From atomic research to a zest for living, Morningside Heights embraces the soundest traditions of our American heritage. In its historic, natural setting, this gateway to the world is a community of cooperation which makes it a gateway to the future.[1]

Without the knowledge or the consent of the official leaders of this community, a youth gang known as the Balkans claimed this same territory as their own turf.

1. Bernard M. Weinberg, 'Morningside Heights, New York' (New York: Morningside Heights, Inc., Publication, 1956).

They went so far as to divide it into divisions. As a gang member put it:

> The Balkans were busted up into block communities, so many members to a block. They [the leaders] know who was on their block, who belongs to the Balkans ... then the Balkans are busted up in divisions. ... The division commanders know each division, but are not sure of their membership. They know the members, but are not sure of the individual persons. ...
>
> Like if a fight came up tomorrow, they'd get in touch with the sector commander. The first sector which is Manhattan between 110th Street and 125th Street could raise 400 guys. The others – I don't know how many they could raise ... they could do a lot better than that in case of a fight, maybe a few thousand.

Land and territory were important to the Balkan gang in both a real and a symbolic sense:

> You have a certain piece of land, so another club wants to take over your land, in order to have more space, and so forth. They'll fight you for it. If you win, you got your land; if you don't win, they get your land. The person that loses is gonna get up another group, to help out, and then it starts all over again. Fight for the land again.

The Balkans first became news after an incident reported in all New York newspapers as 'a quarrel over territory'. In my role as crime-prevention director for Morningside Heights, Inc., the story in the New York *Daily News*, on 11 June 1955, demanded my attention:

NIP 200-PUNK FIGHT
NEAR COLUMBIA CAMPUS

By Grover Ryder and Jack Smee

A flying squad of 25 cops, alerted by a civilian's tip, broke up the makings of one of the biggest gang rumbles in the city's turbulent teen history last night at the edge of Columbia University's campus on Morningside Heights.

Running a motorized dragnet through the area, police rounded up 38 youths from 13 to 18 years old. But those seized were only a fraction of the 200-odd members of six different gangs, who, police said, planned to square off in the shadow of Grant's Tomb.

Later 10 of the boys were released. Five, 16 to 19 years old, were held on charges of unlawful assembly. The remaining 23, all juveniles, were paroled in custody of their parents for a hearing today in Children's Court on juvenile delinquency charges.

A cache of weapons, including a 16-inch bayonet, two hunting knives, a stiletto, seven assorted clubs, and a length of iron pipe, was found in an apartment house hallway just off Riverside Drive. In addition, 16 of the captured youths wore heavy, metal-studded garrison belts.

A Quarrel over Territory

The prisoners were taken to the W. 100th St. police station, where questioning disclosed that the rumble was to decide territorial rights to Riverside Park.

On one side were the Balkans, whose center of operations is Broadway at 115th St. and who claim the park as their exclusive stamping ground. Challenging them were the Villains, who held forth at 130th St. and Amsterdam Ave.

As the battle loomed, the Balkans, 40 strong, recruited reinforcements from the Mighty Hoods and the Politicians, who operate in central Harlem. The Villains sought aid from the Black Knights and Scorpions of the upper west side.

The report of a 'Balkan' gang came as a surprise to our crime-prevention agency. During our first year of operation we had made contact with many gangs and youth groups in the area, and had involved several hundred in athletic-league projects at Columbia's baseball field and basketball courts. We were working with gangs and youths who lived more on the periphery of the Morningside Heights area, in central Harlem and the upper West Side above 125th Street. Despite this, outside my observation of some 'tough-looking' kids on several street corners directly in the Morningside Heights area, we had not heard of the Balkan gang.

I had my first direct encounter with the Balkans on the Monday after the Villain–Balkan skirmish. Leaving my office, I spotted a fairly tough-looking youth swaggering down Morningside Drive. He looked about fifteen, but he was over six feet tall and weighed about 180 pounds.

Defying the manual's directions, which specify an oblique approach, I approached the boy directly and stopped him.

L.Y.: Are you a Balkan?

G.B.: Are you a cop?

L.Y.: No, I work for the institutions here on Morningside Heights. We're interested in the guys in the neighbourhood and want to provide things for them to do to keep them out of trouble.

G.B.: You're a cop.

L.Y.: No. Maybe you know about our baseball league up at Baker Field?

G.B.: Yeah, I heard about that.

L.Y.: Well, we want to help guys in the neighbourhood stay out of trouble if we can.

G.B.: It's too late to help us; we're all messed up. Some of our guys are locked up and we're going to get the bastards who did it.

The youth, who introduced himself as Nicky, seemed troubled, perhaps because his brother was one of the boys locked up. Nicky had escaped being arrested on the night of the rumble and was now apparently in the process of regrouping his forces to get the Villains and Scorpions.[1]

He agreed to come into my office and talk – in part to check out his cop hypothesis regarding me. We talked for about an hour and, although he was fairly guarded, I was able to get some clues about the origins and development of the Balkans. I learned that Duke, the president, had just been released from jail: 'If you talk to him he knows about the whole Balkan club. He'll talk to you maybe.'

I saw Nicky the next day on the corner of La Salle and Broadway wildly wrestling with about a dozen other boys, a standard gang 'fooling around' activity. There were shrill shrieks as three boys pushed and dragged one boy along the ground for no apparent reason. In another clique a boy was being pulled down a flight of concrete stairs, with his head bouncing unmercifully on the tenement

1. As nearly as I could assess it during my entire research, the so-called Villains and Scorpions were close brother gangs and used these names interchangeably. Hereafter I shall use the name Villains when referring to this 'combine'; except, of course, where both or one is used in a verbatim quote.

stoop. I couldn't understand how he could get up so easily, obviously faking unconcern about the beating he had just taken.

No one, especially Nicky, paid any obvious attention to me, standing awkwardly and out of place, watching the group at 'play'. Yet they were all aware of my presence, and seemed to wait for my move. Although he had been fairly cordial when we had adjourned the day before, Nicky was not admitting he knew me. I addressed him directly and asked if I could talk to him for a few minutes. He said, 'What about?'

'Well,' I replied, 'you know, like we were talking yesterday – I'd like to meet Duke and all and see if I can help you guys.'

At this point two boys came over and asked Nicky if I was bothering him. It was clear they were willing to do something about me if I was. One was about five-feet-ten, 200 pounds, chunky and muscular, his arms flexed and folded across his chest, with his sleeves pushed high to reveal as much muscle as possible. This was Duke.

The other, Pedro, was a Puerto Rican youth about twenty, thin and surly looking. He moved in as if to second anything Duke would say. Nicky mumbled an introduction, referring to me as 'This is the guy I told you about, from Columbia.' I extended my hand and received a moist, flabby handshake.

I told the boys of my interest in their current gang problems and volunteered any help I could provide. Most of my comment was heard with a complete lack of expression. I pushed the situation to a yes-or-no response by inviting them to my office to discuss the problem of 'their boys in jail', the forthcoming trial, and the possible prevention of further conflict with the Villains.

I later discovered that Duke decided to co-operate because he saw some possibility for using me in court. Pedro and Nicky followed him along to my office.

The central theme of our two-hour discussion was their investigation of me and Morningside Heights, Inc.: 'Who is in back of all this?' 'How come you're doing this work?'

'Do you deal with the cops?' 'How come you're tearing all those houses down on 125th Street when they're still good?' 'How can you help us?' I answered all questions honestly and directly.

Pedro and Nicky remained 'tough', but a remarkable change came over Duke. He shifted from the brusqueness of a corner gang leader to an almost pleasant, friendly demeanour, which for the next several years never left his behaviour when he was around me. From that point on, Duke became almost a co-researcher into himself and the Balkans, ready to work with me in exploring and analysing them and their activities. The only clue to his conversion I ever received was a comment made about a year later: 'I liked you right away and decided you were a pretty good guy who wanted to help, not hurt. So I figured why give you a hard time?'

During the next year of studying and working with the Balkans and Duke, I had to go back to the street-corner meeting to remember him and his cold-blooded demeanour, which was probably the only side of him seen by his gang and others.

The Rumble over Territory

My discussions with Duke, Pedro, and Nicky revealed that the June gang war had many more dimensions than those revealed in the press. Because the rumble was in the heart of Columbia 'territory', the Morningside Crime Prevention Committee requested and received a report. My account of the gang fight presented here was originally written as a memorandum on 20 June 1955 about a week after my preliminary analysis:

GANG FIGHT BROKEN UP BY POLICE

On 10 June 1955 at approximately 7.30 p.m., twenty-seven youths were arrested for unlawful assembly. They were arrested in two groups: one group of eleven was arrested at 115th and Riverside Drive, and the other group of sixteen was apprehended in the vicinity of 120th Street at Grant's Tomb. The first group was composed of four youths who lived near 115th and Riverside Drive and was identified as Balkan gang members. They were accompanied by seven boys, members of a central Harlem fighting gang called the Politicians. The opposing gang, arrested in the vicinity of Grant's Tomb, was composed of boys who came from the vicinity of 130th Street and Broadway. They were known as the Scorpions and Villains.

I began working on the problem Saturday morning, 11 June. Following is a summary of the background of the event based on my observations and discussions with the police captain, arresting police officers, many of the boys on the scene, the hearing in Children's Court (where I appeared), talks with citizen volunteers who knew the boys, interviews with parents of the boys involved, and information from other local youths. I cannot be certain about parts of this account, since participants in emotional events of this kind often unconsciously exaggerate and distort versions of the situation.

The newspaper and police accounts state that the event occurred as a fight for the rights to Riverside Park. This, according to reports I received from the boys, is an oversimplified explanation. The Scorpions and Villains frequent Riverside Park, and regularly 'beat up' boys from the 115th-116th Streets and Riverside Drive area. In retaliation, a group of about four or five youths, known trouble-makers in the Morningside area, formed the gang now known as the Balkans. The event also emerged as a result of the aggressive needs of several disturbed youths from the area. Mainly, however, the rumble was scheduled between the Balkans and the Scorpion-Villain gangs (brother gangs) as a consequence of the Balkans' feeling that they 'had taken all of the push-around by the uptown clubs that they were going to'. Through one of their leaders the Balkans contacted the Politicians, a known fighting gang who would show up at this, or any other gang war, possibly for 'kicks'. The battle did not come off, as both groups were stopped cold by the effective action of the police. This has ended hostilities, at least temporarily.

Leaders of the Balkans were arrested. Several gang members are still in custody. An older gang leader (eighteen) [Duke] was released. On his being released from jail, I contacted him and he came to my office for a conference. In our talk, he agreed that the battle was senseless and that we could work out a solution to possible future hostility. The leader of the Balkans agreed to the following plan to curb future gang wars:

He was amenable to a meeting at which the Balkans would

attempt to talk over their differences peacefully with the Scorpions and Villains. Negotiations are under way for this 'peace meeting' with the other groups, possibly to be held in my office at 90 Morningside Drive.

The leader welcomed the opportunity I offered the Balkans to participate in our baseball league. Initially, I will personally 'manage' this team.

Another action taken was that the 24th police precinct and police youth divisions have been contacted on the matter and have been informed of our moving in on the situation. They agreed to notify us immediately if they hear of any gang-war activity between these groups. We, of course, will in turn alert them.

The twenty-seven youths arrested in the gang war appeared in court under two different legal categories. Twenty juveniles (under sixteen) were held in Youth House and arraigned in Children's Court. The remaining seven were arraigned in 'Youth Part' court for youths over sixteen. At the trial I was consulted about some of the boys by the judge. Police and gang testimony did not reveal what actually happened. The boys all said they were either going to play stickball or they just 'happened' to be in the neighbourhood. The collection of weapons in the hallway was never adequately explained. Duke was among the boys arraigned in the upper youth court where the charges were dismissed for lack of evidence. Though all of the boys on trial had some prior arrest or previous brush with the law, most of them were placed on probation.

For the next several weeks I met almost daily with Duke and Pedro. We seemed to have overcome all resistances to communication about the Balkans, and their version of the rumble with the Villains poured forth with little inhibition. Part of their involvement seemed to be related to a personal interest in finding out their own motives for gang action. The two boys permitted me to tape-record most of our discussions, and I accumulated about fifteen hours of tape. They were permitted to hear, and seemed to enjoy, a playback of our discussions at the end of several sessions.

The many emotion-laden perceptions of the 'gang war' puzzled me. The newspaper reports, my memo on it, the police report – all conflicted somewhat with one another. It gradually became clear that the Balkans, prior to the rumble, had only a limited degree of organization. Perhaps the most 'accurate' report was made by the gang boys 'on the scene':

DUKE: One reason we got together is that a group of guys around 122nd Street used to play most every day – and Scorpions come down and the Villains would come down and steal money from them, steal watches, rings, they'd go walking up and say how much money have you got to the kid and take all the money he had and if he said anything back, he'd have his head handed to him. And these kids came down to 115th Street one day and that's how they knew us, they'd known us for about three weeks and they were being chased by the Scorpions again. When the Scorpions tried to pull that on our block and we told them to stay off. And then it was about a day after that they decided to go see these kids getting robbed on their own block, so we told the Scorpions to cut out.

They threatened to fight one day when we came up there – about eight of us came up there and met with a group of guys on that block. They never came around from that day on, they stayed away, but that's one of the main reasons – they never went after big guys. They'd go after small guys, robbed them, take a bike – they catch them riding around their blocks to grab a bike and steal money or break into a house or something and blame it on the kids in our neighbourhood. In that way the kids would get the blame. They didn't care or anything. They had nothing to lose.

At this time the Balkans were merely a scattered collection of youths involved in petty individual deliquencies. But they were becoming increasingly unhappy about the invasions:

PEDRO: We were really getting pissed off – these guys, Blackie and them, coming down pulling all this stuff. If I had a gun I'd have shot them all.

The boys revealed some preliminary efforts at retaliation prior to the mass rumble of 10 July:

DUKE: When Mike got beat up – he was the most popular guy on the block. Three guys went up there to Villains' territory about ten o'clock at night to find some Villains and get even for it. Three of us met – we were just going to beat the hell out of this guy Blackie for what he had done to this friend of ours and teach him a lesson. We figured that when fifteen guys jump one guy for a quarter that was pretty bad and we were going to get even for it so we went up. We didn't find any Villains or we didn't find any Scorpions, well, we figured let it lay and came back. We walked up – we weren't scared – just mad. We felt like if we saw a Villain or a Scorpion we weren't going to give them any fair one, the three of us were going to jump him. We just talked about how we hoped to hell we could find a Villain or a Scorpion or any of their friends – we'd teach them a lesson once and for all to leave us alone.

We figured this was going too far, that the guys couldn't walk on their own blocks without being jumped. . . . We only knew this one guy – Blackie was one guy who had beaten up Mike. We wanted to just put him in the hospital.

With all of the invasion threats and counterthreats in the air, Duke was going through some personal traumas that further charged the atmosphere. He talked about his 'emotional condition' before the battle:

DUKE: They [Villains] always came down to steal money – they never let anyone alone – they always picked on small kids. They always liked to beat them up. They always threatened people, especially if they had a family they always come out and go after them and I've been beaten up and robbed twice by them for no reason; my friends have been beaten up. . . . No, I wouldn't have fought them if my grandfather hadn't died. I used to talk to him about the situation all the time. He always used to advise me and keep me cool-minded and tell me what the right thing to do was and he never got excited. Then, when he died, you know, I sort of went to pieces and I figured that I just had to get even for something. That was too much. I had nobody to turn to then. I couldn't talk to my father, so that's when I decided that the Villains would have to pay for what they done.

In his dilemma Duke seemed to feel that his problems

could be solved in an all-out gang war to 'teach everyone a lesson once and for all.' As the build-up to a mass rumble developed, Duke and his boys attempted to line up 'brother gangs' as allies for defence. According to Duke they sent word out to the so-called Harlem Syndicate for help against the Villains. The Syndicate was presumably an alliance of all gangs in the central Harlem area. According to Duke, he had a contact with a member of the Syndicate who was going to help out:

We called up this guy Tate, and the Harlem Syndicate showed up. Two days before the fight we met all the guys from the Syndicate in my basement – all of the Presidents. We could take on the police department. So we wanted to get the Villains and they would help out.

They sent word up to the Syndicate that there was going to be a fight with the Villains. Since the Balkans are very friendly with the El Quintos, all the Harlem Syndicate and their brother teams came around. They came down from 85th Street up to 156th Street. There were teams coming from the Bronx, Brooklyn and Queens. [What were the names of the teams in the Syndicate?] Diablos, Corona Dukes, Young Lads, Fordham Baldies, Fordham Eagles, Centurians, Golden Guineas, Seminoles, Young Sinners, Dragons, Navahos, Young Bishops, Tiny Tims, Englishmen, English Morocco's, Copians, Turks. Some showed up, but not all.

L.Y.: So then you had all of these other gangs to help – how many did you figure you had in all these groups that you could count on?

DUKE: We never bothered figuring it out – we didn't know how many we would need – we didn't know how many we had ourselves. The day the troops caught us there were lots more than they thought there were.

L.Y.: How many guys were there that day?

DUKE: About five thousand.

PEDRO: In the neighbourhood there were about a thousand, but they said there were other guys coming up.

L.Y.: How many guys did you actually see?

DUKE: I saw the guys that came across the street that I got picked up with. That's all I saw – fifteen or twenty guys.

PEDRO: I went to Palisades Park because I figured plenty were

coming up and I didn't want to get in trouble. I'm on probation now; I would say there were guys from 72nd Street to
150th Street.

DUKE: From Westchester.

L.Y.: Sounds like an invasion by the Martians, but how many
guys did you actually see?

DUKE: I didn't see them all. But after I got out of jail every
time I saw a guy, he said he was there ready to fight. I would
say about five thousand.

L.Y.: You figured there might have been five thousand? But
there were only thirty guys picked up.

DUKE: That's right.

PEDRO: I saw plenty of guys when I came back from Palisades
Park. I heard about the fight and I went to Palisades Park
because I didn't want to get picked up. You know, I'm in
trouble now – When I came back, I see many guys running
from the park, about ten o'clock – there were about a hundred
guys running down the street. I stopped one of them and
asked them what had happened. They said the cops were
crawling all around Grant's Tomb. They threw guns and
everything away.

DUKE: That's right, guns, knives, everything.

Duke gave the following account of his actions the night
of the rumble:

L.Y.: Duke, how would you describe the fight that night? This
is for my information only. What happened from your point
of view?

DUKE: I came out around six. I didn't think anything was going
to come off, but the guys [the Syndicate] told me that they
were gonna be around and I said yeah, sure [*unbelievingly*].

L.Y.: You weren't expecting them?

DUKE: It seemed kinda impossible for two guys to come from
the Syndicate and say that they were going to show up. They
said they were going to bring their men over and they sure did.

L.Y.: How did you know the Villains [the enemy] were going
to show up?

DUKE: Blackie, the Villain Captain told us they were gonna
come down and fight. He called it 'on'.

L.Y.: At what time?

DUKE: Eight o'clock. I wasn't sure whether it was coming off
or not. I was told by guys in the Syndicate that they were

going to come up and it was gonna be about six o'clock, and when they didn't show up yet I figured, oh, the hell with it. I told everybody to stay home. I was going to go to the movies.

L.Y.: You were the president – right? And you didn't know what was going to happen?

DUKE: That's right – up until the last minute when I saw these guys coming across the street about seven o'clock.

L.Y.: What guys?

DUKE: I saw the Politicians and the Tims from the Syndicate coming across the street.

L.Y.: How many?

DUKE: The guys that got picked up – about fifteen. Then I saw a lot of police around there and I figured the cops were down. Then I went upstairs to eat for about fifteen minutes and came back down again. Then the cops were grabbing all these coloured guys [from the Syndicate] and searching them.

PEDRO: But they had already thrown everything they had in the hallway – bayonets, guns, and everything.

DUKE: We seen the Politicians walking down the street – no packages, no nothing. We saw the police search them and they were clean and when we got down the block I walked away from them and then those cops came running over and start to search them all again. And then I crossed the street and the minute I crossed the street the cops picked me up.
. . .

L.Y.: Did the cop ask you whether you were president or belonged to the club?

DUKE: He just took me in. I didn't tell them a thing. They asked me if I was a member and I said no.

L.Y.: So then, all you guys got busted [arrested].

DUKE: They took me to the Tombs [jail].

The organization of the Balkans prior to the Villain-Scorpion rumble, and the reason we knew so little about them prior to this event, are here revealed by Duke:

L.Y.: What happened at the police station?

DUKE: Oh, they asked us lots of questions and lined us up and all that. Asking us our names.

L.Y.: Did you give your right name?

DUKE: Yeah, but no gang name.

L.Y.: Why not?

DUKE: Oh, we give 'em a name, but not at first. See, we didn't have a name then. No names, just guys we knew. No leaders, no nothing.

L.Y.: Well, when did you get your name . . . it was in the paper all right?

DUKE: You mean when the name started? . . . It was when the guys got picked up by the police, until that time there was no name.

L.Y.: You mean on 10 June when you got picked up?

DUKE: Yes, that's right. Up until that time there was about ten different names the guys were trying to start. That was when the name started.

L.Y.: What were they?

DUKE: Espionage, Four Aces, American something-or-other – what's all the others? All I know is Aces and Balkans. Yeah, Aces and Balkans.

L.Y.: You mean that's how the name started?

DUKE: Yeah, it was in the police station.

L.Y.: You told the cops Balkans?

DUKE: No, not me. I think it was Jay; he kept saying, 'Call us Balkans, call us Balkans.' He liked the name. At that time we didn't even have one. At that time it wasn't even a club; it didn't have any leaders. We were in the middle of naming leaders.

Later interviews with 'Jay' revealed that he thought of the Balkans' name because at the time he was studying the history of the Balkan States in school. He claimed, in his own fashion, that their gang was in an embattled military position similar to that of the European Balkan States at a particular time in history, 'locked in by enemies'.

The gang now had its leaders and its allies. They were on record with the police, the courts, and they even had a social agency attempting to work with them. They also had some clear-cut enemies to the north – with whom they were still in conflict over territorial rights. The Balkans were now a full-fledged bopping gang.

The Balkans Expand and Attack

Duke and his boys were now in the spotlight. Not only did they have recognition as a bopping gang – adversary to the Villains – but they also had been 'acclaimed' in the press. This notoriety was a source of pride, and most of the boys carried wrinkled and torn news clips of their press notices.

Notoriety also seemed to have an effect on gang size. According to Duke:

We mushroomed mainly because of the publicity we got in June and well, that was it, mainly – the publicity got Jerry and his friends and then guys all over the city started to join up. Up until that time in June there had been thirty-eight at the very most and only about fifteen were actually on the team itself.

This was a period during which I attempted to learn as much as I could about Duke, Nicky, Pedro, and Balkan gang organization. The boys joined in with my efforts. In part their co-operation was related to the fact that having an agency concerned and working with a gang seemed to give it rep in gang circles. As a gang leader once told me: 'Having a worker makes you a real "down" club. All "bad" clubs have a "man" trying to change them.'

Now that I was accepted, Duke and Pedro were responsive to any and all questions about Balkan organization. They were in my office daily, and I toured the streets with them on foot and, more to their liking, in my car. Though the boys knew I was opposed to their assaults, rumbles, and thefts, during this period I felt that information about their natural activities flowed more easily if I was not restrictive.

Apparently the conflict with the uptown groups was still simmering. In part because the police and our agency were watching the situation closely, a mass all-out rumble between the factions didn't seem feasible. However, less dramatic gang violence continued.

DUKE: I was standing on the block when about five or six of them [Villains] came down and I saw them beat up a few Balkans. All of them had guns – I didn't. As I was walking away, one of them came over and took a swing at me. So I got mad and told Animal [a Villain] I would meet him at one o'clock that day. I told him I'd meet him, just him and I –

no gang or anything else – just he and myself at one o'clock at Grant's Tomb. He agreed to it.

I found out that he was coming down with Chino, president of the Uptown Villains-Dragons and ten or twelve other guys. I run into about six Balkans and they told me that they would come up with me. As we were going up I picked up about seven or eight more Balkans just to be on the safe side.

We went up to Grant's Tomb and nobody was there. As we started to leave we ran into about twenty or thirty Villains and Scorpions. It was decided that I and two of the boys would fight against Chino, Animal, and this boy Lefty. The others would be peaceful.

So we went up to 132nd Street under the viaduct to fight it out and that's when we found more Villains waiting for us and Lefty pulled a gun and told us that Marcus – the boy Chino was fighting – either lost or he would be killed. And the boy I fought, either he won or this other guy would be killed. So naturally, all three of us lost.

This type of somewhat confused conflict was almost a daily occurrence for the Balkans during this period. These situations revealed the Balkans were no longer simply responding to Villains and Scorpions attack; they were on the offensive. The Balkans engaged in what gangs called 'Japs'. These were quick sneak attacks on another gang – with a prompt withdrawal from their territory.

Duke described the various levels of gang war to me one day as follows:

One is when we go on a 'stomp'. That's when three or four guys will jump one, for no reason at all. . . . They go down and grab a guy for any reason at all. They'll sometimes beat up a guy on their own team – it doesn't make any difference – they just want to stomp someone.

Second kind is a 'Jap'. That's when a group of guys, two guys or three guys, go down to a different club's territory, get in fast, beat up one or two guys and get out. The thing is not to get caught. They can do that with fists or they go in sometimes with guns, knives, depends on the group they're fighting.

Third is a 'bop'. That can be a small group, five, ten, twenty guys from one team, having it out with the same number from a different team. It doesn't make any difference; it doesn't mean that those two teams are actually at war with each other, it's just that, well, it's just one of the clashes.

The *fourth* is a 'rumble'. That's when both clubs are getting everybody they can – brother gangs and all – to go out and fight. It's an all-out gang war. . . .

Guys sometimes say when they're gonna rumble, that they'll give you a *fair one*; that's when one guy from one team will meet another guy from another, and it's supposed to be just between those two groups. Just two guys, nobody else is supposed to butt in.

At times when Duke and his boys described various angles of their gang organization to me, I had the uneasy feeling that I was inadvertently helping them to make more explicit a pattern that originally did not have much definition. Yet Duke, as leader, carried the gang image agreed upon by the gang. This was Duke's view of Balkan gang-war operation as he wrote it out for me:

Pedro is a lieutenant, Nicky is another officer, Jay is war counsellor. When a fight starts with another club, the war counsellor sets a date and place for fighting. It's also up to the war counsellor to decide with the President whether or not the group fights. If you have a crazy counsellor you're always fighting.

Once the fight starts the Captain takes over. This is what the Captain does: (1) The Captain takes half of the group and the Co-captain takes the other half of the group. (2) The Captain sees the other gang to decide whether to use weapons or not. (3) The Captain and the Co-captain may fight the Captain and Co-captain of the other gang in a fair one to stop a large gang war. (4) They [Captain and Co-captain] get weapons for gang war. (5) A Captain or the Co-captain may assign five guys to go beat up a member of the other gang. This is called a 'Jap'. A Jap is a small raid. A Jap is where you hit the other team before they hit you first. Hit first and get out is pulling a Jap. When the Captain tells a member he's out, then he's out of the club – just because the Captain says he's out. Whoever the Captain tells you to fight, you have to. The Co-captain also has the right to tell a guy he's out and can only be changed by the Captain. The Captain and the Co-captain started the club. Whatever the Captain tells you to do as a member, you do it.

When I toured the neighbourhood with Duke and Pedro, it was interesting to note the respect they received from apparent members of the Balkans. There was an element of appreciation reflected in the comments of some younger Balkans:

He [Duke] helped us. Those bastards [Villains-Scorpions] were always coming down and working us over, now things are better – not so much trouble. We got protection.

Other Balkans responded to my question 'Why did you join?' in the following ways:

JOHNNY: Well, I wanted a social club and then to protect ourselves against the bopping gangs that come around and stomped a couple of boys like what's-his-name said before around 122nd – they'd come around in a big bunch and they'd take on a couple of the boys and beat 'em up so we got kind of tired of that after a while. Duke used to come around to see Pedro, and so Duke started the gang and he asked me to join and I said I'd join, why not?

RED: The reason I joined – Duke told me to. Before the Balkans started, the Scorpions and all them guys come down and used to knock us all over the street, so finally we organized to protect ourselves and keep them off our territory – Duke can fight real good and he helps us.

'KING FAROUK': We all used to be on 122nd, playing cards and they come mess us up. One day we were waiting for 'em – we figured they'd come around so, we got on the roofs with ash cans and all that sort of stuff – so then they did come around, you know, we had this rumble and they split. So the next day they came up they had to deal with Duke. He helped us out. Then we all got together and started hanging down on La Salle Street and then Jesús Ramírez, you know, Jay thought up this name, you know, got it out of the history books, Balkans.

Duke's reputation grew and extended beyond the Morningside Heights neighbourhood. He talked repeatedly about organized alliances or affiliations with brother gangs, especially the Harlem Syndicate. The exact nature of these alliances seemed hard to evaluate.

One afternoon I was invited to accompany Duke to central Harlem where he was to have a meeting with some brother-gang members reputed to be in the Harlem Syndicate. We met two fairly tough-looking Negro youths on the corner of 114th Street and Lenox Avenue. One appeared to be about eighteen, the other sixteen. They both spoke very 'hip', and greeted Duke: 'Hello, Duke daddy – what's shakin'? Who's this cat?'

Duke introduced me as a friend who was writing a book on gangs. He assured them that I was OK, that I helped some of his 'people get out of trouble, jobs, and like that'. He told them that they didn't have to worry about me: 'No cop or nothing like that'. The other boys seemed to accept me on Duke's recommendation – somewhat more so when I offered to buy coffee.

We went to a coffee shop on Lenox and 114th Street. Duke reassured them that they could talk freely in front of me, and they launched into an elaborate discussion of gang activities. My presence, rather than inhibiting them, seemed to *expand* their discussion as I felt they were observing my reaction.

At first Duke thanked them for coming through with help against the Villains. (This apparently developed because one of the Balkans had a cousin in the Harlem Syndicate.) Turk, the older boy, responded coolly:

We don't like to see our friends messed up – so when we can help, our boys are ready to move when trouble starts. Jay is a good man – so like – your click is in. We don't fuck around – man, when you want to whip one on, just call. . . . Our boys are always ready.

Duke assured Turk that the feeling was mutual:

We now have about a thousand people because the downtown Saxons have come in with us and we have a few more divisions around the Polo Grounds in the Bronx. Then we have some more people in Queens. 'Cause you know Pedro? Well, his cousin is leader of the El Quintos in Queens and they have about a thousand right there. [Duke glanced at me and seemed to slow down somewhat.] Of course, we're just defensive now – but if the Villains and Scorpions want to turn one on, we're ready. Also, if we can help you guys, we're ready.

The boys listened intently to Duke's grandiose soliloquy; then the other brother-gang leader, called Lucky, launched into a description of his troops, which in total exceeded Duke's estimate of alliance by over 3,000:

Look, man, we're peaceful, but if they want war we'll turn it on. We got a hundred clubs in the Syndicate and maybe five thousand guys. We'll just whip it on and wipe them all out good. So you tell Blackie and all those uptown mother-fuckers the Syndicate's with you, and that's it.

Duke, Turk, and Lucky went on in this vein for about a half-hour. The alliances and size built to seemingly incredible proportions. Each supported the other's gang size and seemed to get satisfaction and security from hearing all about the powerful alliance which had apparently been further cemented by this conference. In the middle of their discussion my presence was apparently forgotten, as the boys intently elaborated their strength and power. I reminded Duke of an appointment I had, and after a short private huddle with Turk and Lucky we parted with them.

On the drive back to Morningside Heights, Duke was in a highly elated, almost hysterical, state. He kept up a steady stream of description elaborating his now reinforced grand alliance with 'the Syndicate'. Peace was his theme, but war would come for defence: 'We're peaceful; we're a social club, but if they want war – we'll really turn it on. Syndicate, brother clubs – we'll wipe them out, once and for all.'

At this point in my relationship with Duke and the Balkans, I was convinced of several things. Duke was a young man of many moods. He could sincerely be friendly with me, help me to understand the Balkans, and perhaps even assist in 'keeping them out of trouble'. He was also equally capable of violent episodes that could produce a gang war with homicidal results. His own potential for committing extreme violence was evidenced by the nature of his involvement in several bloody Japs.

Duke was also something less than a well-adjusted, tough gang leader. His delusions of gang-leader power, alliances for defence, and fears of being attacked by invading clubs apparently had some pathological elements. Despite this, or perhaps because of this, Duke was widely accepted by the Balkans and the Harlem Syndicate as a tough, powerful gang leader, with many others supporting his image in the world around him. There was also clear evidence that a major violent-gang battle with the uptown gangs was still brewing, and we began to work to avert it.

4. The Search for Peace

Baseball and a Jump

'Redirect the gang from destructive to constructive activities' was the prevalent approach of the time. Under this theme New York City spent millions of dollars each year. If we could change the Balkans' activities from bopping to baseball, we might be providing some constructive activities.

Duke and Pedro were, at least on the surface, cast in the role of my helpmates in moving the Balkans into peacetime activities. After six meetings attended by about twenty Balkans in my office, there was agreement about the activities in which they would like to participate. Baseball and throwing a 'jump' (dance) at Columbia were major preferences. Both activities interested the boys in part because they now knew Columbia and the other institutions were in back of our project.

NICKY: We always walk by and see the students. [*Laughs.*] Sometimes we jump them. Then there's all those big walls and the guards chase us and everything. Now you guys gonna let us throw a jump there?

The thoughts of running a dance within the hallowed walls of Columbia University and playing baseball at Columbia's Baker Field were tantalizing to the Balkans. I had no concrete way of knowing whether their ranks grew as a result of these two possibilities; however, I did observe that Pedro and Duke seemed to gain in prestige from their relationship with me and, indirectly, with the institutions on the Heights.

Duke commented on this at one point:

DUKE: If there were any trouble, we could come down and help out.
L.Y.: And that was the main thing that they would belong for?

DUKE: That's right.

L.Y.: Then you had about two hundred guys – how long was this after the [June] fight?

DUKE: About two weeks – no, it was about a month after.

L.Y.: Then what happened?

DUKE: Then we had the dance – that's when a lot of guys joined up. When you got in touch with us. They figured that if they joined up with us they could get sports, dancing – a lot of them joined up to get in baseball and to get into the dance.

The first call for baseball practice brought out about twenty youths, most of whom had been involved in the June gang war. The experiment seemed to flourish. Twice a week the boys would meet on the corner and we would drive them up to the field we had secured for baseball practice. On the way the main conversation revolved around the June gang-war incident and impending problems with the Villains. The boys would generally 'throw their weight around' and brag about Balkan strength. They were impressed with the new recognition they received, not only from the press but also from our organization's interest in them. The discussions further revealed that our project's affiliation with Columbia University and their use of Columbia's Baker Field for baseball gave the Balkans a new-found prestige in the neighbourhood. One reaction to this was expressed by another gang in the area, which felt neglected: 'What do we have to do to get some attention from you guys – go out and kill somebody?'

A partial result of the Balkan baseball project was its shifting effect on gang leadership. Two somewhat marginal gang members, Cisco and Ríos, developed leadership positions because of their baseball skill. Duke and Pedro were poor baseball players and lost prestige – at least in the gang's baseball activity. Duke was an impossible first baseman. He dropped or missed almost every ball thrown to him. Although none of the boys openly said that he should not play on the team, there was a lot of mumbling: 'He'll really screw us up in a game' was the consensus. Pedro also was a failure at baseball. For a short time he became a scorekeeper, but this didn't last long. Although the two boys lost prestige at the ball field, they maintained control of corner activity and gang-war manoeuvring.

About this time Duke and Pedro became more aggressive and beat up several gang members – no doubt to let them know they were still boss. Duke developed a 'shoulder injury' that did not permit him to play ball any more. Pedro openly stopped playing and became (under my guidance) a team manager.

The baseball project lasted about a month and affected the gang in several ways. One important change was a greater (less suspicious) acceptance of our agency. This took the form of almost complete freedom in discussing many things going on in the gang at the time. Another effect of the baseball project was the indicated change of leadership. Finally, the membership of the Balkans seemed to increase.

During the early weeks of the baseball project, a number of the boys who participated at first and were poor baseball players dropped out, while a number of 'baseball players' who lived in the neighbourhood joined the gang. The Balkans as a violent gang continued to hang out together with substantially the same organization.

Our attempt to direct the gang's energies into constructive channels such as baseball did not seem significantly to change the Balkans and their violent pattern. We found that working with them in an attempt to get them to play baseball resulted mainly in bringing some additional 'baseball players' into the gang. The more recalcitrant gang members remained in the back hall, playing cards, or at the old hangouts on the corner.

One night after practice I went home feeling that our efforts with the Balkans on the baseball project seemed merely to solidify and integrate a gang that might otherwise have disbanded. I was not convinced that our moving the Balkans together into baseball or attempting to get them into other constructive activities was the correct approach; but we already had made the move and could not easily shift our commitment to the boys. As one boy said: 'When we met you and we could throw jumps [dances] and play ball, a lot more guys started to join up with the Balkans.'

The Jump

The dance was a major conversation piece for the boys. There were about eight planning sessions, which dealt with such issues as: 'How much should we charge each member?' 'Should we let anyone come who isn't a Balkan?' 'Why should there be cops around?'

Nicky moved into the foreground as a planner of the dance, and Duke seemed to be on the sidelines. This was apparently because Nicky was more of a ladies' man. He had a girl friend and knew how to dance. Nicky was most efficient, and organized the collection of money, bought soft drinks, brought the records, and decorated the hall.

The dance took place in one of Columbia's main dining rooms, which the boys had neatly decorated with streamers. The dance revealed for the first time a contingent of girls from the neighbourhood – a sort of female auxiliary. Although the boys referred to them as Balkan Debs, they appeared to be simply girls who knew some of the Balkans and came to the dance. There were about thirty girls and forty boys present.

There was nothing unusual about the gathering except the fact that all of the boys and girls were tremendously impressed with being at a dance at Columbia University. There was the usual amount of tough-guy behaviour on the part of the boys who were most uncomfortable and could not dance. Duke and Pedro were leaders of this contingent, but since they were big shots in the overall operation they contained themselves reasonably well.

There were rumours that the Villains were coming down 'to bust up the jump'. Duke, Pedro, and several others bragged about what they would do if Blackie, Sonny, or any of the other uptown clubs put their heads in the door.

The main dance was the 'fish'. In its extreme form the couples did not move their feet at all, but merely stood in the same spot and undulated to the rock 'n' roll music.

There was a major controversy with me and other 'chaperons' about how much light would be permitted. If left to the boys (and girls), the lights would all be out.

The majority of youths at the dance considered themselves junior-division Balkans, and consisted of about thirty boys. The seniors, including Duke and Pedro, totalled about ten. There was some measure of disappointment at this, since the boys had expected about fifty seniors. According to Pedro:

Man, if all the seniors showed up, this joint would be loaded. There are at least one hundred around here alone – and then in our brother gang you maybe have at least five hundred. They're probably busy tonight, but Jerry [a senior leader] should show up.

Two 'senior Balkans' showed up briefly and were introduced to me. They were Puerto Rican youths in their early twenties. Introduced by Duke and Pedro, they entered as if they were visiting generals inspecting the troops. 'Cool' and aloof, they shook hands with me, acknowledged the greetings of several of the boys whom they apparently knew, had cokes, and then left. I never saw them again at any Balkan meeting or at any other time.

Jerry, the Balkan leader Pedro had referred to, never showed up at the dance. He was considered by Duke, Pedro, and Nicky as one of the major leaders of the senior division. He would come up regularly in Balkan conversation whenever a gang battle was being planned or discussed. At the dance they commented that if the Villains or Scorpions showed they would call Jerry, 'and he'll come "down" hard with the seniors'.

The dance and talk ran at a high pitch until about twelve, when the building had to close. All – even the 'antifemale' gang members – seemed to enjoy themselves. About ten boys, headed by Nicky, stayed behind to clean up. Everyone seemed to agree with Nicky's comment: 'Man, it was a great jump.'

I walked Duke part of the way home. He seemed pleased that the boys had enjoyed themselves, and he felt

the dance was a success, but mainly the dance to him was
a show of strength:

> A lot of guys showed, but if the seniors weren't busy tonight,
> you would have really seen the Balkans. They wouldn't all fit
> in that one place. . . . Anyway, you met a couple of seniors,
> Ramon and Johnny. It's a good thing the Villains didn't show
> up – we would have stomped them good.

Despite the success of the dance it was apparent that the
major preoccupation of Duke and the Balkans was with
gang wars and Balkan enemies, especially the Villains.

Profile of the Villains

The Villains became known to our agency about three
months prior to the June gang war with the Balkans. Although the Balkans at that time did not report on the
Villains' assaults and extortion tactics, we heard about
them through other sources. Several boys, sons of Columbia faculty, were referred to me as a result of a robbery in
Riverside Park. One victim gave me the following account
of the event:

> We had just finished throwing a ball around down in River-
> side Park when these three fellows came up to us. There were
> about four of us, and we probably could have protected our-
> selves, but this one they called Blackie grabbed the baseball
> bat out of my hand and began laughing about how he would
> crack a few heads if we didn't co-operate. He looked like he
> meant what he said.
>
> We looked to run, but they had Jim cornered and we didn't
> want to leave him. They made us sit on the bench and empty
> our pockets. We didn't have more than $2 or $4 on us altogether,
> but they took it. Another one they called Frenchie pulled out
> a switchblade knife and kept waving it around our faces,
> laughing all the time. He really seemed crazy – he just kept
> laughing and acted as if he was enjoying himself.
>
> Finally, for no reason, they threw our gloves over the wall
> into the park, punched me in the face, and then they left. The
> other one didn't do much – he was quiet. But this Blackie and
> Frenchie really gave me the creeps.

The victim's description did not at that time seem to fit any of the some three hundred boys participating in our recreation leagues, so I checked with Sam, a volunteer citizen worker who co-operated with our agency. Sam had grown up in the neighbourhood and knew most of the problem boys well. He would make contact with the more difficult youths and attempt to provide constructive activities for them through our agency and a local community centre. We would co-operate fully with him by providing activities and some funds for his useful work.

When I mentioned the extortion incident to Sam, he smiled knowingly. The next afternoon he brought about six very wild, 'hip', and tough-looking characters into my office. After Sam introduced us, there was some initial banter back and forth about gangs and general problems in the neighbourhood. The boys, in typical fashion, began to try to find out more about the agency and me. In line with my general policy, I told them anything they wanted to know, very directly. After some talk about our agency, I commented about my role:

L.Y.: The institutions want to help guys in the neighbourhood like you keep out of trouble. Understand? We try to provide activities, like baseball, basketball, swimming, weight lifting, and other things for neighbourhood guys.

BLACKIE: Yeah, I know about the ball league and all that stuff. What's this weight-lifting bit?

I went on to explain the weight-lifting programme we had been operating in the basement of our building. (I did this in part for my own benefit to keep in shape, and I found it was a good gimmick for getting acquainted with tougher youths informally.) I attempted to involve Blackie and his 'men'.

L.Y.: You guys look pretty strong. Did you ever lift weights?

BLACKIE: Oh, man, who's got time for that bullshit. You can be strong without muscles. A 'piece' [gun] makes you the strongest man around.

After some interchange along these lines, Blackie gave the OK and the boys joined me for a weight-lifting session in the basement that afternoon. At first they wrestled around and joked about it, but the concrete act of lifting a particular heavy weight (about 110 pounds) was challenging. Despite his 'skinny' appearance, Blackie discovered he could lift as much weight as anyone else. This sold the project.

About eight Villains then began to participate regularly in the weight-lifting programme about three times a week. We developed achievement charts, and they took to it seriously, although at times they would practically kill one another by joking and pushing when a boy had hoisted up a fair amount of weight. Since I could lift more than any of the boys, they would usually co-operate with my requests to 'knock it off' when they became too wild.

About a month after I knew the boys I mentioned the assault and the extortion situation to Blackie and Frenchie, who regularly attended the session. They smiled slyly, and Blackie commented: 'Oh, man, I don't even know any punks like that. What are you gonna be, a cop about it?'

His remark placed me in a difficult spot and I found myself hedging: 'I'm not going to do anything about it. Just tell me if it's true that you were the guys.'

Blackie and Frenchie then launched into describing the incident in great detail, laughing and joking about the victims' response:

FRENCHIE: They were scared shitless. I just waved my blade in his face – telling him I was gonna shove it up his nose. [*Laughs.*] I felt like throwing the punks over the wall.
BLACKIE: We just needed some bread [money]. You know how it is?

We talked about it for about an hour, but I made no particular dent in their rationale for the extortion: 'Man, we just needed some bread.' I decided to drop the issue, at least for the time being, since I did not want to break off my fairly good relationship with these boys. (My role conflict as an upholder of law and looking the other way on some illegal gang activity was a continuing problem in my work. I never adequately resolved the dilemma.)

During the process of our weight-lifting project, I became fairly well acquainted with both Blackie and Frenchie – at least on the surface. Blackie was clearly the Villain leader. He was a 'hip' eighteen-year-old, who was a model member of the gang, looked up to by most of the boys. He always used jive talk and wise sayings, with his shoulders flexing as he looked at you sideways with a little smile that seemed to indicate he knew something you did not. According to later reports of many Balkans and other victims, Blackie was one of the important leaders of uptown violence. He was quite wild and given to 'sudden outbursts' of violence. In addition to having the boys' respect for his violent abilities, Blackie was 'well liked' by the Villains for other reasons. One day I had Sam record his views on why Blackie was the Villain leader:

When the average gang starts out, they have a leader based on their own characteristics. The guy who talks the most and is most impressive in his speech, the guy they can 'respect' or look up to. In other words, in Blackie as a leader – here is a guy who had a 'bad' way of talking, he was older than the other guys – even though he wasn't as strong and as powerful physically as the others.

Blackie was quite a ladies' man. To these boys who were 'afraid' of girls this was a big deal. He would go out and get women for himself, or at least he would talk about it as if he had. The average kid looks up to a conquest, whether it's physical or anything; that is, a guy beating up another guy or a guy making out with a girl, or a guy stealing money. These things would make the fellow a leader in their eyes. In other words, he was doing or seemed to be doing all the things they wanted to do and couldn't. Blackie didn't do well in school. Before he left town he was pushing and using marihuana quite a bit.

One of the things about the gang was an attempt to make a name for themselves, and they could do this through Blackie. Blackie had a strong need to be a leader, and the Villains and Scorpions wanted him to be their 'leader'.

The other uptown leader in the weight-lifting project, Frenchie, was the Hollywood version of a stereotyped laughing psychopath. He seemed happiest when someone else was suffering. One day on the way up the concrete steps to my office, one of the boys running up the stairs fell, hitting his arm so that it bled profusely. When we picked him up, he appeared to be all right except for some scrapes and the bleeding. I never saw Frenchie happier or laughing harder than when the boy was injured.

Frenchie was also a 'shoulder flexer'. He was usually punching or wrestling with someone and had a pattern of rolling around on top of the smaller boys as he beat them up. Frenchie's favourite and repeated pattern was to point to another boy (any other boy), and comment, 'That faggot eats it.'[1]

Despite our seemingly close relationship in the weight-lifting project, I had no advance notice on the Villain–Balkan June rumble from Blackie, Frenchie, Sonny, or the other Villains whom I saw several times a week. I knew that they had some assaultive incidents with local youths, but my impression was that it was nothing more than the routine battles characteristic of these groups.

For about two weeks after the June rumble the Villains did not show up for the weight-lifting session. They re-appeared on the third week as if nothing had happened. I did not press them. One afternoon we discussed the situation, and Blackie said: 'Oh, we used to knock them around a little, that's all. Then all of a sudden they're big gang men. When that punk, Duke, called it on, we laughed and thought he was crazy. But they did get the Syndicate. As soon as things cool, we're gonna whip it on 'em. We'll get all of those punks – but good.'

The Peace Treaty

At this time, about a month after the June rumble, the

1. One evening about two years after I had lost contact with the Villains, when getting off the subway at 125th Street and Broadway, I heard a shrill feminine voice calling my name. I turned around to find that a very 'swishy' homosexual was the one calling to me. At first I didn't recognize Frenchie, but, sure enough, there he was, attired very fashionably with marcelled hair. The transformation from the tough hood I had known was startling. I talked with him briefly, to find he had become a Forty-second Street homosexual prostitute.

police were still 'down' on all gangs in the area. They would stop and search all boys for weapons. Boys who came in from outside the Twenty-fourth precinct (the dividing line was 125th Street and Morningside Park) were given special attention by the police. In order for Blackie and his boys to get to my office for the weight-lifting (when Sam didn't drive them), I produced a 'letter of passage'. (A similar letter was also carried by Balkans at the time.) The letter cleared the boys with police in the area. On Morningside Heights, Inc., stationery, and addressed 'To Whom It May Concern', it stated:

> [Boy's name] is on his way to my office. These boys are now organized as a social club and we are having a meeting this evening to discuss athletic and social activities. If there is any problem call [phone number].

The letter gave the boys safe police passage through the neighbourhood. If a clique of gang youths without this 'visa' appeared, the police would 'send them home'.

The neighbourhood continued in a state of siege, with daily violence, threats, hostility, Japs, and assaults between the uptown gangs and the Balkans. The essential factor that seemed to hold off another all-out gang-war attempt was the fact that some gang members were still under probation investigation from the June rumble. Baseball, weight lifting, and other activities may have had some impact on keeping the Balkans and Villains in check, but during this period the theme remained one expressed by Nicky: 'We're still gonna have it out with those bastards, especially if any of our boys get sent away. We're just waiting until the trials end and then we're gonna have it out with them once and for all.'

In addition to my discussions at the weight-lifting sessions with the uptown leaders, with this new rumble brewing, I made frequent excursions into Villain territory to explore the potential of another major gang war with the Balkans. From most of their comments I had good reason to assume that they, too, were still seriously considering having it out with the Balkans 'once and for all'.

Another mass rumble seemed imminent, and my continuing efforts at talking the boys out of it by logic did not seem to be effective.

Taking a leaf from the New York Youth Board Manual, I invited the uptown gang's leaders to meet with the Balkans at a peace meeting to arrive at some agreement for preventing another mass rumble. I raised the subject one evening on a drive up the Parkway after a weight-lifting session with Blackie, Sonny, Frenchie, and a boy called Lucky. Their reaction was wild, and they repeatedly joked about 'knocking out the mother-fuckin' punk Balkans once and for all'. Despite this, they expressed some inclination to talk the situation over with the Balkans. Blackie did not believe it would do much good: 'Those bastards need a good working over.' (They never told me why.)

Tension continued high in the neighbourhood, with threats and counterthreats. The emotional reactions seemed to dictate a 'get them before they get us' approach. Each gang's fears seemed to produce more aggressive feelings on the part of the other group. Japs and various assaults became daily events.

Blackie and his 'officers', after much further manoeuvring, finally agreed to meet with the Balkans in my office in an effort 'to work out a peace treaty'. Blackie reflected some scepticism about its success: 'What those punks really need is a few heads cracked.'

At the same time I was negotiating with Blackie for the peace meeting, I was in communication with Duke, who seemed agreeable to the idea. He was more in favour of the meeting, and seemed interested in dealing with the situation peacefully. Duke said: 'We want peace. We can deal with those guys any way they want. But a peace meeting might settle all these problems. We'll be there – only I hope they don't pull anything, 'cause we mean business.'

The meeting was finally scheduled for 7.30 p.m. on a Friday night. Both gangs agreed to send their leaders. About 6.00 p.m. on the night of the peace meeting, I picked up Blackie at Forty-third Street and Third Avenue where he worked as a messenger for a delivery service. ('I gotta work or my P.O. [probation officer] will lock me up.') The first stop, *en route* to my office on the upper West Side, was a candy store where, according to Blackie, his 'lieutenants' were waiting.

On the drive up the jammed East River Drive, Blackie assumed a pose of general lack of concern, although he was obviously nervous about the meeting. He talked primarily about his P.O., the 'geese' (burglary) for which he was on probation, and asked if I could help him get off probation:

BLACKIE: Oh, man, that cat he don't help me none. I mean it wastes my time seeing him. He just says, 'Are you workin'? Keep your nose clean' – all that bullshit. It takes me about an hour to get there and all that – and he just gives me that stuff in two minutes. So maybe you can cut it for me. You know, the geese was nothin', just that market on Broadway.

If I was off probation, I would split this scene and go west – I got relatives there. All this diddley-boppin' bullshit is just a waste, man. . . .

Three leaders of the Villains were waiting in the candy store on Broadway at 137th Street. One was Chino, who claimed to be 'packin''. Another Villain was Ching, an Oriental-appearing Puerto Rican youth whom I had never seen. He seemed ready for action. The other youth in the waiting trio was Sonny. He seemed quieter than the others, and might possibly have been 'turned on' drugs.

We arrived at my office about 7.40 p.m. Chino and Blackie talked wildly and were worked up to a fever pitch for the 'peace meeting'. They seemed to be trying to conceal their fears with brave threats. They all acted the role of tough, violent, and powerful gang leaders.

The Balkans had not yet arrived, and Chino asked for the use of my phone. He called his girl friend: 'Baby, you ought to see me here sitting in this leather chair, like a big shot!' In Spanish he went into details about the big peace negotiation he was about to conclude.

Blackie's mood was a high pitch, considerably different from his quieter tone when we were alone on the drive up-town. 'Where are those mother-fuckin' punks? Let's jump them when they get here.'

By the time the Balkans arrived, the Villains seemed more prepared for a fight than for a peace meeting. Duke arrived for the peace meeting with an older boy named Phil and Pedro. They were obviously nervous.

Chino opened the meeting: 'Come on, you fuckin' punks, we're going to take you out in the park and knock the shit out of you!' Duke rose with a grunt of agreement. I intervened with some success, and the meeting was under way.

The Villains again challenged the Balkans and came close to a battle on the spot. Blackie kept repeating: 'You cats are always talking about getting me. Well, here I am! What are you going to do about it?' Chino's repeated comment was: 'You guys are nothing but a bunch of mother-fuckin' faggots; I think we ought to beat your heads in, have it out right here and now, once and for all.' Ching also threatened, and was prepared for immediate battle. Sonny was the only Villain who sat by quietly and coolly.

The Balkans were less defiant. They had been prepared in advance for this kind of reaction. I had instructed Duke to try to resist reacting aggressively to the expected needling. After about forty-five minutes of the same haranguing, always on the verge of assault, they all agreed to a 'peace treaty'. They requested the following statement, which I typed up in triplicate:

THE PEACE TREATY

24 June 1954

We agree to no more fights and we have a truce.

1.   Uptown boys can come down without being bothered.
2.   If Balkans come up cool, it is OK.

The treaty was signed by all the gang leaders, with Duke and Blackie each receiving a copy. Here, again, there was almost an explosion. One of the agreements was that the

Villains could come down into the Morningside area of Riverside Park if they came down 'cool' (no weapons or assaultive behaviour). The Balkans were permitted similar access to the uptown turf. Duke then said, in a sincere peace gesture, 'We don't care about coming up to your neighbourhood.'

In response to this, the Villains became enraged: 'Oh, you people think you're too good to come up in our neighbourhood, huh. You bastards don't wanna come up in our neighbourhood?' This almost produced another flight.

After this outburst settled down, Chino commented, 'We make a promise, we mean it. So like you guys better watch your step and not break this treaty.' The Balkans agreed they would not break the pact if the uptown clubs co-operated. The 'treaty' did not look too stable; however, it was a recognized agreement.

The group disbanded with the Balkans leaving first. I held on to the Villains for about another fifteen minutes to ensure the Balkans safely getting out of the immediate vicinity. Blackie, Ching, and Sonny were let out of my car at 125th and Broadway. There were several boys waiting, and I heard Blackie's reports. 'We signed a treaty and everything is cool.'

I continued uptown alone with Chino, who was heading for 145th Street near the river. On the drive back with Chino, I felt a small sense of relief. Perhaps they would stick to the bargain and avoid a rumble that might very likely end in a killing. The ride was disquieting as I began to reflect on the depressing situation.

My view on the ride up Broadway, past 125th Street, was a sight of the standard rat-infested broken-down tenements rising on both sides of the filthy elevated subway girders. As we went across 130th Street toward the river, the buildings seemed worse. The desolation of the neighbourhood converged on an old broken-down pier that juts out into the river. In summer the boys in 'Dead End' fashion swam off this pier in the filthy water below. My reaction that night was a strange revulsion and feeling of hopelessness about the boys, the neighbourhood, and the caricature of summitry – the foolish peace meeting with all its hysteria. I felt like a grown-up fool.

In contrast, Chino seemed elated. He kept up a constant chatter: 'I love this fuckin' neighbourhood. . . . These are my people. . . . Any fuckers try to take our turf, we'll burn em. . . .'

He seemed on the verge of cracking off at the end – in his somewhat hysterical effort in part to convince me – but mainly himself – that despite everything he could see with his eyes (a view similar to mine) all was well with his world. Mainly he was talking and asking. It made me think of a similar experience I had recently been involved in, in another part of our agency's programme.

Jimmy Cannon, the news columnist, attended a group-therapy session I ran with a group of parolees in a special project in an uptown courtroom. Rocky Graziano had talked to the group, and several young parolees discussed their problems. In his news column the next day I felt that Cannon had captured the impact and mood of Chino and 'his people'. He wrote:

This is what the city does to so many of its people. It is not only New York but all the large settlements where there are wicked streets. They were heist-guys and junkies and hustlers who didn't know how to make it pay.

Make all the numbers a pair of dice holds. Have all the broads in the neighborhood sparring for you. Zoot yourself and plaster your hair until it looks like a duck's behind. Your pegged pants don't count. Your wise-cracks flop. Nothing goes for you if the rap's right and you're a loser. And these are losers trying to be winners.

There was one kid I felt had made it all the way. He wore a one-buttoned jazzy coat. I'd bet on him. He had the drug habit and had shaken it. You had to be touched by the fierce pride. He stood up there when Yablonsky solicited questions and told them the ring was out of his nose.

There was no con in him. It had shaken him up, aged him beyond his tortured years but he wanted to know why. He explained how he had dug in for kicks but he was asking, asking, asking. He was telling but also wondering and going back over it and attempting to put it together. Why, why, why?

It's poverty but that's not enough, either. It was in all of them, that demand for asking as they told it. They spoke casually. They weren't cheating or why would they come back into this room where their grief had been punished? They wanted to know. . . .

Chino wanted to know that night. I felt that his mood was mine in trying to untangle why and how we had become part of a 'peace meeting' to prevent a violence that no one really wanted – at least when they were sober.

Results of the Peace Treaty

The treaty-signing produced a short period of peace, at least from any major rumbles. Even though it had seemed an appropriate move at the time, I later had some negative second thoughts. The meeting gave a degree of official recognition to the illegal activity planned by a disorganized collection of neighbourhood youth. Moreover, the treaty may have structured a loosely developed conflict. The meeting confirmed the fact that there was trouble brewing between rival groups. Now two 'gangs' had a war truce.

On the other hand, some positive things seemed to result from the peace meeting. It gave the leaders the recognition they sought, the opportunity to blow off steam, and a way out of the battle. They were also given an opportunity to explore their feelings. In addition, I had a chance to assess further the two gangs' organization.

Chino's reactions in my car, inarticulate as they were, gave him an opportunity to explore somewhat rationally the 'why' of his violence. My presence in a somewhat official setting (my office) did bring to bear some of the external official societies' views of the impending gang war. The boys could measure their violent emotions against some representations of the larger society.

The treaty-signing had an apparent measure of success. Although minor skirmishes continued, a major rumble seemed to be prevented. This is the way Duke described his reaction to the meeting about a week later in my office in a tape-recorded interview:

L.Y.: What were your feelings about the peace conference?

DUKE: When I first heard about the peace conference, I thought
it was a pretty good idea. I'd just been picked up and let go
and I didn't like the idea of being pushed around by the
Villains or Scorpions. . . . I spoke to different guys and they
all said that if the Villains and Scorpions agreed to leave us
alone – fine; if they didn't – they'd fight. When we first came
in and saw Blackie, Sonny, and Chino, the first thing we
noticed was Chino was 'packed'. . . . We figured he had a
blade on him, too. Blackie, he didn't have anything I don't
think – I think Sonny might have. Blackie might have had
a knife, but I doubt it.

L.Y.: How did the meeting look to you? Just what happened as
you saw it?

DUKE: We tried to talk to them and they just started to bullshit . . . they said they were going to come down to our block
any time they wanted to and do whatever they wanted to
and we weren't going to come over there. We didn't feel
like fighting there, but, well, we felt that if we caught them
later they sure as hell weren't going to get off on their own
power. . . .

Well, you know, we talked about stopping the fighting –
that three Balkans could go up there at a time, but no more
than three and the same with the Villains and the Scorpions.
They could come down, but no more than a certain group;
that boundaries would be set; that they'd leave us alone and
we'd leave them alone; that if they heard rumours they'd
come and talk it out. If we heard rumours, we'd come and
talk it out and nobody would jump to fight and they'd try
to talk before they fought. That's about it.

L.Y.: What happened after the meeting?

DUKE: A lot of things happened about two weeks after that, or
a week after that. Blackie and Sonny and about six or seven
of the Scorpions came down to 122nd Street. I think to test
the pact between us – they were down about five minutes trying to push some guys around when about fifteen or twenty
Balkans showed up and the Villains saw that we meant it,
and left. About a week after that, rumours went around that
a fight was going to start all over again and me and some
other guys went up to Scorpion territory to see what was
going on. We went up and spoke to Blackie. He agreed to
find out who was spreading the rumours and stop them.

The Balkans agreed to the same. No fight came off and everything was peaceful.

L.Y.: Do you think the treaty worked?

DUKE: Oh, there would have been fighting if the treaty hadn't
been signed. Because of the treaty, there was no fighting. . . .

L.Y.: What did they – the Villains and Scorpions – think of the
treaty?

DUKE: Well, they thought it was a pretty good idea. They said
that they thought it was fair to both sides and they intend
to live up to it one hundred per cent and they said that if
anybody broke it, it wouldn't be them. They thought we
might break it. We told them that if anybody broke it, it
wouldn't be us, so nobody broke the treaty. Chino didn't
have too much to say other than he thought it was fair and
that he thought it would work out; that he thought gang
busting was nothing and he wasn't going in for it any more.

I think signing the treaty was good for those guys. Makes
them feel important and, well, it makes you think the other
person thinks you're important. That's what they wanted
in the first place . . . to feel they're leaders of something. So
I think it's good.

That's what they all want. They want to be somebody and
not just nothing.

5. Prelude to a Rumble

There was a break in extreme talk about a mass gang war from August through September. During the lull guerilla warfare continued as usual, with Japs and assaults from both sides. Much of this, however, was the average daily assault and aggression among the boys in a world where fighting was routine.

I asked Nicky one afternoon, in one of my daily discussion sessions with Duke and his boys: 'Why are you always fighting?' (It was apparent that he averaged about four or five fights a week.)

You gotta keep moving if you slug a guy every so often, they know who's boss and you get the first shot in. That's better than being hit first, ain't it? Besides, we always fight in the house. I always fight with Joey [his brother] and then, you know, I fight with the old man. [*Laughs.*] We really fight. Sometimes we knock down things off the table. Roll around and all that. He beats me all of the time but I'm getting bigger.

Although Nicky 'lost' his fights at home, he won most of his street fights. One week I tried to keep count of his fights, and found some relationship between fights lost with his father and fights won on the street.

Although Nicky was only fourteen, he looked seventeen. He was about six feet tall, weighed about 180 pounds, and on the two occasions I saw him in fights, he packed a wallop. Nicky maintained an aggressive dignity that limited fights to situations he selected himself. Although he was big for his age, he was the smallest one in his family. His older brother, twenty-one, who was in the Marines, was six foot four, and both Joey and his father were six foot two and well over 200 pounds. Despite his general aggression – or maybe because of it – Nicky was well liked by most all of the Balkans.

During this period my relationship with the Balkans deepened. Duke seemed to accept me without reservation.

We would meet at least four times a week in my office. Although he was generally accompanied by Pedro, Nicky, and Jay, we found the opportunity to meet alone frequently.

Duke's demeanour would change when I was alone with him. He seemed less concerned with muscle flexing, and would pour out his inner feelings. He didn't seem to like himself and would keep repeating how he was too stupid to finish high school. His main problem in school was being 'picked on':

The teachers would always pick me out for not doing work or eat me out for something. I mean, if I attended regularly they would find fault with my haircut or something else. Sometimes I felt like strangling them – so I would just cut.

My father's the one who always gives me a bad time. I like him, but I wish he would leave me alone. You can't talk to him – he jumps all over you. My grandfather was the only one I could talk to. He would keep me cool. But when he died that was it.

. . . My mother? Well, she's all right but she keeps comparing me to my kid sister. And, you know, she's real good in school – and I get tired of hearing how she's so good and I'm so bad.

Duke and I agreed to 'experiment' with several intensive discussion sessions to determine why he liked to fight. He was as interested as I, perhaps more, in trying to find the answer – if there was one.

Invariably he would begin discussing his family, and talk would centre on his father. Here he would try to convince me (and himself) how much he liked his father. His reasoning would get shrill; then he would begin an outpouring: 'The son of a bitch never leaves me alone, always going at me. Nothing I do is right. . . .' He told me about several occasions when he felt like strangling him, but was fearful he would really kill him. His mother was apparently the mediator during these battles.

On one occasion I drew a diagram of his family: mother, father, sister, Duke. I then asked him to discuss the relationships.

He said: 'First, you gotta include my grandmother in

the family. She doesn't live with us, but she's really part of the family. [*Laughs.*] My old man is always fighting with her. That's OK, but every time he fights with her, he comes home and fights with me. ...' Duke paused, reflecting, at this point, then continued: 'Then I go out, get my boys, and start turning on a rumble.'

Duke had a strong need to assert himself through the Balkans. Prevailing conditions in the neighbourhood and his personal needs produced a compatible union in the gang. In his inner dreams Duke played the role of a martyr, fighting for the cause of local boys. Duke's need to be a leader in the gang seemed related to the reverse situation of childish behaviour and position in his home.

Some gang leaders' needs to be 'men' in the gang seem to have a direct relationship to their feelings of inadequacy and limited status or prestige in their home situation. This guilding theme as expressed by one gang boy points to this notion: 'Some guys are nowhere at home and school, so they're always trying to show what big men they are with the guys.'

To his father, even though he was eighteen, Duke was still a 'baby', always in trouble, always doing the wrong thing, and unable to make any rational decisions. In the gang, at least in his self-image, his role was one of power, decisiveness, and respect. He visualized himself as a powerful leader of men.

As a result of my many intense discussions with Duke, I had a feeling that he was attempting to relive, in the gang, earlier and current years during which he was weak and helpless in school, at home, and with his peers. Now at eighteen, in his fantasy at least, he 'became' the omnipotent individual he always dreamed of being since he was now a 'big gang man'.

Duke kept a diary that reflected his inner dreams of power.[1] One day, to my complete surprise, he came to my office with a large fifty-page notebook containing his daily reflections as a Balkan gang leader. (It read somewhat like

---

1. The diary came into my hands several months after this period; however, I shall introduce sections at relevant points in this chronicle.

Hitler's *Mein Kampf*.) Here he described his response to a potential gang attack upon the Balkans:

BALKAN REPORT

The fifth division is to be held in reserve unless we need them in extreme need and then they are to be given two weeks' notice. They are seventy strong. The Saints and Anzacs will combine to protect La Salle Street and 122nd Street from attack – combined, they are sixty-one strong and with the X group they are ninety-one strong. The Balkans are now 219 strong in the field for defence or offence and combined with the Anzacs and the Saints they are 280 strong in the field at a moment's notice, but given two weeks' time, they could throw in seventy more at the least from outside divisions which would bring the force in the field up to 350–380. If we called on our brother clubs we could have:

Red Wings – 300 strong, plus 400 Balkans, plus twenty ROD
  Knights
Tiny Tims – 300 strong, plus twenty-one Anzacs, plus thirty
  Seahawks
Politicians – 500 strong, plus forty Saints, plus 100 Dwarfs
Imperial Lords – 300 strong, plus thirty X, plus 150 X
Imperial Knights – 200 strong, plus thirty Iron Dukes, plus
  300 and something, 100 from King Farouk [a Balkan]
Mighty Hoods – 200 strong, plus fifty Jr Turks
Harlem Aces – 500 strong, plus fifty Jr Braves
Total, 2,500

The Villains have three divisions or 150–350 people. The Sportsmen have over 1,200 men. The Englishmen, 300 – the Scorpions, 100; the Viceroys, 600; the El Quintos, 1,600.

The fourth platoon is twenty-three strong with attack points above 125th Street. The third division will join in with the fourth platoon of the first division in attacking all points above 125th Street. They are forty strong; combined they equal sixty-three strong. The first, second and third platoons of the first division are to hold and defend all of the Green from 120th to 125th Street; combined, they equal thirty-eight strong.

The first and second platoons are to hold the approaches, both the upper and lower crossway at 125th Street – combined their strength equals twenty-four strong. The third and fifth platoons in the second division will hold all the approaches to Greenie from 108th to 120th Street – combined they are thirty-three strong. The fifth and sixth platoons combined with the fourth division will attack.

In Duke's world others were always attacking and he and the Balkans were fighting defensive battles. Duke's dreams of glory and defence were somewhat exaggerated conceptions of what most Balkans thought and felt.

Duke's diary at times was more direct and related to the moment. During the earlier baseball period, the diary revealed, I was not as clearly accepted by him as I had thought:

> Yablonsky . . . thinks that he will get away with taking over our club and joining us up with the uptown clubs. I will let him think so for about one more week or until he gets Jim, or whoever else is on probation, off it for good. At the end of that time he is out but good unless he changes his tune fast and only tries to help and not take over. . . . Jim says that the odds are now in favour with the Villains because the Politicians are broken up by the Enchanters but good. . . .
>
> Nellie is the one who copped the stuff from our cellar and now the cops are on the look-out for him. If they find out that he is a lieutenant in our group, we'll all be messed up but good and so either he quits or gets out. Also, have to watch him to see he does not try to get even with us. Jim has been warned to stay away from us for the rest of his parole. We will see what Yablonsky can do about it.

In addition to Duke and Nicky, several other core Balkans, always on the scene, were Pedro, Ape, Jay, and Red. Joey, Nicky's brother, was important in the Balkans at first, but he was sent to Lincoln Hall, a Catholic reformatory, soon after the June event.

Pedro was about twenty and a 'yes man' to Duke. He seemed to lean on him for support. Pedro lived in a local rooming-house apartment, which was notorious for numbers, gambling, narcotics, and prostitution. He spoke of his father as 'a no-good prick who brought me over here from P.R. when I was a kid and then cut me loose'. He never talked about his mother; as nearly as I could assess she was still in Puerto Rico with another family. Pedro worked periodically as a grocery delivery boy, but most of the time I believe he maintained himself by petty thievery. There was also some evidence (which I saw) that linked him with selling marijuana cigarettes. He claimed he was holding the 'tea' for a friend.

Johnny, another core Balkan, was called 'Ape'. (I asked a Balkan one day why they called Johnny 'Ape'. His quick reply was, 'Did you ever take a good look at him?') He was a constant whiner, complainer, and defeatist. The Balkans, according to Ape, were under constant attack and would never survive: 'Although I hang with them for protection, I fuck everybody. They try to burn me, I got my blade, I'll get 'em all but good.'

Red and Jay provided the comic relief for the grimmer, more hostile Balkan core members. They were always laughing and making fun of the whole gang-war scene. For a time – just to keep them busy – I permitted Red and Jay to 'play' with my tape recorder alone, in our back office. This consisted of Red making up spontaneous gang stories that involved a sequence of caricatures about rent collectors and police – all with a violent theme.

Balkan Hangouts

Although my office became a main hangout, the boys constantly were on the lookout for a clubhouse of their own. (This was true of practically all gangs we knew.) They always wanted to have some place they could call their own. This was probably connected with the gang's strong feelings about being 'nowhere' and alienated. Territory was always, at least symbolically, their excuse for fighting:

PEDRO: Well, a lot of times a guy figures he's protecting what's his. In the city, there isn't much to do, they haven't got any playgrounds or centres – they're being pushed around either by a different group; or – because they act bad or try to act bad – by the police, and they get to resent it. So what they do have, or what they think is theirs, they're going to defend against anybody or anything. So if someone comes by their territory or block or candy store, and tries to horn in on it, they'll fight. They think they're defending their personal property.

The Balkans used several hangouts or meeting places in addition to my office, where the boys now felt free to come and go, discuss problems, or, in their words, 'just to bull-shit'. A hangout frequented was the corner of La Salle Street and Broadway (near Broadway and 125th Street). Here the boys would 'hang' on the corner in standard street-gang fashion, discussing conquests, plotting, whistling at girls, or just talking.

The 'corner' is a symbolic expression – since the corner for the gang boy can be a tenement stoop or even the middle of the block. Here is a typical summer day's activity for Red on the 'corner':

RED: I usually get up at eleven or twelve o'clock, you know, I sleep late. And then I will go out and see the guys, sitting on the stoop, you know, doing nothin'. I would sit there with them, and sometimes they will say, 'Let's split and go to a movie', so I would go to the movie with them. Or sometimes we would try and get a game of stickball or somethin' like that. Our block is crowded; we didn't hardly have a chance to play because the busses kept going back and forth, back and forth. We couldn't do nothin'. So that we just sit; then when it got to night time, well, you know, we would go around and say, 'Come on, man, let's go break windows for some excitement', or, 'Come on, man, let's go boppin'.' Then we would go and look for guys to beat up. Then we would come back. And then [*laughs*] we would sit on the stoop, man, and we'd hear a cop car outside and we would all fly up to the roof, or somethin' like that. Then, we just come down and start talkin' and talkin'.

Talking about past, present, and future violence was also primary Balkan activity:

NICKY: You know, ya always talkin', 'Oh, man, when I catch a guy, I'll beat him up', and all of that, you know. So, after you go out and you catch a guy, and you don't do nothin', they say, 'Oh, man, he can't belong to no gang, because he ain't gonna do nothin'.' You gotta do what you say.

Another main conversation piece in the gang is the 'flicks'. Here one Balkan talks about the type of movie he likes best:

Usually I go for horror pictures like *Frankenstein and the Mummy* or things like that. I like it when he goes and kills the guy or rips a guy in half or something like that [*laughs*] or when he throws somebody off a cliff. You know, all them exciting things.

Apart from the 'bull sessions' on the corner, there was a continuing interest in finding a hangout with some permanence. The 'corner', or Grant's Tomb, where the boys ran around, played football, fought, and wrestled with each other, was not sufficient.

The cops or somebody is always chasing us. You go here, they say go there. The super[intendent] chases you off the stoop – Clint chases you out of his store [a coffee shop] – the old man out of the house.

They finally obtained a 'clubroom' in an apartment cellar through a local janitor. It was an extremely dirty, former coalbin with very little light, yet it was considered 'terrific' by the boys. They used it mainly as a place in which to sit and have 'bull sessions'. (In part, I utilized the clubroom for research purposes by observing gang interaction in its 'natural state'. After a while the boys paid little attention to me as I sat in a corner, casually observing their activities and taking notes.)

The clubroom to me was stifling. The space was not much larger than twenty feet by twenty. One weak bulb with a string hung from the ceiling, and orange crates and some abandoned chairs served as seats, but most of the boys used the floor.

To get to the clubroom required a walk through a damp, twisting, unlighted basement hall. On my first visit, while going through the dark passageway, I thought Duke, Nicky, and Pedro had finally decided to do me in. I didn't really believe that we were visiting a clubroom. When I saw it, I repressed my real reaction and complimented them on the several 'cheesecake' pictures that hung on the walls.

Clubroom activities included 'sounding' – the standard needling and picking on one another, wrestling, card playing, and some quiet games, but mainly boasting about violent-gang activities past and future. For this privilege, the boys agreed to levy and pay a tariff of ten cents per meeting. The real purpose, however, for collecting the money was to purchase guns for the gang.

The essential meaning of the 'permanent' clubroom to the gang was revealed by Jay. He would come regularly, pay his ten-cent 'dues', then go and lie down in a corner on the floor and stare quietly at the ceiling. One day I questioned him about what seemed to me to be a waste of money:

L.Y.: Jay, how come you pay your dime and just lie around? Why don't you play checkers or talk to the guys or something?

JAY: Look man, this is the only place in the world they leave me be. Don't bug me. I hang on the corner or the park – the cops boot me. I go home – they throw me out. They don't let me in the [community] centre no more. I hang in my hallway – the janitor yells. I go on the stoop – the neighbours bitch. I get a little peace here – so leave me be.

The clubroom, outside of jail, was probably one of the few places of refuge left to the Balkans. If nothing else, it kept them off the street and out of conflict with the law for a brief period of time.

About this time I made some effort to check the arrest records of the twenty Balkans whose names I knew. Almost all of these members had had contact with legal processes. As nearly as I could ascertain from talking with the boys and checking police and court records, all twenty had been arrested or questioned by the police at one time or another for involvement in some illegal act; about fifteen had Juvenile Aid Bureau cards, received for minor deliquencies, on file with the police. Seven had been arrested and brought into detention or jail custody; two were later committed to long-term institutions. Most of the boys, when closely interviewed, described many specific illegal acts committed for which they were never arrested. All the boys had problems at school; either they were habitual truants or, at minimum, classroom problems.

Street fights, assault, and petty thievery were daily events in this delinquency pattern. Gang warfare and its concomitant talk about violence was, however, the dominant activity of the Balkans. And a new gang-war problem was 'on the scene'.

6. The Dragons Invade

Now that I knew most of the Balkans, Duke and Pedro began by mutual consent to introduce me to other gang leaders and gangs affiliated with the Balkan kingdom. Most of these individuals, according to Duke and Pedro, were gang leaders from the Harlem Syndicate. I met with nine of these leaders in my office and at various luncheonettes in Harlem.

Most of them were Puerto Rican or Negro youths in their late teens or early twenties. Each was introduced with a title: 'president', 'war lord', or 'war counsellor'. Duke would present me as a 'good guy' who was writing a book on gangs and had helped the Balkans. From then on I was on my own. His introduction usually ended with the assurance that I was not a cop.

I was impressed with several things at these conferences. It became apparent that Duke was hooked into and accepted by what were apparently some of the major gang leaders in the city. They treated him with a degree of respect and full acceptance of what seemed to me to be incredible stories of vast gang empires and affiliations. I was also struck by the fact that these leaders all seemed to support one another's stories on what seemed to be fantastic descriptions of gang size and alliances. Some would work themselves up to a fever pitch, while others would coolly discuss their empires, mingling plans for defence with threats of violence to invaders.

One tough-looking twenty-two-year-old Negro youth called Alex described his gang involvements with typical flair. The session took place in my office with Duke, Pedro, and a friend of Alex's sitting silently on the sidelines. (Alex had a bulge by his breast coat pocket. Though he never came out and said it directly, he implied that he was 'packing' by patting the bulge at appropriate points in our discussion.)

ALEX: . . . In the Harlem Syndicate we have about 150 clubs;
there's a couple of thousand guys in all. . . . I ain't afraid of
nobody that walks the street. My club's in this . . . [a gang-
war situation] and I can only get beat once. I want peace.
I'm tired of all this bopping stuff. I don't want any more of
it. They messed up a couple of my boys. The Dragons think
they can get away with picking on these little clubs. One big
club should go up there and wipe them out. . . . On the East
Side they don't mess with us 'cause they know we're too
strong for them and they try to keep cool. . . . I'm gunning
for Frankie Loco . . . when I meet up with him one of us is
gonna go down. . . .

L.Y.: Did your Syndicate ever meet together, all at once?

ALEX [*laughs*]: Man, if we all got together at once, you would
have to hire the stadium. Also, we gotta be cool. Too many
guys, the nabs come down. When we travel, we move in twos
and threes. But when we whip one on – it's all out.

L.Y.: Do you know all of the other Syndicate leaders?

ALEX: Most all – but some of the guys I know only by rep, I
never met them. I heard about Duke here and the Balkans.
Read about them. We met 'cause we wanted to check whether
he's with us or not. The Balkans is in with the Syndicate.

L.Y.: What are some of the other clubs in the Syndicate?

ALEX: Englishmen, Sportsmen, El Diablos, Turks, Latin Gents,
Mighty Hoods, Viceroys. . . . The Viceroys been fightin' those
mother-fuckin' Dragons for years. They [the Dragons] think
they're goin' to take over the city. Well, they're wrong –
'cause we're all getting together. Loco, Bobby, and all of them
are finished!

Alex's comments were typical of the others. They included discussions of gang size, alliances, self-aggrandizement, threats, and weapons. A dominant theme was a
desire for peace and harmony – 'but if we have to fight,
we'll whip it on fast and wipe them all out at once and for
all. . . . You see, man, we're sociable, not looking for
trouble, but if they want it they'll get it.'

The vague 'they' used interchangeably with the Dragons
was a dominant ploy. Also, the raging monologues and
denouncements of the imperialistic enemies would be
cyclical, ranging from abject 'What can we do but fight?'
to an exultant 'We'll wipe them out once and for all.'

Their stories confused me, since the gang leaders mixed many gang names together. Such names as Englishmen, Diablos, Turks, Imperial Knights, and Sportsmen were popular. The Dragons dominated as the main target gang. 'They' [the Dragons] forced them to join forces and defend themselves against a threatened invasion.

Gang size and allies' strength would typically rise and fall from 100 members to 2,000 and back in the same dialogue. The following comment by Duke was seriously listened to by several Balkans and two visiting gang leaders in my office one day:

The Dragons want all of our territory for their own; they ask too much. They want from 125th Street and Morningside Ave. to 123rd Street from Morningside to over to the East Side. If we give in on this we will have to give in on other things, so we gotta stand up to them. War may start again. There has been peace now for past weeks without any trouble and that's great. We have ten divisions with 800 members as it now stands. The first [division] has sixty members, the second has sixty members, the third has fifty and the fourth has fifty. The fifth has seventy and the sixth has thirty. The seventh, eighth, ninth, and tenth divisions give us at least 2,000.

The Balkans and their allies agreed that the Dragons were starting to draft and take over Manhattan, and if they wanted to stay independent they would all have to fight. It was evident that the Balkans were entering another crisis. I began to try to disentangle the nature of the Dragons' invasion threat in which we were all apparently involved. (At one point Loco sent 'the word' to me through Nicky that if I didn't keep hands off, the Dragons were going to bomb my office.)

The name Frankie Loco appeared repeatedly in the boys' conversations. Loco was apparently now president of the East Side and West Side Dragons. Loco, whom I met only once very briefly – he was pointed out to me in a local candy store – was a short, wiry Puerto Rican, about twenty-six years old, with a long career in gang activity. As former head of the notorious East Side Dragons, he was now on the West Side, according to the boys, to force all the West Side clubs to join the Dragon empire. Loco was known, feared, and at the same time ridiculed by many gang members up and down the West Side.

He had a scar down the centre of his head that was the result of a childhood injury. He was called 'Loco' for apparent reasons, and, according to many Balkans, had been under observation at Bellevue on several occasions. The rumour mill and a series of assaults and threats demanding that local youths join the Dragons produced a hysterical condition in the neighbourhood.

Loco and a henchman called Bobby (supposedly a leader of the East Side Dragons) were, according to the boys, intent on expanding the Dragon empire into all of the boroughs of New York City. (Later information from several social agencies revealed that they were attempting to draft gang members up and down the West Side of Manhattan.)

Although their ability to produce the tremendous force of gang members they claimed to have at their disposal seemed questionable, they were still dangerous. Their drafting technique was an interesting process, which usually took place at night. Loco and four or five lieutenants would 'grab' a presumed member of another gang (this could be any boy they met), and assault or threaten him with violence unless the youth and his gang joined the Dragons. They would often assault the boy on the spot to prove 'they meant business':

RED: Loco and those four guys grabbed me – dragged me into this hall; then they punched me in the face. I said, 'Keep your mother-fuckin' hands off me!' I didn't even know these other guys. So they kept saying, 'You better join up, you little faggot – you better join up.' They kept saying, 'The Dragons are taking over the West Side', and like that. So they punched me again. So I said, 'Fuck it', and I joined. . . .

L.Y.: Did they take your name or anything?

RED: They never bothered me again – and I never seen 'em again. I guess they just like to punch people around.

The consequences of the 'joining up' process seemed to

be meaningless in terms of expanding a membership that could be counted upon. Apparently the boys' names were never taken, nor did the Dragons keep a membership list or call on the boys drafted to do anything other than 'join' at the moment of drafting. The meaning of the drafting was probably the act itself. Loco and his boys seemed to get their kicks from this enlistment process. It gave them an opportunity to throw their weight around and gain recognition as supreme commanders of a vast Dragon network.

The Balkans caught in this 'imperialistic expansion' reacted with alarm. Duke described the Balkans' reaction in his diary:

> The situation looks very bad now because the god-damned Dragons insist that everybody join them, and if we do join them we will all be in trouble with the law, and if we don't we will be in trouble with the law another way. Either way we get it, but if the Dragons say that all they want is our territory and for us to become brother clubs with them and then no trouble, so OK, but if they say we have to become one of them we will have to fight. The trouble is that we know the cops know what is going on. If we ask them for help we don't get it, instead we will get busted, because they don't care whether we are trying or not. They're just out to bust us this time and what can we do about it. Dear God, I wish I knew.

The dilemma was complex; if they joined the Dragons, they would get into trouble with the police; if they didn't they would have to fight and get into trouble another way.

The Dragon 'invasion' involved many more 'join up or else' situations. One threat to 'join up' was resisted with no apparent consequences:

DUKE: One day when they came over to us and said that they were taking over, that this was to become a Dragon division and that we were all to become Dragons. We told them bullshit. Nobody was gonna become Dragons. Frankie Loco said that either we were gonna join up with them or there's gonna be trouble. He said that we thought we were rocky characters and he owed us something. We told him that if he ever came around and bothered us again that we weren't gonna fool around with him the next time. So we told him and this other guy that if the Dragons ever came around and bothered us or our families instead of threatening, we'd kill 'em.

This occurred about the same time Nicky reported the rumour that I was to be 'burned' and my office 'bombed' by the Dragons if I didn't 'mind my own business'. I recall laughing about this at the time, but my laugh trailed off a bit at the edge.

To attempt disentangling the situation, I called up a New York City Youth Board supervisor, who presumably had worked with the East Side Dragons for a number of years. He revealed that, according to Youth Board information, there were really only twenty or thirty so-called Dragon members known to them and that they were all on the East Side. He also commented that the Dragons consisted mainly of six leaders, older individuals with strong needs to organize gangs but with no strong backing in fighting members. (Bobby and Loco were mentioned as leaders.) He explained 'the Dragon invasion' as a re-action by many youths throughout the city to the Dragons' 'publicity'. Many gangs thus assumed the Dragon name simply for prestige purposes, even though they had no clear affiliation.

The most tangible evidence I could obtain from talking to the Youth Board, other professional workers, and by cross-checking many boys' stories at the time, indicated that the 'Dragon invasion' was primarily the action of the several disturbed Dragon gang leaders mentioned. These five or six Dragon leaders, including Bobby and Frankie Loco, had the backing of about twenty to thirty youths who might fight with them. The leaders had strong needs to 'organize' gangs because it apparently gave them prestige and a chance to 'throw their weight around'. Their efforts had some concrete consequences in addition to stirring up fear.

They seemed to have effected a consolidation of the Villains and Scorpions under the Dragon banner. Chino and Blackie, the leaders of the Uptown Villains, told me that the Dragons had forced them to call themselves

Villain-Dragons, which later simply became Dragons.
Thus the uptown Villains and Scorpions seemed now to be
attacking the Balkans under the Dragon banner with the
aid and incitement of the later provoker of the Egyptian
King homicide, Frankie Loco.

One night three Balkans were badly beaten by Loco and
his crew. As usual, there was considerable conflict in the
stories of the Balkans who had been attacked. One said
that there were four assailants, another three. One report
was that Red, one of the boys beaten, was bleeding from
the ear. Another boy claimed, 'Red was beaten so bad on
the ear that he was deaf and had to go to the hospital for
stitches.' About all I could get from Red and the others in
my talk with them about an hour after the incident was
that 'some guys came up and hit me. I don't know who
they were. I'm sure they were Dragons.'

About this time, Duke recorded the following version of
this assault in his diary:

11/1
The Dragons raided our territory yesterday and stomped Jay,
Ape, Red, and Mariciano but good. And now the nabs are
swarming all over the place. . . . All divisions must consolidate
their strength for attack or defence.
11/4
If the Dragons come after me they are at their own risk, for
I will knock shit out of any that come near me or my friends. I
will try to get seven guns by next week. [One of these guns was
turned over to me; it was a German Model .22.] I know where
I can get four [guns] for $4 apiece.

These assaultive situations increased the Balkans' panic
and fear to the point of hysteria. An extreme reaction was
registered by Nicky, who ran away from home and requested commitment to a reformatory until the gang-war
threat from the Dragons blew over. His conclusion was
that he would rather go 'to jail' now for a short while
than do life for a homicide he felt was inevitable. The
circumstances under which he ran away from home and
his panic were related to the following situation in which
he attacked his brother Joe. (Joe was home at the time

on furlough from the reformatory where he was serving an indeterminate sentence.)

NICKY: I want to get sent away for at least a year. I'm gonna do something if I stay here and if I do something bad, I'm gonna be away for a long time, maybe die.

L.Y.: Well, what do you think you might do?

NICKY: I might hurt somebody real bad or kill them. I got an urge inside me and when I'm mad at somebody my mind goes blank. You can ask my brother, Joe. The fight we had up the house – it turned into a fist fight and I was getting wiped up all over the place so we were by the fire escape – so I reached back and grabbed the flower pot and hit him across the head with it. He was knocking me off the fire escape and I took a piece of the broken pot and went all the way down his back with it.

L.Y.: I thought Joe was your best friend, isn't he?

NICKY: Yeah [*shaking his head morosely*].

L.Y.: Then what happened?

NICKY: My mind blanked out – like I got an urge – no matter who it is. I could shoot someone – I'm positive I would do that in a gang war. If I see one of the guys getting beat up, I just ain't gonna stand there and watch him get his ass kicked by those fuckin' Dragons.

L.Y.: Well, what does Ape want to do?

NICKY: Ape wants to kill Chino. He's crazy – just like me.

L.Y.: Well, you're not crazy.

NICKY: I am, when I get mad. If I was there to fight and I had nothing on me [weapon] – you see, I'd use my fist but then I'd hit somebody until they couldn't get up.

L.Y.: Well, what can you do to settle this?

NICKY: I figure I go away [to a reformatory] for a year or two, or something like that, the gang war with the Dragons would be over; then I'll make new friends and everything like – you see. I could forget about everything going on around here.

L.Y.: Don't you think we can settle this gang busting?

NICKY: No, not now – not the way it is now – never. A lot of guys are gonna get 'burned'.

L.Y.: What are your plans now? Do you want to go home? [Nicky had been away from home for several days and was sleeping in the local coal-cellar clubroom.]

NICKY: You know, Joe got 'busted' and sent away from the June thing. I must have been in good luck that night – I was about two feet away from the cops at the time – this month, eight Dragons stopped me – they put me on the burning list. So find me a place to go.

L.Y.: Take it easy over the week-end and I'll try to think of something and we'll talk about it Monday.

NICKY: You gotta get me out of here pretty soon 'cause this is gonna go off any day now.

L.Y.: You think you're really going to hurt someone?

NICKY: Shoot 'em, stab 'em, or strangle 'em – what's gonna happen to me afterwards? I figure if I can go away for a year all that stuff will be over with the Dragons – so if I go now I won't have to go for a long time like if I strangled someone. I figure I'd do a year or two now – I don't care. But if I kill someone, I'll get life.

About six Balkan gang-war strategy sessions were held in my office in response to the 'Dragon invasion'. I recorded most of their discussions. About ten gang members were present at this particular meeting:

L.Y.: What's happening on this Dragon deal?

APE: The Dragons, well, they beat up Jay and them guys – like that – my boys got beat up wicked and I don't like it. They broke Jay's ear and he bled and other guys got stomped.

L.Y.: Yeah, but they quieted down.

APE: He [Frankie Loco] came up last night and spoke to me again – he called me a 'hero' and asked me to join up with the Dragons or else. I ain't gonna be a fuckin' Dragon.

L.Y.: Were you there last night when I was in there? [Referring to a candy-store hangout.]

APE: Yeah, he comes there [Loco]. I'm gonna knock his mother-fuckin' teeth in – not with a blade – I don't need my blade. I've got it on me now – I got a button [switchblade knife] on me now – I admit it because I'm 'packing', that's it. I ain't gonna take no fuckin' crap from those Dragons – you'd do the same thing if a cat got after you? I ain't messing with those people. They came up to my house and told my old man that if they catch up with me they're gonna kill me.

L.Y.: They came up and saw your father?

APE: I don't like it – you see, they know where I live. Two guys come axing for you and they're gonna burn you or something I don't like it – my father said that if he catches me out on the street, he's gonna knock the shit out of me and then he went to work.

L.Y.: Maybe you should stay home.

APE: I don't care if he puts me away – them mother-fuckin' Dragons come around here looking for trouble – we were sociable, man, lots of guys around here were sociable. Now that they built up the Dragon division, they want to pick on the Balkans, pick on the 114th Street, and they want to pick on Sportsmen. Like the time they were gonna burn me, I was scared like a dog.

L.Y.: Are they out to burn you tonight?

APE: We just want to talk to them peaceful – they stay on their block, we stay on our block and nobody has any trouble. They better listen to that.

L.Y.: You think they're going to listen?

APE: They better listen to it, because they're fuckin' punks.

At first the main discussion was between Ape and myself. Others arrived and joined in; soon the meeting developed into a wider discussion of the Dragon problem. It was somewhat on the order of a revival meeting, with Loco and the Dragons cast in the role of the devil. The originator of the Balkans' name, Jay, near the end of the session, attempted to summarize the discussion and the relative strengths of the Balkans versus the Dragons:

JAY: The Dragons, they want to take over the whole West Side. They want to take over the projects [public housing developments]. They want to take over all of Harlem. I think the Dragons are crazy because with the Balkans they got the Politicians, the Sportsmen and they got Queens against them; the only brother clubs they got is the Chaplains and the El Quintos from Brooklyn.

Duke's diary at this time describes the hysterical reaction of Balkan warfare defence and attack plans:

Duke's Diary

La Salle Street is to be the first line of defence against the Dragons. All counter-offences will begin at 115th Street. Their strength is at least 250 men and at the most 400 men. Spies will be sent down to 109th Street to see just where they stand. War is expected to be decided in the next two weeks by them. There will be a general sneak attack on them by our divisions. If it can be helped no big rumble will be fought, only Japs. Every method will be used against them, even burnings, to knock them out for good. If we are forced to fight with just local guys the fight will be purely a defensive one with a few offensive movements to keep them guessing. We would prefer not to fight at all but if they are after us what can we do?

Balkan's Report

Ape is to lead a division if war is declared, with Jerry as Supreme Commander of our war forces. He is to bring his division into the Dragons from the rear and flanks and try to either envelop them or destroy them. All of the clubs in the 24th Precinct should fight if they are to stay independent; if they do not they will fall one by one to the Dragons. The Dragons have already taken over from 3rd Avenue and 89th Street to the Drive to 105th Street from 3rd Avenue to the Drive also from 125th Street and 8th Avenue to the Drive to 131st from 8th Avenue to the Drive to 20th Street. Others should also fight with us against this threat to our security. Also the 30th Precinct and after this is done we take over every one of the clubs in our [police] precinct.

Johnny, Ape, and Marciano are to take care of Chino today and so it starts. I just got word that the Dragons moved in on our first division and they start burning today. Well, guess this is it for sure now. Pedro is holding my piece [gun] for me in his room and I pick it up tomorrow.

One reaction to the 'Dragon invasion' was an attempt to shift Balkan leadership. Duke moved Jerry, a more remote leader, into the limelight as president. The shift of leadership was accomplished by several 'public announcements' to the Balkans by Duke: 'Jerry is president now and will handle the fight with the Dragons.' The move seemed to be made in part to give other Balkan members the security of a mysterious, powerful president, and in part by Duke to get himself 'off the hook'.

Jerry was a twenty-four-year-old Puerto Rican with a moon face and a small black moustache. Speaking in a soft voice, he maintained a permanent little smile as he talked about 'his people' with a Latin passion, gesticulating and almost breast-beating as he described his gang. He would often in moments of great emotion clasp his hands to his chest, close his eyes, and tilt his face skyward:

If they [the Dragon invaders] attack we will be ready. Our divisions will fight them on the streets and wherever we meet. If one of our people falls, two will rise in their place to fight on. We will never give in to this enemy. We want peace – but will fight, if necessary. My divisions wait for my command.

Jerry resembled Wallace Beery in the role of Pancho Villa. He looked and talked like the Hollywood version of a Mexican *bandito*. At this point, near the climax of the 'Dragon invasion', Jerry, according to Duke, was 'the supreme commander of our war forces'.

Jerry outdid all the gang leaders I had ever met in his vivid descriptions of overwhelming divisions and alliances. His incredible monologues would last fifteen minutes at a stretch and would only be interrupted by another gang member's comment or mine to check a wild fact or figure.

In one session we were alone in the office, and he launched into a confessional:

I am now going to tell you the real truth about me as a Balkan leader. As you may know, I come from East Harlem. I was once myself high up in the Dragons. [He looked at me at this point for the shocked reaction he received.] At that time Loco and Bobby were nothing – we had a leader whose name I will not reveal. To do so – I might be burned tomorrow.

By the way, he is the only one who can stop the Dragon trouble we now have. I became president of the Balkans to end war and make peace. But I cannot do this without your help. I will have to see the real leader of the Dragons. [I felt at this point that he wanted me to push him into revealing who the leader was, and I did.]

I will tell you but you must swear to secrecy – for my life would be in danger. [I assured him accordingly.] His name is Cherokee, and he is doing ten to twenty at Sing Sing Prison. He is older, about thirty-five. From his prison cell he controls the Dragon movements which are now taking place. The Dragons are organizing to start a citywide drug syndicate.

'Horse' [heroin] will be sold through all Dragon divisions throughout New York.

Well, how can I help?

There is one way. You must get me a special pass to visit Cherokee. I am the only one who can talk him out of it. And he is the only one who can order the drafting and the war to stop.

At this point in my talk with Jerry, I bordered on getting him a pass and the decision that either he or I was crazy. My relationship with the local police captain, Peter Costello, was excellent and we were in close communication on the 'Dragon peril'. Captain Costello later became inspector placed in charge of the citywide New York Police Youth Squad.

In part to check my sanity, I asked Jerry, who was now playing the peaceful-leader role, if he would accompany me to a meeting with the police captain to discuss his story and suggestions. No doubt enjoying the recognition he was receiving, he agreed. I got in touch with Captain Costello, and Jerry and I went down to the Twenty-fourth Precinct headquarters.

In the captain's office Jerry launched into about the same story on his former Dragon leadership and the need to get Cherokee 'to turn off the trouble that is now attacking our neighbourhood'. If anything, this version of the story was more polished and convincing. Captain Costello and I kept checking each other's reaction as the story went on in great detail about the narcotics syndicate. (We later agreed that the presence of another rational person enabled us to stay clear of the convincing web Jerry was able to weave.) The captain and I listened attentively and then told Jerry that we could not arrange a visit for him to see Cherokee but that we appreciated his current efforts 'on behalf of peace in the area'.

Not stymied by his rejection, Jerry launched into an alternative plan of action for preventing 'this threat of mass gang war on our lives':

I have here a book [which he never let us look at] with the

names of all important gang leaders in New York City. My plan for a lasting peace is for me to call all of these gang leaders. We will call one on Friday night, 7.30 at Grant's Tomb. Then you [Captain Costello] have twenty police squad cars come in from all directions. You will then be able to arrest all of New York's major gang leaders and members and we will have peace.

With that he reached for the captain's phone. Captain Costello stopped him from calling, and we both informed him that we would take all of his 'excellent' plans under consideration.

Two days later I heard from Duke that Jerry had left town for California because the Dragons wanted to 'burn' him. I never saw Jerry again, nor did anyone else from the neighbourhood.

In later discussions with Captain Costello, we agreed that Jerry was no doubt 'psycho'. If his plans had not been so incredible, it might have been an interesting experiment to test Jerry's Cherokee and mass gang arrest suggestions. (A later discussion with a Youth Board worker revealed that there had been a Dragon leader called Cherokee, who was serving time at Sing Sing.)

When Jerry disappeared, Duke abandoned him in his diary. Jerry, who was recorded in Duke's diary at one point as 'Jerry, the supreme commander of our war forces', is here described ignominiously:

Our President has turned yellow and will not face up to the Dragons at all. None of our people are inclined to back him up after this. They want to see him face up to Frankie Loco but if he will not face up to him we will abandon him but good this time. If things look too bad we will get Yablonsky to step in and really round up those bastards [Dragons] once and for all. We are now testing the Syndicate to see whether or not they will desert us, in case of bad trouble. *They did.* Things do not look good for us.

At this point the 'Dragon invasion' hysteria had reached what seemed to me to be an absurd level of distortion. A news reporter captured the Dragon fantasy prevalent at the time among the Balkans and upper West

Side gangs. This front-page story appeared in the *New York World-Telegram and Sun* on 30 November 1955:

TEEN GANGS BAND FOR CRIME

by Wm. Michelfelder

The Police Department has uncovered a brazen plan by a syndicate of seven of Manhattan's toughest juvenile gangs to organize all of the city's hoodlum mobs under the leadership of adult criminals, the World-Telegram and Sun learned today.

The toughest and oldest of these gangs, the Dragons, has already absorbed 400 to 600 youngsters from the now defunct Crusaders, Sportsmen, Imperial Knights, Politicians, and three divisions of the Scorpions, also called the Villains. All of these gangs roam the upper West Side from 59th to 165th Sts.

'Charter Signing'

A 27-year-old hoodlum, known only to gang leaders as 'Bobby', recently conducted a syndicate 'charter signing' in a Manhattan community center. More than 60 gang leaders attended, including gang bosses from Brooklyn and Queens who were ready for a citywide syndicate.

For several weeks, this newspaper learned, the Police Department's youth squad and Juvenile Aid Bureau have been watching the syndicate trend.

The motive is still unclear to the police. But the best investigators in the department surmise that the youthful gangs are banding together to end fights among themselves and conserve their energy for a concentrated assault on law and order.

Independents Resist

Recent flareups in YMCA buildings and various youth centers in Manhattan and Brooklyn have been touched off by independent gangs resisting efforts by the syndicate to recruit them into the new organization, one police source says.

The clearest picture the police have at the moment is that the Dragon gang has assumed control of the syndicate. The Dragons started out on the East Side, according to police sources, and gained strength and prestige so quickly they moved across Manhattan and over into Brooklyn.

One police informant said that adult criminals, some with

long records, have been seen hanging around Dragon meetings in some community centers.

60 Leaders Meet

On November 9, it was learned, the 'syndicate' met in the basement of a Manhattan recreational center. At least 60 gang leaders were present. Another 100 youngsters remained on the first floor waiting for instructions that would come from the conference.

Leaders of the Dragons held the floor, under the direction of the 27-year-old Bobby, who has a long police record. The syndicate agreed on the following:

That gang territories would remain about the same. But that territory leaders would not order 'rumbles' without consulting the syndicate.

That all gangs in Manhattan, and later in other boroughs, would be broken up into 'divisions' of the Dragons.

The End of the Affair

The rumours and Japs persisted, along with planning for the 'once-and-for-all rumble' that would rock New York City. Jerry's disappearance and the apparent inability of Duke to produce alliances were the main discussion topics at the meetings held practically every night for the next several weeks. At the sessions the boys continued to assess, evaluate, and hash over their frightening positions vis-à-vis the Dragons. The meetings were scheduled as 'all-out membership and allies' meetings. I was consistently warned that the meeting space I provided would be insufficient for their needs. (Our front office could handle about fifty to sixty boys for a meeting.) Despite these extravagant preliminary plans, no more than twenty boys ever showed up at any of the meetings.

I co-operated fully with the meetings because they proved to be excellent opportunities for tape-recording data on Balkan organization and reaction to the invading hordes. They centred around Duke's plans for defence and attack. He would present Balkan reports on alliances and strategy for defence, based on his diary notations at the time. His plan for counterattack against the Dragons was scheduled in three 'stages':

Stage I

Get control of 115th Street from Riverside to Broadway
Get control of 122 Street from Riverside to Amsterdam
Get control up to 125 Street from Riverside to St Nicholas
Take over the Iron Dukes, Ringoes, Toutons, Four Aces and Saints, Gails, Warriors, Lances, Rams
Take over from 110 Street from 8 Avenue to Hudson up to 115 Street from Hudson to 8 Avenue
Get in with the Harlem syndicate
Join the Harlem syndicate
Crack the Villains' power in their area
Drive Dragons out

Stage II

Get divisions in Brooklyn, Queens, Bronx
Crack Vultures and Downtown Villains and Dragons in that area

Stage III

Get divisions from 70th up to 125th Street and take over all of Dean Street, Prince Street, Polo Grounds, Corona and Queens
Get divisions solidified – those out of N.Y.C. – and clear the Dragons out once and for all

At the meetings several of the more marginal fifteen to twenty gang members always present began to suggest that they were probably the only Balkan members who could really be counted upon 'if war came'. Many became disgusted and disillusioned with the continued discussion of gang size and allies. At one meeting when several 'core' members became carried away with enumerating the many Balkan divisions and thousands of members, Andy, a more marginal Balkan, seemed to reflect many of the boys' feelings: 'I think all you guys are full of shit. I ain't seen no one but the guys here. You keep talkin' big about people. Put your mother-fuckin' people where your mouth is.' No one strongly argued with his remark.

At one session Pedro countered this critique with a

statement about an alliance which 'came through':
'Johnny Ape went and got his people like he said he could.
Him and some Sportsmen went up and stomped the
Villains last night.'

This 'fact' of a brother gang was accepted by the central
Balkans, who were quite elated with at last striking back.
A closer group discussion and check of the facts revealed
that Ape, with the aid of two friends, presumably Sportsmen, had beaten up an eleven-year-old uptown boy, who
apparently had no gang connexions.

At first at the gang-war discussion meetings I played
the role of a neutral observer, neither for nor against any
of the grandiose plans being discussed. As notes of dissent
with some apparent gang fantasies began to develop,
I made the decision to throw my weight with the dissident
faction of the gang.

My strategy became one of exposé. I first began to
expose, then question, then refute many of the gang's
illusions. I began to employ what became a 'you're full of
it' technique.

When the central Balkans – Duke, Jay, Pedro, and
Ape – would launch into their grand claims of size and
affiliation, I would shake my head with a small smile in
disbelief. Some of the boys began to view Duke and Pedro
as 'psychos', and the Dragon threat as a wild rumour. I
didn't discourage this reaction, in fact, I gave support punc-
turing some of what I now believed were fantasy stories.

It became a juggling act to blast Duke in front of his
boys and yet maintain my relationship with him. I was
able to remain friendly with him by seeing him almost
every day alone. About three times a week I had him to
my house for discussion. At what turned into 'therapy
sessions' I would assure him: 'Look, I still think you're
OK and all that – but frankly I think a lot of the Dragon
and ally stuff is B.S. and I'm just going to be honest about
what I think.'

During this phase of my relationship to Duke he began
more desperately to attempt to convince me of the Balkan
empire. He brought around more syndicate gang leaders

to whom I listened attentively. After the sessions when I was alone with Duke I would again register disbelief. He would respond: 'OK, don't believe me, but when the Dragons start burning and a mass rumble happens, don't blame me.'

More of the seemingly 'less disturbed' Balkans began to challenge the leaders and Dragon myth, even when I wasn't present. Red, at this point the Balkan clown, 'produced' a fascinating 'debunking' playlet which he taped and then played for me.

Instead of leaping into peace discussion meetings and organizing gang meetings that gave rumours credence, I instituted a debunking approach that seemed to trim gang rumbles, fantasies, and rumours down to size.

For example, one day during this phase of what seemed to be a levelling off of the Dragon invasion, Red, Ape, and Nicky arrived at my office and excitedly reported an impending rumble for 'Friday night, seven-thirty at Grant's Tomb'. Instead of leaping into the gang-war inferno, I at first hedged:

L.Y.: What did you say?
NICKY: That's it – Friday the Dragons, Villains, East Side and Downtown are all coming in to turn it on. About 1,000 more guys – guns – blades – everything.

The others chorused in excitedly with the same fear and concern. I said 'Hold on a minute; I got to make a call.' I purposely made an inconsequential call related to checking the time and date of a social-worker meeting I had to attend. I role-played being somewhat disinterested in the mass rumble during the call. Then I hung up the phone and addressed the boys directly:

L.Y.: Now what's all this bullshit about a mass rumble?
NICKY: This is it! They're going to turn it on with the Dragons once and for all.
L.Y.: Who told you?
APE: Duke.
L.Y.: Do you guys believe all that crap about the Dragon invasion? When are you guys going to smarten up? Who told

Duke the uptown clubs and Dragons are coming down?
Loco?

NICKY [*sheepishly*]: Yeah, that's right.

We discussed the possible rumble for a while fairly
calmly. I was cool, and my demeanour and probing seemed
to tone the group down. Finally, I turned the discussion
over to the subject of basketball at the Columbia gym-
nasium. The possibility of a rumble was still on my mind.
However, I was not going to rise to bait until they settled
down. My next move was to check the temperature and
fact of the impending rumble a bit farther.

I asked, 'Where are all the guys?'

Nicky said, 'Over at Clint's.'

'OK,' I said. 'Come on – let's go have some coffee.'

We piled into my car and went down to Clint's. About
fifteen Balkans, including Jay and several friendly Villains,
were hanging around. We had coffee. I purposely spoke in
a loud voice to Jay, who was several stools away, also
having coffee. I wanted all of the boys to hear:

'I heard some nonsense about a rumble for Friday. In
case anyone is interested, [all] Captain Costello and his
men from the Twenty-fourth know something is shaking,
and the area is going to be crawling with cops and squad
cars. So, as a friendly tip, if no one here wants to get
busted, I advise you all to be cool.

'Also, if you guys are worried about Loco and the
Dragons, don't be. All local police have his description and
if he shows up with any Dragons, they're going to bust
him cold.'

I then finished my coffee, and left.

Everything I had said was a fact or about to become
fact. I called Captain Costello and alerted the local police
and the Youth Squad. Loco's description had already been
circulated, and he had already in fact been picked up and
questioned on two occasions. Nothing was revealed in the
police questioning, but Loco did stop 'invading' Balkan
turf. (I later found out a 'Dragon invasion' was flaring
around an area at Sixty-ninth Street and Amsterdam

Avenue. An individual who apparently looked like Loco
was the spearhead.)

My critical and direct approach was adopted by our
agency as policy and was used on many occasions. Rather
than leaping into peace conferences and supporting gang
fantasies, we began to attack what we thought was not
fact, but rumour. I later found that many of the more
emotionally stable Balkans had adopted our policy of
debunking and deriding 'on the corner' vis-à-vis gang
rumours. The police were also always informed of potential
problems, and their presence no doubt had its impact.

It was hard to sort out from the complex of factors
those which were instrumental in deterring and ending the
'invasion'. The only fact that could be stated with assurance was that the mass Dragon invasion, despite its
many minor assaults, collapsed as it had arrived –
spontaneously.[1]

One fact can be pointed to with certainty. The total
experience had a major effect on Balkan gang organization
– or, better – disorganization. The Balkans were exposed
by the pressure of the Dragon invasion. The fact of its
shifting and loose definition was brought to light, and the
Balkans as an entity never seemed to recover from this
revelation. The illumination of pursuing facts versus
distorted gang self-image, the technique consciously used
by our agency at the end of the Balkan régime, no doubt
had an effect. It seemed to have considerable impact on
the seemingly less emotionally disturbed peripheral gang
members in dissuading them and extricating them from
gang-war activity. It deflated the prestige of the hard-core
members and leaders and produced a sharp curtailment of

1. At the time I projected several speculations. The police impact, particularly upon Loco, may have cut off the invasion's primary source of
energy. The Balkans' increasing self-recognition of their lack of real strength
and brother gangs may have cut down the rumour mill. This may have been
partially affected by the deflation of Duke and Jerry as 'grand leaders'. It
is conceivable that my attack upon Balkan strength took its toll in cutting
the gang down to 'only you guys here now'. Another possibility is that the
mass conflict may simply have been diminished by the Christmas holidays,
which had just arrived. Whatever the reasons, the Dragon invasion ended
without a mass rumble.

Balkan violent-gang activity. Apart from a few scattered meetings and my continued relationship with several core Balkans, the Balkans as a fighting gang became defunct.

With the disappearance of the Balkan syndrome, as a vehicle for expressing hostility, pathology, and violence, other patterns of 'acting out' emerged for the members as a replacement, since nothing intensive had been accomplished with the individual boy's disturbed needs for this pathological group. Duke continued to meet with me several times a week. I later referred him; surprisingly he accepted the psychiatric care he apparently required. Nicky joined his brother in a reformatory. Several Balkans took to excessive drinking. Three in particular shifted from violent-gang pathology to drug addiction. Several Balkans went on to other gangs with other names. To the best of my knowledge the uptown clubs were dormant for a time. The leaders (notably Loco) then resumed the standard gang organization and drafting practices that amalgamated many former Villains and Dragons. On the night of 30 July, about a year later, these youths joined forces with the Egyptian Kings in their fatal march on Highbridge Park.

7. A Final View of Balkan Organization

The 'time of the Dragons' when the Balkans considered themselves at maximum strength seemed an ideal period for assessing their 'real' organization. Given the shifting nature of the gang, I realized there was insufficient time for constructing any elaborate 'research design' to supplement the 'field study' method already in operation. It was at this point that the idea of getting the gang to 'study itself' emerged and was developed.

'The Researchers'

At the height of the 'Dragon invasion' I called a private conference with Duke and Pedro and proposed a 'research project':

'What I would like to do is find out more about you guys and the Balkans. A lot of people are interested in how gangs are organized and why you guys feel you have to bop and all that. I've cleared it and have some money available for research. So, would you guys be interested in working for me as research assistants, at a price?'

Duke and Pedro looked at each other, puzzled, but also apparently interested and pleased. Duke asked, 'Well, what do we do?'

'Not too much more than we have been doing. I'll be asking you and your boys a lot of questions. And also we will make up a list of questions which I want you to get answers to from known gang members.'

Their immediate response was one of great interest, although they were not sure that an actual working arrangement with our agency would look good to their boys. After some skirmishing and assurances from me that I would not broadcast the fact that they were 'employees', they agreed to work for Morningside Heights,

Inc. — 'If the boys don't know, and it's just between us.'
After we had worked out the arrangements, including an
hourly rate of one dollar, which I proposed and they
accepted, the boys seemed excited about doing 'research'
but were still at a loss about how to proceed. (I shared
their feelings.)

At my insistence, the first project we 'mutually' selected was a study of Balkan gang organization. In several
afternoons of discussion Duke, Pedro, and I worked out a
questionnaire they felt was 'OK for us to ask questions
on'.

Appropriate spaces were left for answers. Terms like
'race' and 'guy' were used, as suggested by Duke and
Pedro:

Name of Club .... Age of guy ....
Race ....

1. Date you joined?
2. Why did you join?
3. How did the club begin?
4. What does club do? (For example, bopping, sports)
5. Alliances

    Names   *Number*

6. Leaders (How many?)
7. What other clubs have you belonged to?

    Clubs   *Dates*

8. Why did you quit?
9. What do you think of the Dragons?
10. How many Dragons? (Division and number)
11. How many divisions in your club?
12. How many members?
13. Weapons of club
14. What do you have against other clubs?
15. What other clubs have you fought? (Dates and clubs)
16. Anything else

Armed with this 'schedule' my 'research team' went
out into the 'field' for about three weeks. I met with the
boys daily to check their findings and in some cases to

decipher their writing. They varyingly filled out the questionnaires in their own handwriting at the time of the interview or let the interviewee fill it out himself.

The gang-boy respondents had mixed reactions to Duke and Pedro as researchers. Some boys co-operated fully with them; others felt they were stoolies working for the cops, and some non-Balkans reacted with overt hostility. On one occasion Duke arrived at my office, displayed some obviously fresh lacerations on his face, and claimed he had been beaten and robbed of ten filled-out questionnaires by six unidentified Negroes in central Harlem. He believed that his assailants were 'Dragon agents'. The details of the 'robbery' were incoherent, and I was never able clearly to ascertain what had actually happened. Despite the incident Duke was not deterred from his work. He requested more blank questionnaires and went back into the field. My conclusion about the assault was that five or six tough youths looking for action jumped Duke, who was alone at the time, for no special reason.

In addition to discussing the questionnaires with Duke and Pedro, on several occasions I used a role-playing device to attempt assessing at 'first hand' their interview technique. Their approach seemed to vary between a polite request for information at one extreme and a threatening 'You fill it out 'cause I say so' interview at the other. I tape-recorded several role-playing sessions of their interviews. The transcribed version of one such acted-out interview reveals a somewhat clearer picture of Duke's approach as a 'research interviewer'. I played the role of the gang boy being interviewed.

L.Y.: Well, what's that for?

DUKE: A guy I know is writing a book on gangs and I'm doing it for him.

L.Y.: No, man, I don't know whether I want to do that, 'cause it's liable to get in the papers or liable to get to the cops or something like that.

DUKE: I'm not giving it to the cops or anybody else; this is just for this guy.

L.Y.: How do you know he isn't a cop?

DUKE: Well, you know me – I wouldn't give it to the cops.

L.Y.: Yeah, but I can't be sure.

DUKE: Just don't bullshit me; just fill it out [*getting angry*].

L.Y.: What do you mean, suppose I don't want to?

DUKE: I say you wanna, you do it – you're filling it out.

L.Y.: Well, all right. Any special way you want me to do it?

DUKE: Just put down what you think is true, that's all – just don't put down your name.

L.Y.: Why shouldn't I put my name down?

DUKE: The guy doesn't want anybody's name; he just wants the opinions of the members of the clique, that's all.

L.Y.: I'll put down anything that comes to mind.

DUKE: Well, you just put down what you think is true, that's all.

L.Y.: How do I know what's true? It says here how many divisions of this and how many divisions of that – I don't know for sure.

DUKE: Just put down what you think.

Though Duke's interview technique was 'forceful', he had a talent for getting information. He confirmed the role-playing session as being close to many of his actual interview situations, and Pedro concurred. Given this somewhat less than ideal 'research' technique, the boys interviewed 126 different gang members. Fifty-one of these were identified by Duke, Pedro, and the respondents themselves as Balkan gang members. The balance of the questionnaires were filled out by sixteen Sportsmen, twelve Politicians, six El Diablos, and the rest by youths with various other gang designations.

The Balkans' Self-image

An appraisal of the fifty-one questionnaires with Duke's and Pedro's help revealed pertinent information about how the Balkan organization viewed itself. Of the fifty-one individuals who claimed membership and identity in the Balkan gang most lived in the area of Balkan turf. These were 'live' members known on a face-to-face basis by Duke and Pedro. The Balkans interviewed were identified according to 'race' as follows:

Spanish (Puerto Rican)	22
White	15
Negro	11
Other	3
Total	51

The 'white' boys, according to Duke and Pedro, included boys from 'Italian', 'Irish', and 'Polish' backgrounds. The issue of when a Puerto Rican is dark enough to be considered Negro was never clearly settled by our discussions.[1]

Balkan age distribution was revealed as:

Age	Number	Age	Number
12	7	19	10
15	8	20	2
16	5	over 20	5
17	10		
18	4	Total	51

The fifty-one responses to the question 'How many members?' varied within a range of eighty to 5,000. About twenty boys reported between 400 and 600. Most Balkans admitted that they did not know all the other Balkan gang members. Many youths indicated no knowledge of the number of members in the gang. Another typical vague response on membership was: 'It's about a few hundred or a thousand – lots of divisions.' With reference to alliances or brother gangs, there was no consensual reply. The boys expressed extremely different estimates of names, numbers, and size of 'brother gang' divisions. The range went from five to twenty allies, and their membership ranged from 500 to 6,000.

Duke and Pedro were listed as leaders on almost all of the responses. In addition, on this question there were several names of leaders I had never heard of before. (Some were even unknown to Duke and Pedro.)

There was general agreement (forty-eight out of fifty-one) that fighting and 'defence' were the main gang

1. This complicated issue will be discussed in Chapter 11.

activities, with sports and dances listed next in frequency. Most Balkans joined for defence, or, as one stated, 'Because I like to fight.' Most members did not know how the gang began; several indicated: 'Because Duke and Pedro started it', and the balance commented in various ways that it began for defensive reasons. In response to the question 'What do you think of the Dragons?' the general response consisted of a terse scurrilous remark. Their estimate of the Dragons' strength ran from about a hundred men and five divisions to 5,000 men and fifty divisions. Balkan weapons listed included knives, guns, chains, and belts.

The questionnaire data collected by the 'researchers' on other gangs in the sample were generally consistent with our findings on the Balkans. In particular, each gang member seemed to have his own unique image of the gang. The wide variations of response tended to refute the widely held image of the violent gang as a cohesive, tightly organized group – the one so prevalent in the literature.

A Capsule View of Balkan Gang Organization

A synthesis of field observations and notes, various spontaneous and structured taped interviews, Duke's diary, the Balkan gang leaders' 'research' and self-inventory revealed an overall view of Balkan gang organization that was representative, at least in general structure, of most other violent gangs we encountered and studied during the four years of gang research on Morningside Heights.

Balkan gang size was always a difficult factor to pin down because the exact number of Balkans claimed as members, beyond the fifty-one whom we were able to interview, ran into the thousands. They seemed to use gang size as a means of demonstrating power. Estimates of size would range from one hundred to thousands of members, depending on the gang's needs for strength at the time. When gang-war life was quiet, size lowest; during threats of invasions gang size expanded.

Duke's comment about the confusion of size and its shifting nature is revealing:

L.Y.: It appears as if all these [responses] are confused, that is, out of the fifty-one Balkans that answered the questionnaire, there were so many different answers as to numbers.

DUKE: Well, each guy wasn't sure of his own membership or who else was on the team, so they naturally weren't sure of their alliances. Each one had a different idea as to the organization of the Balkans. . . .

Despite this characteristic of gang size, the Balkans whom I actually observed to meet together consistently both in street-corner hangouts and in my office consisted of about twenty-five regular members, and I never saw more than thirty-five together at once. The three main leaders in the Balkans (individuals who maintained a formal leadership position such as 'president', 'captain', or 'war counsellor') were Duke, Pedro, and Jay. The Balkans adhered to a standard prescription for gang-leader categories, which an Egyptian King had succinctly described:

First, there's the president. He got the whole gang; then there comes the vice president, he's second in command; then there's the war counsellor, war lord, whatever you're gonna call it – that's the one that starts the fights; then there's the prime minister – you know, he goes along with the war counsellor to see when they're gonna fight, where they're gonna fight. And after that, just club members.

Duke was no doubt president, with Pedro in a supportive vice-president role. Other reputed leaders, such as Jerry and Ramón, were less tangible, even though they were mentioned on the questionnaire. (Such 'fantasy' leaders appear to be a characteristic part of violent-gang organization.)

The Balkans had a graduation division. Their 'first' and 'second' divisions were interchangeable with 'senior' and 'junior'. The first division was presumably the old group, composed of individuals roughly from the age of seventeen up. The second division was the group whose ages ranged from about twelve to sixteen. Although the gang discussed two divisions, the second division, the juniors, was the most tangible unit. My observations and the questionnaires revealed that the juniors comprised about twenty, or the majority, of visible members. The visible seniors were apparently the nucleus of the somewhat mythical first division of the gang, the contingent exaggerated by junior gang members as a sign of strength.

The pseudo-existence of the seniors was indicated on several occasions. When the Balkans held their dance at Columbia, the majority of gang members present were the twenty-five to thirty members of the second, or junior, division. Only a few seniors attended. During the 'Dragon invasion' most of the first division could not be produced for warfare or even a meeting. This led the Balkan juniors to agree finally that the senior Balkan division was more 'bull' than fact. Yet the 'division myth' was an important aspect of the Balkans' strength, since it served as a means of bolstering their courage under stress. The pseudoleaders and mythical divisions served as a 'reality', readily available as weapons for 'defence'.

Two levels of Balkan organization and membership participation seemed to cut through the entire gang. About twenty-five boys formed the 'core' group characterized by a more intense interest and concern with being identified as Balkans. Their activities stressed perpetuating the group, increasing membership, fighting for the gang's honour and turf, wearing Balkan jackets (which they purchased prior to the Dragon invasion), and selling the myth of large size and fighting power to anyone who would listen.

Other, more 'marginal', members of the Balkans were less involved with the gang. They were not always paying verbal homage to the strength and glory of the Balkans; sometimes they were even critical (for example, the gang-size debunkers during the invasion were marginals). Although they had some feeling of 'belonging', they could not be counted on in a fight.[1] (Under the pressure of the

1. Several specific categories of marginal members will be discussed in Chapter 13.

Dragon attack, many marginal members quit the Balkans
with a 'shrug of their shoulders'.)

The vast gang size and its divisions may be viewed as
marginal Balkans of pseudo-membership dreamed up by
Duke and others in fantasy and perpetuated by the core
gang members' needs to be part of a vast fighting army. Of
course, they were not complete fantasy, since on occasion
such gang members would appear briefly as marginals,
only to drop out of the gang the following day. Also to be
included in this Balkan category of membership were the
non-gang youths living in the neighbourhood who were
pointed to as Balkans by the strong needs of core Balkans
under stress. (In fact, these neighbourhood boys had no
idea they 'belonged' to the Balkans, and would laugh
when informed of their 'status'.) The gang alliances and
affiliations discussed continually by core Balkans comprised a mythical membership that might be viewed as a
part of the gang's 'normal' structure. Such a contingent
of mythical members that glorified Balkan alliances was
continually recorded by Duke in his dairy. In one section
he constructed a system of mythical envoys whose counter-
parts in the foreign service might be ministers or am-
bassadors:

Envoys for the Balkans

Duke is envoy to Villains for us. Also Devils. (Devils are now
    Balkans.)
Duke is envoy to Rams for us. Also United Dukes. (Rams are
    now Balkans.)
Johnny is envoy to Apaches for us.
Andy is envoy to Dwarfs for us, also Huns.
Marcus is envoy to Turks for us. Also Queens.
Gilbert is envoy to Copeans for us.
Peat is envoy to El Diablos for us. Also Anzacs.
Baby Face is envoy to Tiny Tims and Politicians for us.
Red is envoy to Road Knights for us.
Charlie is envoy to Sea Hawks for us.
Flortey is envoy to Saints for us. (Saints are now Balkans.)
Carlos is envoy to Gaels for us. (Gaels are now Balkans.)
Tex is envoy to Amboy Dukes for us.

Andy is envoy to Jr Braves and Jr Rebels for us.
Phil is envoy to Red Wings for us.
Portuguese is envoy to Saxons for us, also to Cavaliers.
Terry is envoy to Saxon Tots for us.

Some members of these alliances and affiliations actually
did appear at the June gang war. However, it was apparent from observing the Balkans, and having them
identify these constantly shifting alliances and affiliations,
that when other random boys did appear, they would do
so mainly as curiosity seekers. These core Balkans combined with the marginal category of highly prevalent and
aggressive gang boy – always looking for trouble and gang
action – formed most of the personnel of the Balkan 'war
machine'.

The 'research' carried out by Duke and Pedro supple-
mented and supported my views in revealing the Balkans
as a partial pseudo-community that despite its guiding
fictions (or perhaps because of them) was valuable to its
members. This 'self-analysis', combined with my debunking approach, was no doubt instrumental in helping
to cause the demise of the 'Balkan Empire'.

Social-psychological Perspectives on the Gang

8. A Historical View of Gangs: Past and Present

Adult Gangs

An early form of the American violent gang appeared around the latter part of the nineteenth century on the Bowery in New York City. Adult gangs of this type, called the Dusters, the Plug Uglies, the Dead Rabbits, the Five Points gang, and even some all-female gangs, were reported in Herbert Asbury's colourful book *Gangs of New York*. Asbury reports in close detail instances of the 'gang wars' of that period:

The gangs of the Five Points and the Bowery, by far the most turbulent of the city's inhabitants, took advantage of the opportunity to vent their ancient grudges against each other, and engaged in almost constant rioting. Scarcely a week passed without a half dozen conflicts. . . . Led by the Dead Rabbits and the Plug Uglies, all of the gangs of the Five Points with the exception of the Roach Guards began their celebration of the Fourth with a raid on the building at No. 42 Bowery, occupied by the Bowery Boys and the Atlantic Guards as a club-house. There was furious fighting, but the Bowery gangsters triumphed and drove their enemies back to their dens around Paradise Square . . . a few Metropolitan policemen who tried to interfere were badly beaten. The Municipals [police] said it was not their fight, and would have no hand in any attempt to suppress the trouble.

Early the next morning the Five Points gangs, reinforced by the Roach Guards, marched out of Paradise Square and attacked a resort called the Green Dragon, in Broome street near the Bowery, a favorite loafing place of the Boys and other Bowery gangs. Carrying iron bars and huge paving blocks, the Five Pointers swarmed into the establishment before the Bowery thugs could rally to its defense, and after wrecking the barroom and ripping up the floor of the dance hall, proceeded to drink all of the liquor in the place. News of the outrage reached the Bowery Boys, and they boiled furiously out of their holes, supported by the Atlantic Guards and the other gangsters who owed allegiance to them or loyalty to the Bowery. The gangs came together in Bayard street and immediately began the most ferocious free-for-all in the history of the city. . . .[1]

During this era gangs were apparently in charge of their own territory. When the police finally made an appearance, they were quickly 'subdued' by the unappreciative gangs:

   . . . A lone policeman, with more courage than judgment, tried to club his way through the mass of struggling men and arrest the ringleaders, but he was knocked down, his clothing stripped from his body, and he was fearfully beaten with his own nightstick. He crawled through the plunging mob to the sidewalk, and, naked except for a pair of cotton drawers, ran to the Metropolitan headquarters in White street, where he gasped out the alarm and collapsed. A squad of policemen was dispatched to stop the rioting, but when they marched bravely up Center street the gangs made common cause against them, and they were compelled to retreat after a bloody encounter in which several men were injured.

These early gang wars bear some resemblance to current gang battles: they were territorially divided, and certainly gang members did not shrink from violence in their encounters; however, the extent to which battle involved large numbers of adult citizens and the lack of police control shows some apparent differences when compared with modern gang wars. Of interest, however, is the fact that, comparable to modern gang war, 'from all parts of the city had hurried several hundred thieves and thugs who were members of none of the gangs'. Other differences exist between the groups observed by Asbury and the current violent gang. The formal social framework of direct gang suppression is stronger today. This suppression and condemnation of open violence are maintained not only by the police directly but also apparently by the general population. Most adult residents of gang neighbourhoods, at least on the surface, overtly condemn and

   1. Herbert Asbury, *Gangs of New York* (New York: Garden City Publishing Co., 1927), pp. 112–13.

oppose gang violence. This seems at first glance to contrast significantly with the open pitched battles of the past, where an entire neighbourhood joined in with the violence.

On another level, there is some degree of 'cheering on gang violence' comparable to that which took place by citizens in the early part of the century. Most citizens today, although overtly opposed to gang violence, on closer assessment manifest a degree of aggrandizement and glorification of gang activities. Presentations of crude violence in the press, movies, and television are supported and encouraged by an interested, if not fascinated mass audience.

There are also data that seem to suggest that the current violent gangs have a more pathological 'membership' than the earlier forms. The early gangs appeared to be socially acceptable group structures, at least within the norms and values of the neighbourhood in which they exist. They were not necessarily 'alien groups'. In most cases they were woven into the neighbourhood with such ordinary social patterns as political and national causes, 'business', and a way of earning a living. Although the overall public of the time may have considered the gang's behaviour deviant, it was normative to the particular neighbourhood in which it occurred. Senseless, unprovoked violence for kicks and ego gratification did not seem to be as much a part of the early gang's pattern. The social fabric of illegal liquor sales, theft, and particularly politics was closely integrated with gang activity.

A new era of violence was ushered in by the bootleg gangs of the twenties. These gangs, although illegal, were not alien to the society in which they existed. Despite their bloody inter- and intra-gang murders, they maintained a close affiliation with the social and economic conditions of the times. The gangsters of the twenties were the *henchmen* of political manoeuvrers and the 'big businessmen' of that period, in management–labour conflicts, liquor sales, prostitution, and gambling. Violence was used as an instrument of establishing and maintaining these somewhat 'socially accepted' business ventures. These gangs appeared to have strong ethnic, national, and religious cohesion. According to Thompson and Raymond the pre-prohibition gangs of New York were classified by their national or racial antecedents. They were principally made up of Irish, Italians, and Jews and related together partly by national and partly by neighbourhood ties. The Irish controlled the West, and the East Side belonged to the Italians and the Jews. The lower East Side of Manhattan in the first twenty years of the century was the greatest breeding ground for gunmen and racketeers that this country has even seen.[1]

The myth of the modern 'Mafia' or 'crime syndicate' so heralded today had its origins in this country during this period. Thompson and Raymond present one of the many versions of its beginning in New York City:

> The Unione Siciliane is a secret order, a sort of Italo-American version of the Mafia from which it stemmed. It was founded in this country by Ignazio (Lupo the Wolf) Saietta who was related by marriage to Ciro Terranova, one infamous locally as the 'Artichoke King'. The Unione always had a boss – sometimes several local bosses – but in greater New York, until Joe the Boss Masseria took charge in the 1920's the crown rested on a somewhat precarious head insofar as downtown Manhattan and Brooklyn were concerned. The Unione was not restricted then to gangsters and among its members were some men of respectable reputations and occupations. Occasionally the gates were even opened to non-Italians such as a lawyer who had performed a notable job of acquitting some Unione client of a murder charge. The initiation included that ancient rite of scratching the wrist of the neophyte and the wrists of the members, after which an exchange of blood was effected by laying the wounds one on the other. It made them all blood brothers. . . .[2]

As part of the normal business of the various illicit enterprises conducted by the early gangs of the twenties, homicidal violence was employed as an important and normal activity. More than a thousand gangsters died in

1. Craig Thompson and Allen Raymond, *Gang Rule in New York* (New York: Dial Press, 1940), p. 3.
2. op. cit., p. 4.

New York in the bootleg liquor wars of the 1920s. The murder of a minor bootlegger became an ordinary event.

Rum runners and hi-jackers were pistoled and machine gunned. They were taken for rides on the front seats of sedans and their brains blown out from behind by fellow mobsters they thought were their pals. They were lined up in pairs in front of warehouse walls in lonely alleys and shot down by firing squads. They were slugged into unconsciousness and placed in burlap sacks with their hands, feet and necks so roped that they would strangle themselves as they writhed. Charred bodies were found in burned automobiles.

Bootleggers and their molls were pinioned with wire and dropped alive into the East River. They were encased in cement and tossed overboard from rum boats in the harbor. Life was cheap and murder was easy in the bootleg industry, and those men of ambition who fought their way to the top were endowed with savagery, shrewdness, and luck. The killings by which their territories for trade were consolidated, and their competitors put out of the way, were not hot-blooded affairs at all, but cold and calculated business practice.[1]

The 'enforcers' of these gangs killed in businesslike fashion. Their personal kicks and distorted ego gratifications were secondary to their professional demands. A notable example of this type of violent offender was Abe 'Kid Twist' Reles. Reles admitted committing over eighteen murders himself in the normal course of his work as an agent of Murder, Inc. The unemotional quality of his violence was described as follows to a writer for *The Nation*:

The Crime Trust, Reles insists, never commits murders out of passion, excitement, jealousy, personal revenge, or any of the usual motives which prompt private unorganized murders. It kills impersonally and solely for business considerations. No gangster may kill on his own initiative; every murder must be ordered by the leaders at the top, and it must serve the welfare of the organization. ... Any member of the mob who would dare kill on his own initiative or for his own profit would be executed. ... The Crime Trust insists that murder must be a business matter organized by the chiefs in conference and carried out in a disciplined way.

1. op. cit., p. 100.

Although some contemporary adult 'gangs' organized for criminal objectives continue to be woven into current politics, labour unions, and syndicated criminal activities, such as prostitution, gambling, and drug markets, there are no longer *adult* gangs comparable to the early *openly* violent forms. Contemporary 'crime syndicates' bear little resemblance to such early gangs as the Five Points gang, Bowery Boys, or Atlantic Guards. Also, the criminal boss-dominated gangs – the Capone mob, the Monk Eastman gang, the Dillinger gang – have vitually disappeared from the American crime scene, notably as a consequence of vigorous law enforcement carried out by the F.B.I.

Youth Gangs – Early Forms

Contemporary violent youth gangs have a historical precedent not only in adult gangs, but also in earlier forms of youth gangs. The term 'youth gang' has been used to describe a variety of diverse youth groupings significantly different from current gangs. The same term, 'gang', has described collections of youths organized to go fishing, to play baseball, to steal cars, or to commit a homicide.

One of the earliest applications of the term 'gang' applied to youth groups was made by Henry D. Sheldon in 1898. He classified gangs, according to their activities, as: (1) secret clubs, (2) predatory organizations, (3) social clubs, (4) industrial associations, (5) philanthropic associations, (6) literary, artistic, and musical organizations, and (7) athletic clubs. He maintained at the time that among boys' clubs 'the athletic clubs are immensely the most popular, with predatory organizations a poor second'.[1]

Other early descriptions and uses of the term 'gang' go back to J. Adams Puffer (1905)[2] and Paul Hanley Furfey (1926).[3] Puffer's 'gangs' were essentially boys' clubs and athletic teams:

1. Henry D. Sheldon, 'The Institutional Activity of American Children'. *American Journal of Psychology* (1898), pp. 425–8.
2. J. Adams Puffer, 'Boys' Gangs', *Pedagogical Seminary*, XII (1905).
3. Paul Hanley Furfey, *The Gang Age; A Study of the Pre-Adolescent Boy and His Recreational Needs* (New York: The Macmillan Company, 1926).

The Dowser Glums

This tough gang contained four Irish boys, three French, one American. The members were for the most part seventeen or eighteen years of age, except the man of *twenty-six* [my under-line].

'Met out in the woods back of an old barn on Spring Street. Met every day if we did not get work. Any fellow could bring in a fellow if others approved. Put a fellow out for spying or telling anything about the club. Tell him we didn't want him and then if he didn't take the hint force him out. It had been going for two years; broke up now, I think.

'We played ball; went swimming, fishing, and shooting. Each of us had a rifle. Meet (at night) and tell stories of what we had done during the day. Go to shows. Go and watch dancing class. Sundays we loafed around streets. Sometimes went on a trip in the country. Went shooting. Other days catch a freight and go to W— and L—. Went to B— to shows and circus.

'Purpose of club was to steal; most anything we could get our hands on; fruit from fruit stands; ice cream at picnics. Rob a store and put it in an older barn – revolvers, knives, and cartridges. Work for two or three days, then loaf around and spend our money; spend money for circus. Sometimes folks would make us spend for clothes. Play cards – poker, whist, high low jack. Played in the woods. Smoke cigarettes, pipe, and cigars. Biggest fellow drank; he tried to make the other fellows drink but they wouldn't.'[1]

Puffer found that the sixty-six club 'gangs' he studied were all fundamentally alike. Each existed for the sake of a definite set of activities: 'to play games, to seek adventure, to go swimming, boating, and play Indians in the woods, to make mischief, to steal, to fight other gangs . . .'. As early as 1905 gangs attempted to maintain their turf. According to Puffer: 'Especially noteworthy is the desire of the gang for a local habitation – its own special street corner, its club room, its shanty in the woods'. Puffer concluded that all gangs had a high degree of uniformity and that 'Without doubt, there is a gang-forming instinct set deep in the soul of boyhood'. This earlier conception of the 'normality' of boys' gangs is still

1. Puffer, op. cit., p. 26.

prevalent and has coloured many recent images of the gang.

Early Sociological Conceptions of the Gang

The earlier gang analysts seldom used any complex theoretical categories for describing the gang. Essentially they relied on descriptive appraisals – presenting the gang, so to speak, 'as is'. More recent students of gang behaviour have utilized more abstract analyses. They have attempted to make theoretical generalizations about what causes gangs to emerge in society and the group structural factors that exist.

The sociological appraisals of 'gangs' may for the purposes of the ensuing discussion be separated into two categories. In the first appear the earlier writings (1920 to 1940) of individuals associated (if only in theory) with what might be termed the 'Chicago School'. In the second, arising over the past ten years, are the theoretical gang analysts, who have attempted to construct theories of gangs based on various sociological conceptions.

The earlier group, which would include such pioneers as Thrasher, Tannenbaum, Shaw, McKay, and Whyte, relied heavily on first-hand research data collected directly from the 'boys' in their gangs. The reader in most cases was given the opportunity to draw his own interpretive conclusions, since the data presented were sufficiently 'alive' to suggest their inherent meaning. In general their assessments of the gang-causation problem were essentially tied to theories of the slum community, the disorganized 'interstitial' area. Ganging and delinquent activity were considered a result of what Sutherland later called 'differential association'.

The more recent gang analysts, notably Cohen, Bloch and Niederhoffer, Miller and Cloward and Ohlin, may be viewed as 'theory builders'. They draw heavily on the works of Durkheim, Sutherland, and Merton in the development of their gang theories. Essentially the more recent theoretical gang analysts attempt to examine questions related to the forces in the social structure which produce gang behaviour as an adjustment pattern. The recent theories are not based upon direct research into gangs nor do they attempt to describe the structural aspects of gang formations. Although their theoretical logic is tightly fashioned, their generalizations are not based upon the firm foundation of empirical data – a strong attribute of the earlier Chicago school.

The Chicago School and Gangs

During the late twenties and the depression era of the thirties, a group of sociologists, radiating from the University of Chicago, focused upon various social problems which they attributed to urban social disorganization. Thrasher, Shaw, and McKay, in particular, instituted several delinquency research projects that produced data which remain the backbone of many current conceptions of delinquency and gangs. Their research and writing was heavily based upon case-history material and personal documents obtained from offenders in both institutions and the open community.

THRASHER'S GANGS. Frederic Thrasher may be credited with the first extensive sociological study of gangs. His findings were presented in a classic volume appropriately called *The Gang*. He defined the gang, based on his study of 1,313 cases, as: '. . . an interstitial group originally formed spontaneously and then integrated through conflict'. It was characterized by the behaviour of '. . . meeting face to face, milling, movement through space as a unit, conflict, and planning'. The result of this behaviour is the development of a 'tradition, unreflective internal structure, *esprit de corps*, solidarity, morale, group awareness, and attachment to a local territory'.[1] Thrasher's definition has been the basis for most current conceptions of the gang as found in contemporary theoretical appraisals of the crime problem.[2]

1. Frederic M. Thrasher, *The Gang* (University of Chicago Press, 1926).
2. An examination of ten of the most widely used current college textbooks on criminology reveals Thrasher's appraisal as the basis for their discussion of gangs.

Thrasher presented detailed descriptions of many diverse types of gangs to illustrate his material. A typical 'tough' gang observed by Thrasher were the 'Murderers':

Shortly after the race riots of 1919, residents in the vicinity south of the stock yards were startled one morning by a number of placards bearing the inscription 'The Murderers, 10,000 Strong, 48th & Ada.' In this way attention was attracted to a gang of thirty Polish boys, who hung out in a district known as the Bush.

The pastimes of the boys were loafing, smoking, chewing, crap-shooting, card-playing, pool, and bowling. Every morning they would get together at their corner or in their shack near by to 'chew the rag' and talk over the events of the day. The new members who were taken in from time to time were congenial spirits who had shown ability to elude the police or gameness in a fight. . . .

They broke into box cars and 'robbed' bacon and other merchandise. They cut out wire cables to sell as junk. They broke open telephone boxes. They took autos for joy-riding. They purloined several quarts of whiskey from a brewery to drink in their shack.

Most of them were habitual truants, and they acknowledged their commitments to the parental school [house of detention] with great pride. Many of them had been in the juvenile detention home and the jail. Their 'records' were a matter of considerable prestige in the group.

Although leadership shifted with changing circumstances, the best fighter, who 'knows how to lead us around the corner and pick a scrap,' was usually in command.

A high degree of loyalty had developed within the gang, and its members repeatedly refused to peach on each other in the courts. They stuck close together in most of their exploits, for their enemies were many and dangerous. They used to 'get' the 'niggers' as they came from the stock yards at Forty-seventh and Racine. 'We would hit them and knock them out of the cars.' They claim to have killed negroes during the riots. The police too were their enemies, for the 'cops were always picking on us and we liked to get them going.'

Their chief animosity, however, was directed against the Aberdeens, a rival gang that 'was always punching our kids.' They were forced to defend their sand pile on the tracks against this gang and several others, for it was not only a source of fun but a place where they could pick up coal for use at home. Many a rock battle was waged here and on the streets. They formed an alliance with half a dozen gangs for mutual aid and protection, and they counted an equal number as their special enemies. . . .[1]

The intensity and type of violence committed by the Murderers was primarily restricted to fist or rock fights. They apparently did not use knives, machetes, or zip guns – standard weapons of today's gang warfare.

The Community of the Gang

The Chicago Area Project instituted in the early thirties and currently operating out of the Illinois Institute for Juvenile Research has contributed some of the most significant theories, research, and correction programmes which have evolved in the field of American criminology. The project was described early in its career by its originators as a programme that sought to discover by demonstration and measurement a procedure for the treatment of delinquents and the prevention of delinquency in different neighbourhoods of Chicago, which produced a disproportionately large number of delinquents in the Cook County Juvenile Court. Involvement of the residents of the neighbourhood in planning and operating the programme was utilized. An effort was made to effect changes in the social environment of the neighbourhood by providing the area residents facilities and professional guidance for the development of their own programme of child welfare.[2]

Clifford Shaw and Henry McKay were the prime movers of the Chicago project. Their work over several decades, with the aid of many able assistants, revealed a conception of delinquency that remains currently of major significance. Their basic working assumptions were that delinquency was a normal activity in the slum ('interstitial') neighbourhood, that most offences (about ninety-five per cent) were

1. Thrasher, op. cit., pp. 62–3.
2. Ernest W. Burgess, Joseph D. Lohman, and Clifford R. Shaw, 'The Chicago Area Project', *Yearbook, N.P.P.A.* (1937), pp. 8–28.

committed in association with others in a gang, and that most youths were trained into a criminal career by other offenders from the neighbourhood. In short, that the average offender evolved in the normal course of events as a product of his social training.

In the early stages of the development of the delinquent, according to Shaw and McKay, robbery was a playful act in a kind of game:

When we were shoplifting we always made a game of it. For example, we might gamble on who could steal the most caps in a day, or who could steal caps from the largest number of stores in a day, or who could steal in the presence of a detective and then get away. We were always daring each other that way and thinking up new schemes. This was the best part of the game. I would go into a store to steal a cap, by trying one on and when the clerk was not watching walk out of the store, leaving the old cap. With the new cap on my head I would go into another store, do the same thing as in the other store, getting a new hat and leaving the one I had taken from the other place. I might do this all day and have one hat at night. It was the fun I wanted, not the hat. I kept this up for months and then began to sell the things to a man on the west side. It was at this time that I began to steal for gain. . . .[1]

After the initial gang-play activity, stealing would become a more serious business. Tannenbaum writing in the late thirties describes the next phase of gradation and graduation into larger and more serious crimes by the member of the early Chicago delinquent gangs.[2] The older boy, with more experience, according to Tannenbaum was more saturated in the criminal tradition and went 'robbin'' because it was a game and a source of income. This led to further differentiation and bigger jobs. The youth went from apple stealing to shoplifting, and

1. Clifford R. Shaw and Henry D. McKay, 'Social Factors in Juvenile Delinquency', National Commission on Law Observance and Enforcement, *Report on the Causes of Crime*, Report No. 13, Vol. II (Washington, D.C.: Government Printing Office, 1931).

2. Frank Tannenbaum, *Crime and the Community* (New York: Columbia University Press, 1939).

from that to 'rolling bums'. Then came pickpocketing, car-stealing, hold-ups, and sometimes murder. All of the gradation in crime was carried out in connexion with other members of the gang. It was a collective enterprise that had the approval of this 'play group'. The play group became the criminal gang by slow differentiation and habituation.

Delinquent-trained youths tend to become further pulled into the gang as they begin to 'conflict' with some elements of the community. The gang seems to develop in this fashion almost according to the Toynbee theme of 'challenge and response'. Its increased cohesion was a function of the response it met in the community. According to Thrasher it did not become a gang until it began to 'excite disapproval and opposition'. The opposition could come from another gang or simply any adult representatives of the community; the cops begin to give it 'shags' (chase it); or some representative of the community steps in and tries to break it up. According to Thrasher, this was the real beginning of the gang, for now it began to draw itself more closely together, and became a conflict group.[1]

Tannenbaum broadened Thrasher's conception of delinquent-gang formation to include the youth's conflict with additional elements of the 'out-group' law-abiding community. These forces, he contends, help to sharpen the gang youth's delinquent self-conception. In his conflict with the community there develop two opposing definitions of the situation. For the young delinquent it may be a form of play, adventure, excitement, interest, mischief, fun. 'Breaking windows, annoying people, running around porches, climbing over roofs, stealing from push-carts, playing truant – all are items of play, adventure, excitement.' To the community, however, these activities took on a form of 'nuisance, evil, delinquency, with the demand for control, admonition, chastisement, punishment, police court, truant school'. The conflict arises out of a divergence of values. As the problem developed, the

1. Thrasher, op. cit., p. 30.

situation would gradually become redefined and the community attitude would demand suppression. Under these conditions of conflict the gang became more developed and cohesive.

In revealing how the conflicting forces at work in the community produce a delinquent self-concept and attract a youth into the gang, Tannenbaum indicates how more socially acceptable forces lose out their claim on the youth. He specifies that the delinquent gang wins, not because of its inherent attraction but because the positive socio-cultural forces that might train a youth into socially acceptable behaviour patterns are weak.

Heavy weight was given to family disorganization by the Chicago School as a potentially positive social force that did not fulfil its function. This causal theme, still in vogue, remains a valid rationale for explaining part of the current gang problem. According to Tannenbaum:

> The family, by its internal weakness, may have been a contributory factor. The father or mother or an older brother may have been delinquent, or there may have been a sharp conflict of opinions and attitudes in the family, or constant bickering and incompatability between the parents, or the father may have been dead and the mother forced away from home so that the children were left unsupervised, or an ignorant and poverty-stricken mother may have encouraged the child to bring in food or money whether earned or stolen, or the father may have been a drunkard and given to seriously mistreating the child and breaking down the loyalty and unity which are essential to the slow maturation of systematic habit formation. In these and innumerable other examples that might be cited of family inadequacy we have a source for the acceptance by the child of his payments and gang affiliates *as a substitute for the home*.[1]

The gang emerges as a subcultural refuge from a conflict with the larger society that it opposes, and becomes for a disassociated youth his primary identification group. In this context the gang becomes a basic primary group necessary for self-sustenance, and all outsiders become targets for hostility and aggression. The police, in parti-

1. Tannenbaum, op. cit., pp. 12–13.

cular, tend to be viewed as a symbol of out-group hostility and clearly become an enemy. 'I learned to look at the police as my sworn enemies. All the guys in the bunch looked at them that way. The police were the only ones that interfered with whatever we wanted to do. . . .'[1]

According to the Chicago School, not only are societal forces 'sworn enemies' of the gang, but any youth caught in society's mesh for coping with the offender was socialized farther into a deliquent career. This includes the frequent visit to the reformatory. A degree of status was obtained by the gang member who had a reformatory experience since it was part of his training as a gang member.

The early Chicago School, its theories and researches, have had a lasting impact in the sociological image of delinquency in general and the gang in particular. Their conceptions may be summarized in the following propositions: (1) The youth begins his delinquent career on a thin line of malicious and mischievous play and then becomes more concretely involved in delinquent gang activity. (2) The natural conflict of a youth with the community and its conflicting set of norms and values drives him further into gang activity. (3) The gang emerges as a result of the failure of community forces, particularly the family, properly to integrate many youths into the more constructive, law-abiding neighbourhood society. (4) Loyalty and *esprit de corps* are strong mobilizing forces in the delinquent gangs, and it becomes a cohesive entity. (5) The gang becomes a kind of 'street-corner family' for youth detached, disassociated, and in conflict with the law-abiding community. (6) The gang in this context becomes a school for crime that provides both the opportunity, the training, and the motivation for a criminal career in association with others. (7) A youth enmeshed in the delinquent gang as a primary group gets driven farther into a delinquent career by the negative effect of society's institutionalized patterns for dealing with a problem. (8) A youth thus moves up in the delinquency hierarchy, and as a result of his criminal associations and

1. Shaw and McKay, 'Social Factors in Juvenile Delinquency'.

training becomes in his later years a recalcitrant criminal.

The Chicago School's characterization of the gang's development and structure was a logical foundation for Sutherland to specify his classic theory of 'differential association' written in his 1947 edition of *Principles of Criminology*:

A person becomes delinquent because of an excess of definitions favorable to violation of law over definitions unfavorable to violation of law. This is the principle of differential association. It refers to both criminal and anti-criminal associations and has to do with counteracting forces. When persons become criminal, they do so because of contacts with criminal patterns and also because of isolation from anti-criminal patterns.[1]

'*Street Corner Society*'

The Chicago School had the impact of spurring other studies of street gangs. A major participant-observation study made by William Whyte tended to reinforce many of the speculations revealed by the earlier Chicago studies. Whyte moved into the Italian neighbourhood of a large eastern city near Boston, which he called 'Cornerville'. He learned Italian and 'hung out' with the 'Norton Street Gang', the focus of his study. For three years he participated in the activities of the gang, developed friendly relations with the leaders, and, with their co-operation, studied the group's structure.[2]

A primary factor about the Norton Street Gang was that it was a product of the depression. Most of the members were in their twenties, and normally would have been working if jobs had been available. The 'gang', according to Whyte, emerged because the boys could accomplish more together than separately. The gang gave its members a feeling of solidarity, or belonging. They participated in constructive activities, engaged in athletics, helped each other financially (when they could), and discussed mutual

1. Edwin H. Sutherland, *Principles of Criminology*, 4th ed. (Philadelphia: J. B. Lippincott Company, 1947), p. 6.
2. Whyte's analysis of criminal influence and politics was also a major contribution of this book; however, this theme is not discussed here in any detail, since the focus is upon youth gangs.

problems. The Norton Street Gang was a co-operative formation, beneficial to its membership.

The Norton Street Gang pattern of essentially constructive interaction was in considerable contrast with the mutual hostility, aggression, and violence found among contemporary violent gangs. In addition to a high degree of co-operative action and *esprit de corps,* Whyte found the characteristics of permanence and cohesion in the corner gangs he studied:

> The corner-gang structure arises out of the habitual association of the members over a long period of time. The nuclei of most gangs can be traced back to early boyhood, when living close together provided the first opportunities for social contacts. . . . The gangs grew up on the corner and remained there with remarkable persistence from early boyhood until the members reached their late twenties or early thirties.
>
> The stable composition of the group and the lack of social assurance on the part of its members contribute toward producing a very high rate of social interaction within the group. The group structure is a product of these interactions.
>
> Out of such interaction, there arises a system of mutual obligations which is fundamental to group cohesion.[1]

Whyte's comments on gang leadership further support an image of the Norton Street Gang as a constructive organization:

> The leader is the man who acts when the situation requires action. He is more resourceful than his followers. Past events have shown that his ideas were right. In this sense 'right' simply means satisfactory to the members. He is the most independent in judgment. While his followers are undecided as to a course of action or upon the character of a newcomer, the leader makes up his mind.
>
> When he gives his word to one of the boys, he keeps it. The followers look to him for advice and encouragement, and he receives more of their confidence than any other man.
>
> The leader is respected for his fair-mindedness. . . .[2]

1. William F. Whyte, *Street Corner Society* (University of Chicago Press, 1943), p. 255.
2. Whyte, op. cit., p. 256.

Not only did Whyte's studies support the earlier images of the Chicago School, they also fostered conceptions of the gangs dealt with in the postwar era of the forties.

Youth Board 'Bopping Gangs'

About 1946 New York City was struck by the emergence of violent youth gangs that committed a number of seemingly senseless and vicious homicides. Workers were sent into the streets to deal with them in a special project that became known as the 'detached-worker programme'. The mayor later developed a permanent social agency called the New York City Youth Board to carry out work along these lines with such gangs. The Youth Board in a series of manuals and books based on their work developed a concept of the gang that has become an accepted diagnostic image for many similar programmes in urban areas throughout the country:

Structure of the Clubs

The gangs with which we worked were surprisingly well organized, on both a formal and informal level. Each club was divided into several divisions, usually on the basis of age. These divisions were called the Tiny Tims, Kids, Cubs, Midgets, Juniors, and Seniors. Nine to 13-year-old boys usually belonged to the Tiny Tims, while young men over 20 were members of the Seniors division. These divisions regarded themselves as autonomous groups; at the same time they had a strong feeling of kinship with each other. As the boys grew older they 'graduated' from one division to another – a feeding process which insured the continued life of each club. The divisions were in a hierarchical relationship to each other, the older groups having more power, status, and influence than the younger groups. . . .

Each division had its own officers including a president, vice-president, war counsellor, and 'light-up' man. The gang president played a central role in coordinating the group's activities, in exerting discipline, and in determining club goals. In addition, he frequently represented his group in its dealings with other clubs. The war counsellor contacted enemy gangs with whom fights were to take place; he arranged the time and place for these 'rumbles' and the weapons to be used. He also planned strategy and tactics.[1]

The Youth Board, at least on the basis of their writing, seemed to accept fully the stories of gang organization and leadership operation presented to them by violent-gang members. An appraisal of Youth Board publications reveals their conceptual view. According to the Youth Board, current gangs generally possess the following character-istics: (1) gang behaviour is 'normal' behaviour for youths; (2) all gangs have a high degree of cohesion, *esprit de corps*, and organization; (3) gang size or membership is measur-able; (4) the gang's role patterns are clearly defined; (5) gangs possess a consistent set of norms and expectations clearly understood by all members; (6) all gangs have a group of clearly defined leaders who are respected by gang members, distinctly specified and vested with a direct flow of authority; and (7) gangs have a coherent organiza-tion for gang warfare. The Youth Board's image of the modern 'bopping gang' was apparently greatly influenced by the earlier work on gangs described by Thrasher, Shaw, McKay, and Whyte. More recent empirical research raises some serious doubts about the Youth Board's conception of the violent gang.

1. Welfare Council of New York City, 'A Report on the Central Harlem Street Clubs Project', *Working with Teen-Age Gangs* (1950).

9. The Gang in Recent Sociological Theory

Several significant efforts have recently been geared to relating a variety of general sociological concepts and theories to explain the emergence and organization of gangs. Notable work in this direction has been presented by Cohen,[1] Bloch and Niederhoffer,[2] Miller,[3] and most recently by Cloward and Ohlin.[4] Although the gang theories presented are based upon limited direct empirical research, the constructs are logically reasoned and draw from relevant sources in the general field of sociology.[5] These several sociological positions on gangs will be presented here in a condensed form, with special emphasis on those theories which are most relevant for a later effort to develop a theory about *violent gangs*.

The Gang as a Subculture

Albert Cohen in his book *Delinquent Boys* views the gang as a subculture with a value system different from the dominant ones found in the inclusive American culture. 'Working-class' children, according to Cohen, use the delinquent subculture (the gang) as a mode of reaction and adjustment to a dominant middle-class society that indirectly discriminates against them because of their lower-class position. The thesis developed is that working-class youths, trained in a different value system, are not ade-

1. Albert K. Cohen, *Delinquent Boys – The Culture of the Gang* (Glencoe, Illinois: The Free Press, 1955).
2. Herbert Bloch and Arthur Niederhoffer, *The Gang* (New York: Philosophical Press, 1958).
3. Walter Miller, in W. C. Kvaraceus and W. B. Miller, *Delinquent Behavior* (Washington, D.C.: National Education Association, 1959).
4. Richard A. Cloward and Lloyd E. Ohlin, *Delinquency and Opportunity: A Theory of Delinquent Gangs* (Glencoe, Illinois: The Free Press, 1960).
5. It is strongly urged that each of these significant contributions to the development of a theory of gangs be examined at first hand in their entirety. At best, the condensations presented here are incomplete summaries.

quately socialized to fulfil the status requirements of middle-class society. Despite this differential socialization and subculture value condition, they are unfairly exposed to the middle-class aspirations and judgements they cannot fulfil. This anomaly or conflict produces in the working-class youth what Cohen has termed 'status frustration'.

In a 'reaction-formation' to this problem they use the gang as a means of adjustment. In the gang such youths act out their status frustrations in 'non-utilitarian, malicious, negativistic' forms of delinquency, which according to Cohen represent their way of reacting against the described status dislocation of the social system.

Cohen provides illustrations of the working-class boys' difficulties in such middle-class dominated settings as the school and community centre. Here the working-class youth finds himself exposed to generally middle-class agents of the society (for example, teachers and social workers). Their efforts to impose such middle-class rules as orderliness, cleanliness, responsibility, and the virtues of ambition upon him are met with sharp negativism. Cohen specifically presents nine cases of middle-class values, which are rejected by the working-class child. These include the following notions: (1) ambition is a virtue, (2) an emphasis on the middle-class ethic of responsibility, (3) a high value on the cultivation of skills and tangible achievement, (4) postponement of immediate satisfactions and self-indulgence in the interest of achieving long-term goals, (5) rationality, in the sense of forethought, planning, and budgeting of time, (6) the rational cultivation of manners, courtesy, personality, (7) the need to control physical aggression and violence, (8) the need for wholesome recreation, and (9) respect for property and its proper care.

Cohen contends the lower-class child in a 'reaction-formation' to these unfair impositions substitutes norms that reverse those of the larger society: '... the delinquent subculture takes its norms from the larger subculture, but turns them upside down. The delinquent's conduct is right by the standards of his subculture precisely because it is wrong by the norms of larger culture'.[1] The dominant theme of the delinquent subculture is the explicit and wholesale repudiation of middle-class standards and the adoption of their very antithesis. In this 'negative polarity' of 'just for the hell of it' vandalism and violence, working-class youths attempt to adjust their 'status frustration' and hostility toward the larger society's unfair imposition of middle-class values upon them.

The gang is implicitly defined by Cohen as a cohesive collection of working-class youths pursuing their delinquent activities in consort with one another. The individual delinquent is more 'the exception rather than the rule. . . .'[2]

Cohen's position on the gang's relation to the community and the family parallels the conceptions of the earlier Chicago School.

> . . . Relations with gang members tend to be intensely solidary and imperious. Relations with other groups tend to be indifferent, hostile or rebellious. Gang members are usually resistant to the efforts of home, school and other agencies to regulate, not only their delinquent activities, but any activities carried on within the group, and to efforts to compete with the gang for the time and other resources of its members. It may be argued that the resistance of gang members to the authority of the home may not be a result of their membership in gangs but that membership in gangs, on the contrary, is a result of ineffective family supervision, the breakdown of parental authority and the hostility of the child toward the parents; in short, that the delinquent gang recruits members who have already achieved autonomy. Certainly a previous breakdown in family controls facilitates recruitment into delinquent gangs. But we are not speaking of the autonomy, the emancipation of *individuals*. It is not the individual delinquent but the gang that is autonomous. For many of our subcultural delinquents the claims of the home are very real and very compelling. The point is that the gang is a separate, distinct and often irresistible focus of attraction, loyalty, and solidarity.[3]

1. Cohen, op. cit., p. 19. 2. Cohen, op. cit., p. 46.
3. Cohen, op. cit., p. 31.

In summary, the delinquent subculture described by Cohen represents a collective effort on the part of the youths to resolve adjustment problems produced by dislocations in the larger society. In the gang the norms of the larger society are reversed so that 'non-utilitarian' deviant behaviour (especially violence) becomes a legitimized activity. The gang thus provides a legitimate 'opportunity structure' for working-class boys to strike back at a larger society which produces their 'status-frustration' problems.

The Gang in a Cultural Context

THE ADOLESCENT STRIVING FOR MANHOOD. Bloch and Niederhoffer, in an interpretation somewhat different from Cohen's, view gang behaviour as a universal and normal adolescent striving for adult status. The ganging pattern may be found, if looked for, in all cultures, as a vehicle for achieving manhood. The gang pattern, they maintain, is more pronounced in cultures where youths are normally cut off from the possibility of manhood for a prolonged period. Their hypothesis is reached by the utilization of considerable cross-cultural material that attempts to reveal the differences and similarities of the adolescent condition in a variety of societies. Their basic position is presented in the following concise statement:

The adolescent period in all cultures, visualized as a phase of striving for the attainment of adult status, produces experiences which are much the same for all youths, and certain common dynamisms for expressing reaction to such subjectively held experiences. The intensity of the adolescent experience and the vehemence of external expression depend on a variety of factors, including the general societal attitudes towards adolescence, the duration of the adolescent period itself, and the degree to which the society tends to facilitate entrance into adulthood by virtue of institutionalized patterns, ceremonials, rites and rituals, and socially supported emotional and intellectual preparation. When a society does not make adequate preparation, formal or otherwise, for the induction of its adolescents to the adult status, equivalent forms of behavior arise spontaneously among adolescents themselves, reinforced

by their own group structure, which seemingly provides the same psychological content and function as the more formalized rituals found in other societies. This the gang structure appears to do in American society, apparently satisfying deep-seated needs experienced by adolescents in all cultures. Such, very briefly, is our hypothesis.[1]

In their analysis they attempt to assess adolescent cross-cultural behaviour attached to such cultural patterns as 'puberty rites', 'self-decoration', and 'circumcision'. An emphasis is placed upon relating the 'rites' of other cultures to American adolescent 'rites in the gang'. Attention is focused upon symbolic evidence of the 'urge for manhood'. The gang and its machinations are thus viewed as a vehicle for accomplishing the assumed highly desired status objective of manhood.

According to Bloch and Niederhoffer, gang structure has a high degree of stability. In their criticism of Thrasher and others who attribute characteristics of flux and 'movement' to gang organization they argue:

> Observations of gang behavior in various neighborhoods of New York City, for example, seem to reveal just the opposite to be true. In fact, one of the outstanding characteristics of numerous gangs which have been observed appears to be their highly non-mobile and stationary nature, a fact to which many exasperated shopkeepers and building custodians, as well as the police, can amply testify. Gangs, thus, might just as well be characterized by an absence of movement since, for the most part, they frequent the same corner or candy store for hours on end, every day of the week.[2]

Bloch and Niederhoffer strongly emphasize the highly controversial point that delinquency is a 'characteristic of all adolescent groups' and that organizational structure of all adolescent groups (delinquent or not) are similar:

> In respect to the type of organizational structure, there is little to distinguish, in one sense, between middle and lower class adolescent groups. Although middle class groups of teenagers are not as apt to have the formal, almost military,

1. Bloch and Niederhoffer, op. cit., p. 17.
2. Bloch and Niederhoffer, op. cit., pp. 6–7.

structure characteristic of certain lower class 'war gangs' . . . they do have similar and well-defined informal patterns of leadership and control. Even here, however, the distinctions become blurred and, upon occasion, almost indistinguishable when one recalls the ceremonial designations and ritualistic roles performed by college fraternity functionaries.[1]

Using data about adolescents from such diverse groups as the Mundugumor, Manus, the Kaffir children of South Africa, the Comanche and Plains Indians, and a tightly knit delinquent New York gang, Bloch and Niederhoffer attempt to draw the inference that the 'ganging process' provides symbolic evidence of the urge to manhood. At the end of their analyses they conclude:

(1) Adolescent gangs may be profitably studied by using as a frame of reference the theory of power.

(2) The gang's attempt to gain status and power through the domination and manipulation of persons and events is a collective representation of the individual gang member's guiding fiction which is 'to prove he is a man.' In passing it is worthy of note that Alfred Adler's system of psychology is 'tailor made' for the analysis of the gang since it is principally concerned with the struggle for power and the 'masculine protest.'

(3) The presence of the gang, real, constructive or symbolic, gives the individual member ego support and courage. He gains a psychological sense of power and manhood which he does not possess at all when he is on his own.

(4) If single gangs can pose a threat to the peace and safety of the community – and they certainly do so – then the well meaning efforts to organize several gangs into a confederation may be a very grave error. Without significant changes in behavior and values on the part of such gangs, this maneuver may only multiply to extremely dangerous proportions the looming menace which even now we find extremely difficult to control.[2]

LOWER-CLASS CULTURE AND 'NORMAL' DELIN-QUENCY. Using cultural concepts in a somewhat different fashion, Walter Miller projects a lower-class adolescent theory of gangs. He maintains (in a fashion somewhat

1. Bloch and Niederhoffer, op. cit., p. 9.
2. Bloch and Niederhoffer, op. cit., p. 217.

similar to Cohen's position) that the values of lower-class culture produce deviance because they are 'naturally' in discord with middle-class values. The youth who heavily conforms to lower-class values is thus automatically delinquent. He lists such a set of characteristics of lower-class culture that tend to foster delinquent behaviour:

Trouble: Concern over 'trouble' is a dominant feature of lower-class culture. .... 'Trouble' in one of its aspects represents a situation or a kind of behavior which results in unwelcome or complicating involvement with official authorities or agencies of middle-class society. .... For men, 'trouble' frequently involves fighting or sexual adventures while drinking; for women sexual involvement with disadvantageous consequences. Expressed desire to avoid behavior which violates moral or legal norms is often based less on an explicit commitment to 'official' moral or legal standards than on a desire to avoid 'getting into trouble,' e.g., the complicating consequences of the action.

Toughness: The concept of 'toughness' in lower-class culture represents a compound combination of qualities or states. Among its most important components are physical prowess, evidenced both by demonstrated possession of strength and endurance and athletic skill; 'masculinity,' symbolized by a complex of acts and avoidance (bodily tattooing, absence of sentimentality; non-concern with 'art,' 'literature'; conceptualization of women as conquest objects, etc.); and bravery in the face of physical threat. The model for the 'tough guy' – hard, fearless, undemonstrative, skilled in physical combat – is represented by the movie gangster of the thirties, the 'private eye,' and the movie cowboy.

Smartness: 'Smartness' . . . involves the capacity to outsmart, outfox, outwit, dupe, 'take,' 'con' another or others, and the concomitant capacity to avoid being outwitted, 'taken,' or duped oneself. In its essence, smartness involves the capacity to achieve a valued entity – material goods, personal status – through a maximum use of mental agility and a minimum of physical effort.

Excitement: For many lower-class individuals the rhythm of life fluctuates between periods of relatively routine or repetitive activity and sought situations of great emotional stimulation.

Many of the most characteristic features of lower-class life are related to the search for excitement or 'thrill.' Involved here are the widespread use of gambling of all kinds. . . . The quest for excitement finds . . . its most vivid expression in the recurrent 'night on the town' . . . a patterned set of activities in which alcohol, music, and sexual adventuring are major components.[1]

Miller, in a similar vein to Bloch and Niederhoffer's position, suggests that gang activity is, in part, a striving to prove masculinity. Females are exploited by 'tough' gang hoods in the 'normal' process of relating. They are as he specifies 'conquest objects' utilized to prove and boost the masculinity of the street-corner male.

Miller further theorizes that the gap between levels of aspiration of lower-class youths and their general inability to achieve produces different types of lower-class categories, the different patterns he contends reveal the degree of delinquency proneness of a youth:

1. '*Stable*' *lower class*. This group consists of youngsters who, for all practical purposes, do not aspire to higher status or who have no realistic possibility of achieving such aspiration.

2. *Aspiring but conflicted lower class*. This group represents those for whom family or other community influences have produced a desire to elevate their status, but who lack the necessary personal attributes of cultural 'equipment' to make the grade, or for whom cultural pressures effectively inhibit aspirations.

3. *Successfully aspiring lower class*. This group, popularly assumed to be the most prevalent, includes those who have both the will and the capacity to elevate their status.[2]

Emphasis is placed on the fact that lower-class youths who are confronted with the largest gap between 'aspirations' and possibilities for 'achievement' are most delinquency-prone. Such youths are apt to utilize heavily the normal range of lower-class delinquent patterns of 'toughness', 'shrewdness', 'cunning', and other devices in an effort to achieve prestige and status.

1. In Kvaraceus and Miller, op. cit., pp. 68–9.
2. Kvaraceus and Miller, op. cit., p. 72.

... toughness, physical prowess, skill, fearlessness, bravery, ability to con people, gaining money by wits, shrewdness, adroitness, smart repartee, seeking and finding thrills, risk, danger, freedom from external constraint, and freedom from superordinate authority. These are the explicit values of the most important and essential reference group of many delinquent youngsters. These are the things he respects and strives to attain. The lower-class youngster who engages in a long and recurrent series of delinquent behaviors that are sanctioned by his peer group is acting so as to achieve prestige within his reference system.[1]

The Gang as a Delinquent Opportunity System

In *Delinquency and Opportunity: A Theory of Delinquent Gangs*, Cloward and Ohlin 'attempt to explore two questions: (1) Why do delinquent "norms," or rules of conduct, develop? (2) What are the conditions which account for the distinctive content of various systems of delinquent norms – such as those prescribing violence or theft or drug-use?'[2]

In dealing with their first question they focus more upon the emergence of delinquent norms and behaviour systems than upon the 'analysis of delinquent acts or the careers of individual delinquents'. In their descriptions of types of delinquent adjustment patterns they attempt to explain the social conditions which produce three types of delinquent norms – namely, violence, theft, and drug use. Each of these dominant themes they contend provides the focal concern of three basic gang types: (1) conflict gangs, (2) criminal gangs, (3) retreatist gang drug users. Cloward and Ohlin rely heavily in their classification of gangs upon the subculture concept. In their view:

A delinquent subculture is one in which certain forms of delinquent activity are essential requirements for the performance of the dominant roles supported by the subculture. It is the central position accorded to specifically delinquent activity that distinguishes the delinquent subculture from other deviant subcultures.[3]

1. Kvaraceus and Miller, op. cit., p. 69.
2. Cloward and Ohlin, op. cit., p. ix.
3. Cloward and Ohlin, op. cit., p. 7.

Utilizing their concept of 'subcultures', they more explicitly define the three dominant kinds of subcultures or gangs; the 'criminal', the 'conflict', and the 'retreatist'. The delineation of these different subcultures, according to Cloward and Ohlin, refers essentially to a kind of ideal type. They recognize that 'the extent to which the norms of the delinquent subculture control behavior will vary from one member to another'. Because of this factor their descriptions of each subculture is stated in terms of the 'fully doctrinated member rather than the average member'. According to Cloward and Ohlin, therefore, the three dominant types of delinquent gangs are more explicitly described as:

The '*criminal gang*' – devoted to theft, extortion, and other illegal means of securing an income; some of whose members may graduate into the ranks of organized or professional crime.

The '*conflict gang*' – where the participation in acts of violence becomes an important means of securing status.

The '*retreatist gang*' – the most enigmatic group, where the consumption of drugs is stressed, and addiction is prevalent.

The central explanation presented by Cloward and Ohlin for the emergence of such delinquent gangs is derived from the 'goals, norms, and anomie' theories of Durkheim and Merton. Their basic view is '. . . that pressures toward the formation of delinquent subcultures originate in marked discrepancies between culturally induced aspirations among lower-class youth and the possibilities of achieving them by legitimate means'.

Cultural goals become an important aspect of the Cloward and Ohlin thesis as derived from Durkheim. In describing two categories of need, physical and social, Durkheim makes the point that physical needs are satiable, whereas social gratification is 'an insatiable and bottomless abyss'. Given this condition Cloward and Ohlin state that when men's goals become unlimited the 'norms no longer control men's actions' and a state of 'normlessness' or anomie exists.

Using Merton's elaboration of Durkheim's basic postulate,

Cloward and Ohlin attempt to account for the different patterns of deviant behaviour. In Merton's speculation anomie (normlessness) and the breakdown of social control emerge not because of 'insatiable goals' alone but because of a lack of fit between the goals and the legitimate means for acquiring the goals of society. As Merton specifies, 'Aberrant behavior may be regarded sociologically as a symptom of dissociation between culturally prescribed aspirations and socially structured avenues of realizing these aspirations'.[1]

Merton's formulation, according to Cloward and Ohlin, helps to explain the existence of a larger proportion of law violators among lower-class youth. In the social hierarchy, because they are denied equal access to normative social opportunity, a greater strain toward deviance develops. This theme is specified by Cloward and Ohlin:

> The ideology of common success-goals and equal opportunity may become an empty myth for those who find themselves cut off from legitimate pathways upward. We may predict, then, that the pressure to engage in deviant behavior will be greatest in the lower levels of the society.
>
> Our hypothesis can be summarized as follows: The disparity between what lower-class youth are led to want and what is actually available to them is the source of a major problem of adjustment. Adolescents who form delinquent subcultures, we suggest, have internalized an emphasis upon conventional goals. Faced with limitations on legitimate avenues of access to these goals, and unable to revise their aspirations downward, they experience intense frustrations; the exploration of nonconformist alternatives may be the result.[2]

In their discussion of various barriers to normal success placed in the path of lower-class youths, Cloward and Ohlin attempt to account for the gangs as an alternative road to social 'success-goals'. Alienated youths band together in the collectivity of the gang in an effort to resolve mutually shared problems. The same theme is used to ex-

1. R. K. Merton, *Social Theory and Social Structure* (Glencoe, Illinois: The Free Press, 1957), p. 134.
2. Cloward and Ohlin, op. cit., p. 86.

plain the different normative patterning of gangs: the conflict, criminal, and retreatist. A youth's selection of one type of gang over the other is related to the degree of availability of these illegitimate 'opportunity structures' in different socio-cultural settings.

To explain this emergence of different gangs Cloward and Ohlin develop their central 'hypothesis of differential opportunity':

We believe that the way in which these problems are resolved may depend upon the kind of support for one or another type of illegitimate activity that is given at different points in the social structure. If, in a given social location, illegal or criminal means are not readily available, then we should not expect a criminal subculture to develop among adolescents. By the same logic, we should expect the manipulation of violence to become a primary avenue to higher status only in areas where the means of violence are not denied to the young. To give a third example, drug addiction and participation in subcultures organized around the consumption of drugs presuppose that persons can secure access to drugs and knowledge about how to use them. In some parts of the social structure, this would be very difficult; in others, very easy. In short, there are marked differences from one part of the social structure to another in the types of illegitimate adaptation that are available to persons in search of solutions to problems of adjustment arising from the restricted availability of legitimate means. In this sense, then, we can think of individuals as being located in two opportunity structures – one legitimate, the other illegitimate. Given limited access to success-goals by legitimate means, the nature of the delinquent response that may result will vary according to the availability of various illegitimate means.[1]

Cloward and Ohlin tend to minimize the importance of individual personality factors and characteristics. As they specify, '... the social milieu affects the nature of the deviant response whatever the motivation and social position (i.e. age, sex, socio-economic level) of the participants in the delinquent subculture'.[2]

1. Cloward and Ohlin, op. cit., pp. 151–2.
2. Cloward and Ohlin, op. cit., p. 160.

Criminal subcultures or gangs, according to Cloward and Ohlin, are most likely to occur in the somewhat stable slum neighbourhoods which provide a hierarchy of criminal opportunity. In some conflict with Cohen's description of gang behaviour as 'malicious, negativistic and non-utilitarian', Cloward and Ohlin argue that for many youths in this type of neighbourhood the desire to move up in the neighbourhood criminal hierarchy may cause them to 'overconform' to delinquent values and behaviour in order to demonstrate or show off their criminal ability. Such 'criminal overconformity' Cloward and Ohlin maintain accounts for rash 'non-utilitarian' delinquent acts.

About the emergence of criminal subcultures Cloward and Ohlin conclude:

. . . the criminal subculture is likely to arise in a neighborhood milieu characterized by close bonds between different age-levels of offender, and between criminal and conventional elements. As a consequence of these integrative relationships, a new opportunity structure emerges which provides alternative avenues to success-goals. Hence the pressures generated by restrictions on legitimate access to success-goals are drained off. Social controls over the conduct of the young are effectively exercised, limiting expressive behavior and constraining the discontented to adopt instrumental, if criminalistic, styles of life.[1]

Conflict subcultures, according to Cloward and Ohlin, tend to arise in disorganized slums that provide no organized hierarchy for criminal development. They maintain that these slums offer both limited legitimate or illegitimate 'opportunity structures' because of a 'present' oriented high degree of disorganization. The social disorganization of such slums contributes to the breakdown of any adequate social control. The problem of anomie is, however, offered as a central explanation for the emergence of the 'conflict gang':

The young in such areas are also exposed to acute frustrations, arising from conditions in which access to success-goals is

1. Cloward and Ohlin, op. cit., p. 171.

blocked by the absence of any institutionalized channels, legitimate or illegitimate. They are deprived not only of conventional opportunity but also of criminal routes to the 'big money'. In other words, precisely when frustrations are maximized, social controls are weakened. Social controls and channels to success-goals are generally related: where opportunities exist, patterns of control will be found; where opportunities are absent, patterns of social control are likely to be absent too. The association of these two features of social organization is a logical implication of our theory.[1]

The lack of opportunity in these avenues cause such youths to seek it in other ways. They contend: '. . . adolescents turn to violence in search of status. Violence comes to be ascendant, in short, under conditions of relative detachment from all institutionalized systems of opportunity and social control'.[2]

The retreatist subculture emerges, according to Cloward and Ohlin, as an adjustment pattern for those lower-class youths who have failed to find a position in the criminal or conflict subculture, and have also failed to use either legitimate or illegitimate opportunity structures. They suggest '. . . that persons who experience this "double failure" are likely to move into a retreatist pattern of behavior'.[3]

Some youths who either drop out of other types of gangs or find the conflict or criminal gang no longer functional may also resort to the retreatist pattern. Cloward and Ohlin conclude that limitations on both legitimate and illegitimate opportunity structures produce intense pressures towards retreatist behaviour. All three types of gang behaviour are viewed by Cloward and Ohlin as adjustment patterns that utilize the most available 'opportunity structure' provided by the 'anomic' social system.

1. Cloward and Ohlin, op. cit., pp. 174–5.
2. Cloward and Ohlin, op. cit., p. 178.
3. Cloward and Ohlin, op. cit., p. 181.

10. Toward a Theory of the Violent Gang

The Need For a Definition of Gangs

Emile Durkheim, writing on 'The Observation of Social Facts' in his classic volume *The Rules of Sociological Method*, exhorts the sociologist to '. . . emancipate himself from the fallacious ideas that dominate the mind of the layman; he must throw off, once and for all, the yoke of these empirical categories which from long continued habit have become tyrannical'.[1]

Not only is a freedom from preconception urged; Durkheim's second canon is the necessity for being explicit:

> Every scientific investigation is directed toward a limited class of phenomena, included in the same definition. The first step of the sociologist, then, ought to be to define the things he treats, in order that his subject matter may be known. This is the first and most indispensable condition of all proofs and verifications. A theory, indeed, can be checked only if we know how to recognize the facts of which it is intended to give an account.[2]

The term 'gang', as revealed by the foregoing review of the literature, has been employed with considerable imprecision. It is readily apparent that Asbury's Five-Points gang, Puffer's Dowser Glums, Whyte's Norton Street Gang, Bloch and Niederhoffer's Comanche adolescent group, Cohen's 'delinquent boys', and Cloward and Ohlin's 'retreatist subculture' are all somewhat different orders of data. Yet each in the literature has been placed under the overall conceptual umbrella of the 'gang'. In the more recent presentations of gang literature it is difficult to ascertain whether the subject of reference is a

1. Emile Durkheim, *The Rules of Sociological Method* (Glencoe, Illinois: The Free Press, 1938; reprinted 1950, 1958), p. 32.
2. Durkheim, op. cit., pp. 34–5.

collection of 'tough hoods' or delinquents, youths simply hanging out on the corner, a violent gang, or a collection of delinquents joined together to carry out one or a series of burglaries. Cloward and Ohlin's effort to classify gangs as subcultures is a move in the right direction. However, based on my direct appraisal of over one hundred gangs, their description of the 'criminal' and 'retreatist' gangs conflicts with the live evidence.

CRIMINAL GANGS. Cloward and Ohlin's classification and description of 'criminal gangs' is based to a great extent on the older images of gangs and criminal hierarchies which apparently existed in some of the more stable criminal-producing slums of Chicago in the twenties and thirties. Current delinquents, with the exception of a few minority groups, have no opportunity to graduate in any 'criminal gang' hierarchy. What was true in the old Chicago School of gangdom no longer seems to apply in the current 'dis-organized slum'. Cohesive collections of youths band to-gether into gangs for delinquent pursuits; however, this type of gang provides no next step in the criminal world 'class system'. The current 'delinquent-gang' youth, with some rare exceptions, operates in the 'here and now'. He has a limited concern with rising into any adult criminal gang, and his delinquent acts in association with others have the limited goal of a 'quick score' for profit.

RETREATIST GANGS. The 'retreatist subculture' of the addict is simply not a gang in any sense. As Cloward and Ohlin indicate,[1] and as Chein and other researchers reveal,[2] drug addicts have limited gang status and are essentially discarded by the gang when they become addicted. My own research indicates drug addiction as a highly in-

1. Richard A. Cloward and Lloyd E. Ohlin, *Delinquency and Opportunity: A Theory of Delinquent Gangs* (Glencoe, Illinois: The Free Press, 1960), pp. 185–6.

2. Isador Chein *et al.*, *Studies of Narcotics Use Among Juveniles* (New York University, Research Center for Human Relations, mimeographed, January, 1956).

dividualistic activity with few group implications.[1] As one 'long-term' addict revealed: 'You're always alone – even if someone else is there. The only time I ever got together with anyone in the last twelve years was to steal or make a connexion to get a fix.' Most drug addicts are isolates, and their human relations have limited group characteristics. Moreover, a gang – with any stability of organization – or successful delinquent organization can not afford to 'carry' an irresponsible, unpredictable drug addict.

The drug addict is generally not interested in participation in any type of gang. Most research reveals that, with rare exception, the drug addict only is concerned with his last 'shot' and getting 'bread' (money) for his next 'shot'. The delinquent gang doesn't want him because the addicted personality is unreliable and may hinder rather than help in 'pulling a job'. He is also not interested in the violent gang, since through drugs he is getting his kicks in a new fashion.

Many youths become addicts when the violent gang is no longer available or suitable to them as a compensatory vehicle. The youth who becomes addicted gets on the drug-seeking treadmill. His aim in life is to go 'on the nod' with the shot he has just taken, or pursue the next shot he begins to need desperately. His concern with anyone else is simply as a 'mark', a victim to be conned or cheated – possibly a criminal accomplice in a 'quick score' for acquiring drugs. The flux of the addict's life condition provides no stability for any group formation – even one with very limited cohesion. Drug addicts, as social isolates, may be in some physical proximity to each other, but their lack of ability to relate even minimally makes a social group almost impossible. The 'retreatist subculture' can thus not be rationally regarded as a category of gang.

With these considerations in mind, modification of the 'criminal gang', rejection of the 'retreatist gang', and the

1. I am here essentially referring to the extreme 'main-line' heroin addict. The marijuana smoker or 'joy popper' (occasional user of heroin) is not the concern of this analysis, since this type of individual can function with some adequacy in group activity.

addition of another prevalent form, the 'tough social gang', an attempt will be made here to develop a gang classification system. Although three types of gangs will be described, emphasis will be placed more specifically on defining the *violent gang*, the category central to this book.

THE CLASSIFICATION OF GANGS

Three types of gangs appear most persistently in 'gang neighbourhoods': (1) delinquent gangs, (2) violent gangs, and (3) social gangs. Although these prototypes seldom appear in a pure form, the following will attempt to describe the structure and behaviour of the 'ideal type'. Summarily, the *delinquent gang* is dominated by delinquent patterns of activities characterized by such direct illegal behaviour as stealing or assault with material profit as the essential objective; the *violent gang*'s activity is dominated by sociopathic themes of spontaneous prestige-seeking violence with psychic gratification (kicks) as the goal; the *social gang* is a social group comprised of tough youths who band together because they believe and find their individual goals of a socially constructive nature can most adequately be achieved through their gang pattern.

Although these gangs, as indicated, seldom appear in a pure form, they have a central characteristic that distinguishes them, and most of their behaviour revolves around this central theme. There are, of course, youths who belong to one or more types during their gang career; and some youths belong to several simultaneously. The gangs' central norms, behaviour patterns, and personality characteristics of the membership tend to distinguish each gang type. Type I is socially-dominated, Type II is delinquency-dominated and Type III is violence-dominated.

Category I: Social Gang

This form of gang is a relatively permanent organization that centres around a specific stable location such as a hangout, candy store, or clubhouse. All members are intimately known to one another and there is a sense of comradeship and 'we' feeling. Members belong in a clear-cut way. They may wear a club jacket or sweater with an insignia, which identifies the members to the external community.

Activities are 'socially dominated', and require a high degree of responsible social interaction in the group. Their activities include organized athletic participation, personal discussions, organizing dances, and other socially acceptable activities characteristic of youths. Membership is not based upon 'self-protection' (as in the violent gang) or on social athletic prowess (as in a pure athletic team) but upon feelings of mutual attraction. The basic aspect of cohesion is the feeling that through the group the individual can lead a fuller life. Members are willing to submerge individualistic interests to agreed-upon and pursued group activities. Leadership is based upon popularity, constructive leadership qualities, and generally operates informally. The leader is apt to be the idealized group member. (For example, Doc, of the Norton Street Gang.)

This type of gang seldom participates in delinquent behaviour, gang warfare, petty thievery, except under unusual conditions. They may become involved in minor gang clashes but only under great pressure. The social gang has considerable permanence. Its members often grow up together on the same block and develop permanent lifelong friendships that continue when they leave the 'corner' and move into adult-life patterns. Whyte's Norton Street Gang most aptly fits this category of 'social gang'.

The social gang is closely associated with and acts in terms of the values of the larger society. It draws its membership from the most emotionally stable and socially effective youths in the neighbourhood. These are youths most closely influenced and involved with norms and values of the more inclusive society. The social gang and its members are most closely intertwined in their interests with community centre, school, athletics, and the socially acceptable activities operative in the neighbourhood. Thus, the social gang is in the form least disassociated from the overall society.

Category II: The Delinquent Gang

stable youths - out for profit - small close-knit group (handwritten annotation)

The delinquent gang is primarily organized to carry out various illegal acts. The 'social' interaction part of the gang's behaviour is a secondary factor. Prominent among the delinquent-gang behaviour pattern is burglary, petty thievery, mugging, assault for purposes of profit – not simply kicks – and other illegal acts directed at 'raising bread'. It is generally a 'tight clique' – a small mobile gang that can steal with maximum effectiveness. It would lose its cohesive quality and the intimate co-operation required to be successful in illegal ventures if it became too large. Membership is not easily achieved and is generally approved by all gang members.

The delinquent gang has a tight primary group structure. The members know each other under face-to-face circumstances and heavily rely upon each other for co-operation in their illegal enterprises. They are groups that have some duration and lasting structure. This usually continues in action until interrupted by police arrest or incarceration. Members arrested and removed are often replaced. The leader is usually the most effective thief, the best organizer and planner of delinquent activities.

Often members of these cliques participate in the activities of the violent or some of the previously mentioned 'gangs'. However, participation in other gangs is more of a 'sideline', since their basic allegiance and life direction is hinged to acting out within the delinquent gang for profit-making objectives.

With few exceptions, deliquent-gang members are emotionally stable youths. Their delinquency is more a reflection of being 'socialized' into accepting delinquent patterns for behaviour, rather than a reflection of emotional disturbance. The emotionally disturbed delinquent is more apt to steal or assault on his own in a bizarre way. He would lack the social ability required to belong to the organized delinquent gang.

In summary, the delinquent gang is comprised of a cohesive group of emotionally stable youths trained into illegal patterns of behaviour. Violence may be employed as a means towards the end of acquiring material and financial rewards; however, it is rarely an end in itself – since the goals of the gang are profit-oriented. The delinquent gang accepts the materialistic success goals of the society, but rejects the normative ways of achievement.

Although the earlier-described Chicago School 'criminal gangs' are similar in structure to the current delinquent gang there are some differences. A major difference is the lack of a criminal hierarchy in which the young offender may rise in a criminal 'class system'. The delinquent-gang member is restricted to 'present-oriented' delinquent 'success'. The only criminal career he may look forward to is the possibility of learning a good criminal trade (for example, safe-cracker, policy number-writer). Generally, however, the delinquent-gang member from a disorganized slum is 'present' oriented and does not concern himself with his future criminal life. He accepts his later criminal life as it develops, without any significant future planning.

Category III: The Violent Gang — emotional outlet, violence - [ ]

In contrast with the other gang types, the violent gang is primarily organized for emotional gratification, and violence is the theme around which all activities centre. Sports, social, even delinquent activities are side issues to its primary assaultive pattern. The violent gang's organization and membership are constantly shifting in accord with the emotional needs of its members. Membership size is exaggerated as a psychological weapon for influencing other gangs and self-aggrandizement. Small arsenals of weapons are discussed and whenever possible accumulated. These caches include switch-blades and hunting knives, home-made zip guns, standard guns, pipes, blackjacks, and discarded World War II bayonets and machetes. The violent-gang entity is thus essentially organized around gang-war activities, although occasionally certain youths will form delinquent cliques or subgroups within the overall violent gang.

Membership characteristics are unclear in the violent

gang's structure. Leadership and leaders are characterized by megalomania, strong needs to control, and an emotionally distorted picture of the gang's organization. The image of the leader is often exaggerated and glorified by gang members to enhance their own self-concept. There are strong power drives in the violent gang. This is demonstrated by attempts to control territory. Pseudo-territorial disputes are a constant source of intergang conflict.

Because of the misty, unclarified nature of its structure, the violent gang has a chameleon characteristic. Its organization shifts with the needs of its members and is always in a state of flux. Relationships and conflicts with other groups go on constantly either in discussions or in actuality. Affiliations are made with brother gangs who are allies one day and enemies the next, according to the whims of disturbed gang members and leaders.

A considerable amount of the gang boys' time is spent sounding, a pattern of needling, ridiculing, or fighting with other members; consequently a great deal of their 'social' participation is of a negative nature. The underlying theme of these street-corner sounding sessions is an attempt to prove one's self and to disprove and disparage others. There is a continual verbal and sometimes physical attack and defence going on, regardless of the subject. In most discussions the underlying theme is one of hostility and aggression.

Since the violent gang is the primary formation under analysis here, the following description is presented in more specific summarized detail in order to clearly reveal its structure and function.

VIOLENT-GANG ORGANIZATION

Gang Origins[1]

Violent gangs appear to emerge spontaneously, without any special plan. There is seldom a systematic

1. On the matter of 'Gang Origins' I am not dealing here with the larger social context that affects the emergence of the gang in American society. My emphasis is on describing various dimensions of the gang as they

development of the gang's organization. The boys occasionally go through some formal motions of electing officers and defining some membership characteristics. However, essentially the group's organization emerges spontaneously.

The usual overt rationale given by gang boys for the origin of the gang is related to their felt needs for defence and protection. Although this is the usual surface reason given, on a deeper level of analysis it is revealed that the gang serves as a vehicle for adjusting the gang boys' personal problems and feelings of inadequacy. The gang helps to provide a sense of power, especially for the gang leader. It also provides a channel for expressing aggression related to other emotions and difficulties such as a response to discrimination or an acting out of racial prejudice itself. Thus many youths in an effort to cope with a variety of personality problems act them out through the gang. The sociopathic youth who seems to enjoy fighting and violence for its own sake under any conditions uses this gang as a vehicle for violent expressions. In summary, violent gangs appear to originate in order to adjust individual emotional problems, for reasons of 'self-protection' and defence, for channelling aggression, in response to prejudice, because of the peculiar motivations of disturbed leaders or because of a combination of these factors mixed with special external conditions produced by 'enemy gangs'.

Gang Membership Characteristics

Joining most violent gangs is a relatively easy process. The main criterion for membership is a proclivity towards violent behaviour. A youth may voluntarily join by approaching the 'assumed gang leader' and requesting membership. The leader practically always accepts the applicant, since a large membership helps to strengthen him and his gang's prestige. There is a mythology built up

---

appear and exist on the neighbourhood level of assessment. The larger issue, the 'gang's emergence', is dealt with in the next chapter on community factors.

around initiation rites, such as the requirement that a potential member steal something or assault someone, but these entrance demands are seldom fulfilled or really expected to take place. Another method of membership recruitment involves assault upon a youth combined with a 'join up or else' threat. The 'victim' member can resign by his own volition through simply keeping clear of the leaders.

Gang membership has little formal or permanent character. A youth can terminate 'belonging' by simply saying 'I quit'. A 'member' may also be thrown out of the gang at the whim of the leader without the rejected youth even being informed that he no longer belongs. These non-defined characteristics of membership reflect the degree of responsibility and lack of clarity of the gang member's role in the violent gang. There is little precise definition of role behaviour in the gang. If qualifications for membership were more precise and definite, most gang members would be unable to participate since they usually lack the social ability to relate to another, the ability necessary for assuming responsibilities in more structured social systems. Violent gangs thus have limited membership integration and cohesion outside the few core members. Under pressure from without, most members easily leave the gang, although leaders and core gang members seldom resign.

Leaders and Leadership

Gang leaders are essentially self-appointed. They attempt to satisfy their emotional needs through the manipulation of other youths into aggressive action and by committing acts of violence themselves. Gang leaders are the more permanent and core members of the gang because they start it and are at the centre of its organization. The leaders are often glorified by gang members as a reflection of their own desired aspirations, and invested with many attributes the member himself does not possess. The image of the leader, who is often not concretely available, is thus distorted to fulfil the gang member's own aspirations.

Gang leaders conjure up vast networks of gang alliances (some real, some imagined) to fulfil their own needs and those of their gang's members for power. Gang members want to believe, and thus do believe, that their leaders control vast networks of gang relationships that can be called forth for gang warfare and defence purposes, even though their assumptions are not valid.

Many gang leaders manifest paranoid delusions of persecution and grandeur. In some cases they are attempting to compensate and adjust serious personality disorders through acting in the role of powerful but pseudo-leaders. Their wild dreams of glory often serve their pathological needs and those of the gang. Despite considerable fantasy, there is some anchorage of reality to their distortions of the world around them. They do not live in a complete fantasy world, since their pseudo-community is shared by many others in the world of the gang and the 'legitimate' larger society.

The group pattern of violent expression appears to be a more acceptable and legitimate social form for acting out pathology than is individual violent behaviour. The 'consensus factor' of the group seems to permit a wider range of 'legitimate' abnormal behaviour. A disturbed youth may therefore cloak his pathology in the immunity of a socially accepted leader role.

Many gang leaders appear involved in an attempt to relive earlier years when they were disturbed, insecure, and unhappy youths in their contemporary 'power' role of gang leader. At this later period in their lives (approximately between the ages of eighteen and twenty-five) they regress to an earlier life period to act out the 'powerful' role they could not achieve when they were young.

Gang leaders have limited leadership ability which can be translated into the expectations of more clearly defined and constructive social systems. As indicated, they have limited social ability, the requirements for assuming any responsibility to another person in a legitimate relationship.

Alliances and Affiliations (Brother Gangs) — *non-existant virtually*

Gang members and leaders project and perpetuate a myth of vast networks of gang affiliations in part to compensate for their insecure feelings and lowly self-concepts. They are generally flexing artificial muscles and flaunting powers they do not possess. Brother gangs are thus used as artificial weapons to impress gang enemies and to give the gang members themselves a feeling of security. Gang alliance 'contracts' are usually mutual distortion associations. Using this technique, gang leaders attempt to convince each other of their respective powers by exaggerating the vast numbers of brother gangs they can bring to bear in a gang war. On occasion, these alliances and affiliations are produced for a gang war; however, when they do appear, it is generally a spontaneous action.

Gang Warfare — *relieves hostility emotions + aggressiveness*

Gang warfare usually has no clear purpose of consensus of definition for all participants. For most youth gang members it is an opportunity to channel aggressions and hostilities they have about other personal matters. Gang wars originate over trivia in many cases. Territory, a 'bad look', an exaggerated argument over a girl, or a nasty remark may be the basis for stirring up a large collection of youths into gang-warfare action. These picayune reasons are exaggerated and spread through gang networks in distorted ways to inflame many gang members into battle. Such surface provocations give disturbed youths a *cause célèbre* and a legitimate banner under which they can vent hostilities related to other issues. The gang members' emotions are fanned through interaction and produce a group contagion. What starts out as a 'bad look' from one youth towards another can thus develop into a major battle. Each youth who becomes involved can project into the battle whatever angers or hostilities he has towards school, his family, the neighbourhood, prejudice, or any other problems he may be living through at the time.

As indicated, an important facet of the mass gang war is the negotiation and manipulation of alliances and affiliations as demonstrations of strength. Many agreements and contracts are made in the process of putting on the rumble. These are generally pseudo-bargains, which serve as the means for gang members to flex muscles they are unsure they have.

At the 'actual' gang-war event, most youths on hand have little or no idea of why they are there or what they are expected to do, except assault someone. Leaders, gang members, citizens, and sometimes the police and the Press are caught up in the fallout contagion of gang-war hysteria. Although violent-gang members may not be clear about their motives or their gang's organization, the gang war can develop a mob situation which results in homicide. In fact, the confused nature of the gang with its fantasy qualities helps to make it a highly destructive instrument of violence.

GANG THEORY AND RESEARCH

A significant requirement of adequate theory is a firm foundation of data logically derived from direct empirical research. 'Long-distance' views about gangs emanating from outdated research findings or from research related to delinquency in general rather than to the gang in particular are prone to theoretical misconception. Cohen recognizes this latter problem as it relates to the paucity of data on 'delinquent subcultures' *per se*. He attributes the situation to the inherent difficulty of obtaining data from violent gangs but also partly to '. . . the fact that the data at hand have been gathered with other objectives, theoretical and practical, in mind'.[1]

Current theoretical gang conceptions still (consciously and unconsciously) rely heavily upon the wealth of live data contributed by the early Chicago School. This despite the apparent fact that a degree of social change has set in

1. Albert K. Cohen, *Delinquent Boys – The Culture of the Gang* (Glencoe Illinois: The Free Press, 1955), p. 170.

over the past thirty years which would alter the socio-cultural causal context and consequently the type of gang structures that result. The use of personal documents, case materials, and 'live interviews' characteristic of Chicago School research approach are still valid; however, drawing conclusions about contemporary gang structures using such older gang patterns as models demands modification.

The further development of an adequate gang theory at this point requires a market-basket type of research which would gather a wealth of documentary data about gangs. A model for current gang research might very well be the anthropological field study approach generally reserved for more 'exotic' cultures. The researcher, literally moving into the neighbourhood and experiencing the various social forces operating, would be in the most ideal position for gathering the wide range of data that would currently prove most useful towards the development of gang theory. Such data would include information about various types of corner 'gangs', leadership patterns, the meaning of membership, activity analysis, violence patterns, gang language, and gang-youth personality types. Some start has been made, but much more data of this kind gathered in the manner prescribed is required.

The reasons behind the limited amount of live research exploring gangs directly in the fashion recommended has been alluded to earlier. The generally suspicious cop-fearing gang member is not easily approached. More than that, the rapidly changing gang and its membership tend to elude the net of 'formal sociological research'. The development of a design for systematically studying the gang problem remains a challenging and formidable research problem.

Despite the varied problems described, the development of gang theory requires a wider base of live research evidence. The importance of such research to adequate theory building and the pitfalls of not carrying out such empirical investigation are cogently expressed by Merton:

... empirical research *initiates, reformulates, refocusses, and clarifies* the theories and conceptions of sociology. And in the measure that observation thus directs and fructifies the development of theory, it is evident that any theorist who is remote from all research, of which he learns only by hearsay as it were, runs the risk of being insulated from the very experiences most likely to turn his attention in fruitful directions. His mind has not been prepared by experience. He is, above all, removed from the type of disciplined empirical observation which sometimes leads to serendipity, the discovery through chance by a theoretically prepared mind of valid findings which were not sought for. Weber may have been right in subscribing to the view that one need not be Caesar, in order to understand Caesar. But there is a temptation for sociological theorists to act sometimes as though in order to understand Caesar, it is not necessary to study Caesar.[1]

The Theoretical Propositions for Analysis

In the light of the current state of direct knowledge about gangs (including my own), it is premature to specify anything as grandiose as a 'theory of gangs'. The goal in the ensuing analysis of the violent gang will be to blend my findings about such gangs with the relevant theoretical and research material that constitutes the current stockpile of knowledge about gangs. The material utilized in the analysis will necessarily be selective, and thus subject to my own biases about the relevance of various theoretical and research contributions. Given these conditions, the type of analysis that appears most appropriate for my data is what Merton has described as 'post-factum sociological interpretation':

It is often the case in empirical social research that data are collected and then subjected to interpretive comment. This procedure in which the observations are at hand and the interpretations are subsequently applied to the data has the logical structure of clinical inquiry. The observations may be case-history or statistical in character. The defining characteristic of the procedure is the introduction of an interpretation 'after'

1. R. K. Merton, *Social Theory and Social Structure* (Glencoe, Illinois: The Free Press, 1957), p. 12.

the observations have been made rather than the empirical testing of a predesignated hypothesis.[1]

To most effectively structure the 'clinical inquiry' that will follow, it seems appropriate to array the data presentation plan in a logical form and sequence. The specification of the right questions has been pointed to as an important prerequisite towards developing a relevant theory. As Merton states: 'They are questions so formulated that the answers to them will confirm, amplify, or variously revise some part of what is currently taken as knowledge in the field'. Out of the broad range of possible questions for analysis related to violent gangs, the following seem most pertinent towards the development of a theory of violent gangs:

1. What set of socio-cultural factors operative in the community fosters the emergence of the violent gangs as an adjustment pattern?

2. Given other possible deviant opportunity structures, why do certain boys living in the type of community which fosters deviant adjustments specifically select participation in the violent gang as a vehicle for 'acting out'?

3. What structural and functional characteristics of the violent gang make it an ideal-type adjustment structure for the youth who joins?

The more detailed analytic discussion which will follow in the next chapters in answer to these three core questions will be an elaboration of the following set of interrelated theoretical propositions:

1. Varied negative socio-cultural dislocations exist in the disorganized, rapidly changing urban slum area.

2. These dislocations produce dysfunctional gaps in the socialization process that would properly train the child for normative social roles.

3. Children not adequately socialized develop asocial or sociopathic personalities.

4. The resulting sociopathic personalities are essentially characterized by: (A) a lack of social conscience, (B) a limited ability to relate, identify, or empathize with others

1. Merton, op. cit., p. 90.

except for egocentric objectives, (C) manifestations of impulsive, aggressive, and socially destructive violent behaviour when impulsive, immediate needs are not satisfied.

5. The sociopathic individual because of his personality
deficiences cannot relate adequately to more socially demanding groups (including 'delinquent' and 'social'
gangs).

6. Individualized emotional outburst is more stigmatized, considered bizarre, and to some extent more
unrewarding than group pathological expressions. Such
individualistic expression in the violent gang is considered
more socially 'legitimate'.

7. The malleable 'near-group' nature of the violent gang
makes it a compatible and legitimate vehicle for adjusting
the emotional needs of the sociopathic youth, an individual
unable to relate adequately in more demanding social
groups.

The foregoing preliminary propositions are closely interrelated. Because of this fact the ensuing analysis, which
will enlarge upon each of the specified propositions in
greater detail, will proceed in a direct flow – without
necessarily delineating each area of specific analysis from
the other.

A CASE IN POINT: JOSÉ

In the pursuit of theory through the further explication of
a set of relevant propositions, the case of the live gang boy
emerging from his social milieu must not be overlooked.
The actual and representative live case needs to be kept
squarely in the forefront, if the theoretical propositions
that attempt to account for its existence are to have
significance or meaning.

The beauty of the writings of the Chicago School was
that one could experience the totality of social forces con-
verging upon the youth and his gang. The final delinquent gang product seemed logical when the causal factors,
their relative force, meaning to the youth, and time sequence were revealed in their natural rhythm. Although

abstract analysis is vital for a systematic understanding of the regularities of the violent-gang problem, the totality of the problem should be kept firmly in mind in its natural process of evolution. For this purpose, prior to proceeding into the amplification and closer analysis of the specified theoretical propositions towards the development of a theory of the violent gangs, the following composite of the gang problem is presented in its more natural descriptive sequence.[1]

José's Community

José's first reaction to New York City was to the climate and dirt. 'It's always summer in Puerto Rico' was one comment he made on the difference. Although he lived in a rundown slum called La Perla in San Juan, it was 'heaven' to him compared to the slum he now lived in on Manhattan's upper West Side. José could step out of his shack on the island into sunlight and a countryside not far from his home and greet many friends and neighbours. In New York City he would leave his tenement to enter a hostile gang world of indifferent strangers.

On the island José was somebody. Although they were poor, the Pérez family had honour and dignity appropriate to their Spanish background. The Pérez name meant something, and José sought to live up to it. His family and friends identified him as an individual – he had a position in a community, even though he was a child. Everyone in the huddle of shacks where he lived knew everyone else and had some concern about one another.

In New York he was at first shocked, and later became defiant, when he found out he was 'different'. The first time he was cursed at school as a 'dirty Spick' he became severely upset. This reaction slowly changed, under a steady barrage of the same thing, to some acceptance of inferiority mingled with constant anger. His response became aggressive; he retaliated, and began to attack other

1. Although the 'hero' of this 'portrait' to be presented is Puerto Rican, it should be readily apparent that no ethnic, religious, or racial group has any priority. Over the years, as the literature has indicated, various diverse backgrounds have produced deviant gangs.

children without provocation in anticipation of insult. ('They all kept calling me a Spick. That goes deep down inside me.') 'Outsiders' were not his only antagonists. He was 'picked on' by other Puerto Ricans who had lived longer in New York City. To them he was a foreigner, a 'tiger'.[1] He embarrassed them because he was a Puerto Rican greenhorn and reflected negatively on these other individuals who had become assimilated. Other Puerto Ricans, suffering from self-hatred about their lot, took out their sensitivity to being discriminated against themselves on someone they needed to feel was even more inferior.

José had a good school record in Puerto Rico; however, in New York he hated school and became a habitual truant. His newly discovered self-difference as a 'Spick' was accentuated by his inability to speak English. The teacher tried, but, overwhelmed by a large number of students with various problems, she was of limited help. Her students' personal problems, combined with their language difficulties, made teaching subject matter almost impossible. The one available school 'guidance counsellor' (for some thousand students) tried to talk to José; but by that time José was considered an 'impossible problem', and getting worse. His hatred for school became more intense each time he 'played hookey'. Going back seemed increasingly difficult, if not impossible. He withdrew into movies, when he could raise the money by petty thievery, or simply sat and daydreamed. He felt weak, inferior, and alone. His favourite cartoon hero was Mighty Mouse:

You know he's a mouse – he's dressed up like Superman. He's got little pants – they're red. The shirt is yellow. You know, and then he helps out the mouse. Every time the cats try to get the mouse, Mighty Mouse comes and helps the mouse, just like Superman. He's stronger than he acts. *Nothing can hurt him.*

His reverie alternated between withdrawal, fantasy, and

1. The *Marine Tiger* was one of the boats that early in the Puerto Rican migration carried many Puerto Ricans to New York City. The term was shortened to call newly arrived greenhorns 'tigers'.

direct acts of violence – often delivered on undeserving and unsuspecting victims. Lectures and threats to have him sent away to a reformatory by an overworked school attendance officer and others meant little to José. He already knew from a friend that Warwick (the state reformatory) was 'all filled up, and they ain't going to send you there for just playing hookey'. Roaming the streets produced other delinquent activity, including petty thievery and vandalism. These plus a developed pattern of purse snatching, involving a greater emphasis on violence than on financial gain, helped build the necessary requisites for his being sent to the reformatory.

It was not so much what happened to José that caused his unfeeling asocial behaviour to grow; it was what was not happening. In his world there was a vacuum of law-abiding youths or adults from whom he could learn any social feeling towards another person. People to José became 'things' you manipulated to get what you wanted. He discovered that 'being nice' was often useful, but only if it helped get what you wanted. When caught stealing, 'sometimes if you hung your head down right and looked pitiful, you could avoid punishment'.

The main social example missing from José's world was someone feeling for another person without the object of 'getting something' in return. Everything José saw was a 'con' game. The two most successful types of behaviour were manipulation and violence. When one did not work the other one would. José found violence and its threat most effective, since as his rep for sudden violence grew, others would respond and comply to his wishes. José 'naturally' learned to manipulate others and to use violence 'properly'. He never learned to feel affection for anyone, not even his family. No one ever taught him or set any example for such human feelings. In the hostile and asocial world that surrounded him, he learned the most effective adaptation, and his 'sociopathic' personality became more rigid with each day's experience.

José's family was of little help to him in New York. Their rules, language, and appearance were 'old-fashioned'.

Also, his parents and older brothers were busy battling
their own enemies in the city. José's family was generally
not around. He sometimes dreamed with fondness about
distant pleasant evenings of the past in Puerto Rico with
his family. They went to a park near their home in the
evenings. Mostly the children would play and the adults
would sit around and discuss the day's events. Children
and adults at these times even talked to each other. In
the old days, José had the opportunity and would discuss
his personal troubles with his parents and older relatives.
It was even pleasant to be criticized, since it gave José a
secure feeling to know someone was concerned. In the
park not only his own parents but also relatives and other
adults took an interest in children. One man took the boys
swimming; a group of older men from a social club formed
a baseball league for the younger boys. José belonged to a
community.

All of this changed in New York. His father, an unskilled worker, was also Puerto Rican. Getting a job that
paid a living wage was difficult. Some labour unions made
special contracts with employers to provide employees at
the lowest minimum wage, selling out the worker. José's
father, when he worked, earned about $50 per week. He
was periodically unemployed. During these periods, quar-
rels and conflict developed between his parents. Beset
with their own overwhelming problems, the parents sometimes unfairly attacked their children, who became to them
increasingly a burden.

There was no one for José to talk to about his feelings.
His father began to drink excessively, to escape from immediate realities he could not face. The more he drank,
the more violent he became. In his seemingly senseless
rages he beat José's mother and often attacked José for
no apparent reason. Senseless violence surrounded him, and
José became indifferent to his family. About his father he
said:

I'll ask him to take me boat-riding, fishing, or some place
like that, ball game. He'll say 'No.' He don't go no place. The

only place where he goes, he goes to the bar. And from the bar, he goes home. Sleep, that's about all he do. I don't talk to my parents a lot of times. I don't hardly talk to them – there's nothing to talk about. There's nothing to discuss about. They can't help me.

Family trouble was compounded by the need for José's mother to take a menial job to help support the family. This removed her farther from the home. Rents were exorbitant. The family was discriminated against, hence barred from moving into certain neighbourhoods. In any case their erratic income was insufficient for a steady monthly rental in a more stable apartment. The family of six continued to live in a crawling two-room, hotel-apartment they had moved into originally on a temporary basis. They shared kitchen facilities and an outside toilet with eight other families and paid a rental of $25 per week. Close quarters intensified the family conflict. José increasingly resolved his problems outside the home.

At one time José became friendly with Juan, an older youth from the neighbourhood who took an interest and attempted to help him. Juan was a leader in a social gang called the Braves. This group was well organized, participated in sports, ran dances, and belonged to the local community centre. The Braves were tough, but did not go in for 'bopping', gang wars, or violent activity. Most members of the Braves, although they got into an occasional fight or a petty act of thievery, stayed clear of mass rumbles and participated in more socially accepted activities. Juan tried to get José into the Braves, but with little success. José was voted down because the Braves felt he was a 'wise punk' and they didn't want him around. José did not meet the requirements needed for being a member of the Braves. He was, according to their members, too wild, too crazy, and they clearly rejected him.

José one day met a violent-gang leader called Loco. Although many neighbourhood youths, including the Braves, thought he was crazy, his reputation for sudden violence through the use of a knife or a zip gun made him greatly feared. Loco, at the time, as part of his usual gang-leader activity, was 'organizing' a West Side Dragons Division. José was accepted without question and was appointed a war counsellor by Loco after he saw him 'in action'. Loco saw José stab a younger boy on a dare.

José and other Dragons enjoyed the exciting stories Loco told about Dragon gang divisions throughout Manhattan. José learned and began to make brother-gang pacts of his own. Also, as a war counsellor for the West Side Dragons he could legitimately go on a Jap almost every night. His sudden temper and quick use of a blade increased his rep. With Loco he organized a brother-gang pact with another gang on the upper West Side called the Egyptian Kings. Although José did not have the ability to belong to the Braves, he became an exceptional member of the violent Kings. The Kings did not really give José a 'feeling of belonging' or provide 'a natural way of life'. The violent gang 'resolved' his anxieties and troubles in the same way alcohol 'resolves' life for the alcoholic and drugs 'help' the drug addict. It served to destroy him further.

The Kings provided a vehicle for expressing much of the hatred, disillusionment, and aggression that existed in José. It was also a group compatible with his unfeeling and manipulative personality. Violence was expressed at the right opportunity, or opportunities were created. Also, the gang helped minimize feelings of guilt and anxiety about violence at the rare times such feelings existed. Acting out violence with gang compatriots was more satisfying than doing it alone. Any limited concern he had with feelings of worthlessness were diminished by the recognition that there were others as 'low' as himself. In the Kings there were other 'down cats', and 'Everyone puts you down', 'Get your kicks now – make it today' were violent-gang slogans for life. 'Sounding' on and 'putting people down' were central King activities, and José became an expert member.

The violent gang gave José a feeling of power. He was a core member and accepted the mutually supported gang fantasy that he was now a 'leader of men'. In the position of war counsellor he enjoyed the gang's violence. He found it gratifying and exciting to strike out at others, for whom he had no feeling in any case. Violence was a useful instrument for him, and he was well trained for this activity. Quick, senseless violence gave him a rep. Success, prestige, and fame were achievable through the quick stroke of a knife.

On the night of 30 July, when José went to Highbridge Park, the trip was merely another gang foray. It had all the usual elements of gang-war activity: talk about violence, about 'what we are going to do', 'getting even', 'being a big shot', 'It makes me feel good', 'What else is there to do?' José's post-killing comments, 'They called me a dirty Spick' and 'We fought for territory', were rationales. All of José's social deficiencies converged the night he plunged a bread knife into Michael Farmer's back. As one Egyptian King reported about José: 'The guy that stabbed him in the back with the bread knife, he told me that when he took the knife out of his back, he said, *Thank you.*'

11. The 'Community' of the Violent Gang

The Modern urban gang is a distinctive development, and is the outcome of a distinctive complex of attitudes, opportunities, conditions, and means. To expose this complex, to reveal it in its particular operation, and also in its gestation, this is the kind of problem that in its endless varieties continually challenges the student of social causation.[1]

The community of the gang is composed of a blend of negative physical and social forces. The physical nature of the slum that surrounds the gang provides a different image, depending on the vantage point of the observer. To the average citizen coming into New York on a train bound for Grand Central Station, there is a shifting view of red brick tenements, 'bombed-out' slums, and new housing projects. The sight can be easily avoided by becoming engrossed in a newspaper. To a young mother, a 'welfare client' in *The Inhabitants*, a book on slums by Julius Horwitz, another side of the same scene appears that cannot easily be avoided:

I went out into the hallway and I thought I had stepped into some East Harlem pit. There were women screaming and a lot of drunken men and you could smell marijuana as thick as incense. The stairs seemed to be crawling with babies. The toilets were flooded. I saw a dozen faces high from dope. One tried to grab me but I got rid of him by telling him I had to phone St Luke's Hospital for the baby. . . . It doesn't seem that people live here. There was broken glass on the stairs. I saw two men passing heroin. Then one of the girls told me that the checks had come in the morning. She said it's like this on the third and eighteenth of each month.[2]

1. Robert M. MacIver, *Social Causation* (Boston: Ginn & Company, 1942), p. 385.
2. Julius Horwitz, *The Inhabitants* (New York: The World Publishing Company, 1960), p. 84.

In his 'fictional' portrayal of the upper West Side (home of the Kings and Balkans) Horwitz provides a probing and sharply accurate account of the violent-gang slum of the sixties. His vital statistics and descriptions are in close accord with my own observations. Here a welfare worker in *The Inhabitants* describes the 'scene':

> The building has five floors, each floor has twenty rooms and two toilets. . . . One hundred separate families live in the hundred rooms. Every other room has children, from one child just born into the world out of our secret hatching places to more than one child, two, three, and if the building inspector doesn't come or if he turns his eyes toward his own denuded salary check, four children. The roaches in Jowitt's building have already begun the first step toward the insect domination of the world. The slow stately contempt with which they move over the children and the sleeping tubercular drunks would chill even the housing authorities. . . .[1]

The buildings from which most violent-gang members come are corroded on the inside. The toilets are broken, and each building is shared by several families. On the average, fifty men, women, and children will cook and feed off one stove and sink at the end of a hall, called 'the kitchen'. The infestation is an experimental ground for exterminators to try new insecticides and rat-killer formulas that work for a while until the species inevitably builds up its resistance. Despite these conditions, it is not easy for the welfare worker to locate such one-room apartments for a family on public assistance. At a $25–$35-per-week rental they remain overcrowded and in a constant state of change.

The operators of the slum traps are generally considered the villains of this 'community'. Here Horwitz presents their side of the problem through a 'fictional' building owner:

> If they killed their cockroaches, if they used the toilets for what toilets are supposed to be used for, if they spent five minutes washing a window, they would see the park. . . . I give

1. Horwitz, op. cit., p. 162.

them a clean room, I give them a park, and in twenty-four hours you can't walk into the room. They shit and piss in everything but the toilet bowl. Let me tell you what some other landlords won't tell you. I took over this building eight years ago. There were old ladies living in here. Old ladies and old men and some people who still went to business. And then they got out as though they were running from a fire. . . . New York City, if I read my newspaper correctly, has two hundred thousand children and mothers on relief. Two hundred thousand women and children. One hundred and fifty thousand babies. . . . And who makes the babies? These babies who would be better off if they were strangled now instead of later. Who makes the babies? The men who come here at night to sneak into the rooms, who leave babies like they leave their dirty underwear.[1]

The physical muck of these neighbourhoods has its own brand of impact – but this condition in itself is not the total destructive force. The surface appearance is disturbing essentially because it is a representation of the underlying human decay and barrenness. This slum is a 'community' of strangers. The people live in unbearably close physical contact in a vacuum of meaningful human relationships. The violent gang emerging from this type of asocial community forms a bizarre replica of the 'community' that spawned it.

The slums of the past, amply described in the literature, were characterized by a high incidence of crime, delinquency, assault, alcoholism, and mental illness. Despite this, within many of these older slum areas there was a 'sense of community'. The early gang's turf was not simply a thin rationale for a fight as it is for today's violent gang; it meant something to a youth, and his neighbourhood was part of his identity. The earlier 'high-delinquency' neighbourhoods of New York – the Lower East Side and Harlem – had severe problems, but theirs was a 'community' with some degree of cohesion.

Although the unstable type of slum 'community' appears to be most prevalent, in some cases the physical separation of it and the more stable slum is not clearly

1. Horwitz, op. cit., pp. 81–2.

marked. Some 'poor' neighbourhoods tend to have both forms of slum conditions operative in a composite form. The Lower East Side of New York is an example of a mixture of both stable and disorganized slums. Its *bodegas* (Spanish groceries), kosher delicatessens, and pizzerias exist side by side with each ethnic or religious group in different stages of flux and stability.

The rate of delinquency, as well as its typology, seems to be affected by the movement from the stable to the disorganized slum. (José's shift of behaviour may be accounted for largely by the shift from a 'poor' community to a 'non-community'.) The effect of this community condition is implied by a recent report contrasting the Puerto Ricans' movement from such a slum in Puerto Rico to a disorganized neighbourhood in New York City. Professor Robert MacIver, Director of the New York Mayor's Juvenile Delinquency Evaluation Study, found that 'juvenile delinquency among Puerto Ricans in New York may be twenty times as high as in Puerto Rico' – and specifies that the cause appears to be tied to the 'new' slum condition:

. . . rejecting any conclusion that Puerto Ricans or Negroes were more prone to delinquency, the [MacIver] report said that in Puerto Rico in July, 1956, officials had listed 2,539 children under 18 as delinquent or vulnerable to delinquency – out of a total of 1,173,000. This was a little more than two in 1,000.

'There are no strictly comparable figures for Puerto Ricans in New York City, but there is reason to believe that it would be perhaps twenty times the rate just mentioned. . . .'

Obviously, the correlation is not between delinquency and Puerto Rican background but between delinquency and neighbourhoods characterized by all sorts of social problems.[1]

The two types of slum described also appear to produce different deviant patterns: the stable slum creating a more normative delinquent adjustment and the disorganized slum a higher rate of violent behaviour. With particular reference to gangs, the stable slum appears to produce more 'delinquent' and 'social' gangs, and the disorganized

1. *New York Times*, 11 July 1961.

neighbourhood 'violent' gangs. It should be re-emphasized, however, that purely 'stable' or 'disorganized' slums seldom exist. Thus, currently, there seems to be a composite of these slum conditions, with the disorganized slum becoming the prevalent condition.

DISORGANIZED SLUMS AND THE VIOLENT GANG

There are some particular characteristics inherent in the disorganized slum that seem to foster the development of gangs in general, and violent gangs in particular. A closer inspection of the social dynamics of this type of slum, especially as it affects children being socialized (or asocialized) under these onerous conditions, helps to reveal the problem.

RURAL-URBAN TRANSITION. A dominant theme of the current disorganized slum is that it is heavy with formerly rural populations that have flowed into the large urban area in pursuit of greater social and economic opportunities. One effect of this flow has been to chase more stable lower-class and middle-class families, who can afford to move, toward the suburbs. The result is a diverse population of newly arrived individuals ill-equipped to cope with the many-faceted problems and new values of city living in the disorganized slum.

The new urban situation tends to have the impact and characteristics of what Niles Carpenter has called 'city-shock'. He maintains that 'the migrant encounters such starkly new conditions of life in the city that the situation produces in him a state of shock'.

The large population movement to the city produces heavy collections of such families and individuals all concentrated in one area. Two notable examples of this recent transition are the movement of Southern Negroes to the North and the migration of Puerto Ricans to New York City. There is some evidence that this type of large-scale movement of rural populations to urban areas is not restricted to the United States, but is taking place inter-

nationally. A *New York Times* article reporting on a recent
International Social Work Conference describes this trend:

Social workers from forty-two countries completed a week-
long study today of numerous problems arising out of twentieth-
century living conditions.

The topics of chief concern were social imbalances deriving
from expanding and shifting populations in the advanced as
well as the under-developed countries. . . .

. . . attention was focused on a world-wide wave of juvenile
delinquency caused partly by the enormous movement of youth
from farms to cities in almost all countries.

The large-scale movement from rural areas to the cities, with
consequent disruption of traditional family ties and authority,
is causing an 'explosive' situation among youth, the commission
found.[1]

The newly arrived populations bring with them values,
norms, and patterns of behaviour often inconsistent with
the demands of the new society. Adults, but especially *the
children* caught in this situation, are exposed to a set of
conflicting values: those presented by the new society and
the more traditional ones brought from the old community. Professor Thorsten Sellin has described this problem as 'culture conflict'.[2] It consists of a condition where
the individual is caught between a crossfire of norms in
conflict. The youth newly arrived in the large urban area
is often barraged by conflicting standards for 'correct'
conduct. Conflicts may arise between the different norms
supported by his parents, the school, and those operative
in the neighbourhood.

The Breakdown of Social Controls

One of the circumstances which negatively affect the proper
socialization of youth in the disorganized urban condition
is the breakdown of old social controls without any
adequate replacement for these forces that would tend to
curb deviance. By 'social controls' the main reference here

1. *New York Times*, 7 December 1958.
2. Thorsten Sellin, *Culture, Conflict and Crime* (New York: Social Science
Research Council, 1938).

is to defined and clearly expected responses in the social system that tend to inhibit or control deviance. These elements of social control are the basic devices for maintaining human behaviour within expected social boundaries and are of special significance for controlling the behaviour of relatively unsocialized youths. Their breakdown in the disorganized slum tends to affect delinquency rates. McKay describes the relationship between social change, social controls, and deviance in a recent statement presented to a congressional subcommittee investigating delinquency:

> Briefly stated, it is assumed that most juvenile delinquency is a product of social change. While perfect conformity probably never is achieved, stable societies are bothered little with violative behavior. In contrast, when the rate of change is high, as in the modern American city, delinquency and other nonconforming behavior appear in such volume as to be highly destructive.
>
> The relationship between social change and the disruption of community institutions is easy to follow. Institutions through which the child is socialized and through which the values of the group are transmitted lag behind technological developments in periods of rapid change.
>
> As a result these institutions do not function effectively in meeting the needs of the people and fail to furnish the framework within which social life is ordinarily organized and integrated. In addition, during periods of rapid change new problems arise for which there are no institutional solutions. The cumulative effect of this imbalance is seen both in the fact that socialization of children is imperfect and in the weakening of ordinary types of control.[1]

The breakdown in the adequate functioning of the socialization and control process in the 'new slum' is largely a result of the demise of parental control. The more cohesive community, for example, relied heavily upon a strong matriarchal or patriarchal figure for control.

1. U.S. Congress, Senate Subcommittee to Investigate Juvenile Delinquency, *Hearings, Juvenile Delinquency*, 86th Cong., 1st Sess., 1959. Paper submitted by Henry D. McKay, reprinted by Department of Public Welfare, State of Illinois, p. 2.

The youth now finds himself in the new situation with few others to help his social growth. This is partially due to the necessity of the father or mother to work longer hours away from home. However, the breakdown of the necessary dominant and stable personality of the parent under the extreme conditions of their more difficult, new way of life is another significant element.

Since the youth has limited opportunity under these conditions to learn feeling for others or how to relate or empathize adequately with others, he tends towards a pattern of self-satisfying, impulsive, egocentric reactions. The youth emerging from this vacuum of effective socialization forces for training him into adequate social roles is often an asocial or sociopathic personality.

Another factor that affects the child, even when the parent attempts adequately to fulfil the role of socializing agent, is a new expectation of the parental role. The youth's parents will seldom equal the idealized images created in the ads, the movies, or television plays. His mother seldom fulfils her role as adequately as the stereotyped American 'mom' on TV. The youth exposed to the new models of parents may on a covert level be dissatisfied in his new situation with parents who might have appeared adequate to him in the former community. In a kind of disenchantment he may now confront his parents with dissatisfaction, indifference, and a degree of shame about their being 'greenhorns'.

Another factor of social control that diminishes in the new urban condition is the force of 'family honour'. In the prior community the family name may have had distinction or prestige; in the urban area of transition it is relatively meaningless to others, if not identified negatively with low social status. The youth who formerly took pride in his family name and its honour is deprived of another possible social control.

The presence of known others who bring community pressure to bear on the youth, providing another element of social control, are generally non-existent in the new slum. In the cohesive community conditions, a youth was likely to be under the constant surveillance of others who knew him well. In the new urban condition of anonymity, he can commit an atrocious assault or robbery on one block and easily disappear into a crowd of strangers a block away. No person of significance to the youth would know anything about his illegal act. A youth can thus lose himself in the anonymity of the large urban area and avoid any community forces of control.

The absence of elements of social control helps prove a fertile social milieu for producing the type of asocial individual who gravitates towards violent-gang structures. Both the social and delinquent gangs make demands upon their membership. The members of these more cohesive gangs (as in the delinquent gang) have some comprehension and learned ability to fulfil social expectations, even if they are illegal. In order to fulfil their social expectations they can respond in some measure to the requirements of social control. In the violent gang, however, the demands of actual conformity requiring 'social ability' are minimal. Thus, the nature of the disorganized slum, with its vacuum of social control and expectation, is a breeding ground for the development of the sociopathic youth who finds the malleable, shifting violent gang a convenient pattern of adjustment.

The Adult-youth Schism

An issue affiliated with the shift from 'community' to disorganized slum deserving closer attention is the sharp breakdown of adult–youth association and communication. McKay cogently describes several aspects of the problem:

One of the consequences of change is the breakdown of communication between adults and children which arises out of the fact that they live in such different worlds. When the behavior of children is incomprehensible to adults and when adults are not able to make what they do or think comprehensible to children, conflict and stresses are created within the family.

In this situation adults, frightened by conduct which they do not understand, often attempt to explain the delinquency of children in terms of movies, radio, television, comic books, jazz music, and many other such characteristics of modern social life, or, on the other hand, by looking backward and charging that the misbehavior of youth is due to lack of respect for parents, or to the absence of the harsh punishments which characterized earlier eras. While there is no evidence to support these particularistic explanations, it is easy to see how they develop.[1]

The breakdown of a meaningful relationship between violent-gang youths and the only adults who have even a minimal interest in them is affirmed by considerable evidence. A typical Egyptian King response to the question of how he gets along with his parents is: 'Why should I talk to them? There's nothing to talk about. They can't help me.' Another King relates his reason for not talking to his mother:

If I tell her I've been beaten up, she hits me. You know, my mother is divorced and she keeps talkin' about what a rat my father is and then she hits me. She don't give me a chance to explain or say nothing. I can't tell her anything. (*How about your father?*) Who, him? I never see him any more.

Emanating from feelings about their own parents the attitude towards adults in general becomes: 'Why should I tell *you* anything? You don't really care and you don't understand anyway.' This negative attitude displaced on to all adults, partly as a result of specific experiences and conclusions derived from primary relationships with their own parents, often takes an aggressive or violent form. (Although the evidence is inconclusive, there are indications that violent-gang attacks upon adult 'strangers' are a displacement of aggression towards the youth's own parents. I ran a series of role-playing sessions with a violent-gang youth who apparently 'enjoyed' mugging and purse-snatching from old women. At one point the boy commented that the women he selected '. . . all looked like my old lady'.)

The evidence of a breakdown of interaction between

1. McKay, op. cit. p. 3.

adults and youths (part of, but not exclusive to the disorganized slum) is seen also in the language of youths, a
language little understood by most adults. One reason
why gang boys are especially cryptic when adults are
around is that this enables them to talk to each other and
hide feelings, ideas, and attitudes from the adult population, whom they tend generally to distrust.

The special speech of the violent-gang boy was interestingly assessed by Murray Kempton, a *New York Post* reporter present throughout the Egyptian King trial:

> As he mumbled his name, there was a sudden shock of recog-
> nition of how exactly alike these children are. Vincent Pardon
> was like every other ward of the Children's Court we have seen
> over the last seven days. He had, as an instance, the same hair,
> drawn back with some care with a wide-toothed comb, and
> then splattered at the forelock with concentrated devotion.
>
> These children even talk the same way. There is a voice of
> 152nd St and Broadway which is different from the voice
> further up on the Heights. It is a voice without reference to
> ethnic origin. Children named Lago, O'Kelly and Pardon have
> the same precise inflection. They say 'cluck' for 'clock', and
> 'Reeversyd' for 'Riverside'. It makes no difference whether
> their parents be Irish or Spanish; they do not talk like their
> parents. It is as though they did not learn to talk from parent
> or teacher, but from other children; as though they had no
> homes, but only streets called Amsterdam and Broadway.[1]

In reverse of the gang youth's feeling about adults, the
adults' generalized perception of the gang youth is often
emotional and stereotyped. To many adults any youth
becomes a disturbing representation of their own parental
neglect. The appearance of any youth may cause guilt and
anxiety. In particular, the parent of the gang youth, beset
by the myriad problems of trying to find his way in a
new, transient, and difficult world with little time properly to socialize his child, reacts to his own guilt about this
failure by a type of hysterical or quick aggression towards
the child whenever he appears. This furious response in
many cases is a projected feeling of guilt for not having

1. Murray Kempton, *New York Post*, 21 February 1958.

assumed a more adequate parental role. Thus the adult's guilt and negative attitude about his own child is displaced on to children in general.

Adults vis-à-vis youths are a majority group; they still hold the reins of power and, of course, in sheer numbers are the larger population. In this context youths are often treated as a 'minority group' in American society, subject to various kinds of discriminations and stereotypes. Typical of this attitude was the following incident reported to me by one black-leather-jacketed, surly-looking gang boy: 'I was walking across the street and this old lady started to run. I didn't do anything. I just looked at her and she started to run as if she was scared to death. [*Laughs bitterly.*] She almost fell down running away.'

Some adults upon seeing 'tough-looking' youths automatically refer back to some of the violent headlines they have read in newspapers, react with fear, and stereotype all youths, even many innocent ones, as 'minority-group hoods'. Similar to a 'minority-group' victim, youths are easily identified, have a low self-concept (perpetuated and reinforced by the dominant adult group), and are in a subordinate position to adults in American society. Consequently, youth is often subjected to the same type of discrimination received by other minority groups.

In an unconscious recognition of their own deficiency as parents, many adults tend to blame youths other than their own for the delinquencies and gang activities of their children. This manifests itself in the platitude found in high-delinquency areas and elsewhere: 'He runs around with bad company!' The comment often reflects a projection of blame and shifting of responsibility from the parent himself on to boys other than his own. This is apparent, particularly in suburban neighbourhoods, where adults tend to take an ostrichlike approach to local delinquency. They don't recognize the degree of delinquency, because the admission that their children are delinquent is tantamount to admitting a degree of 'self-delinquency'.

The adult–youth schism characteristic of the disorganized slum can be an important determinant of

violent-gang organization. The gang can become not only a
channel for generalized hostility, aggression, and 'prestige
for the youth', but also a structure through which he can
retaliate against adults.

Under this condition of adult–youth conflict and disassociation in the disorganized slum, a functional gap is
produced in the social structure. The gang youth who
spends most of his time with his peers has no relevant
means for learning the normative adult behaviour patterns
dictated and expected by the overall society. It is not
logical to expect youths to grow up to be law-abiding
socialized adults unless somewhere in their social experience
such adults exist and are in communication and interaction with the youth. In the disorganized slum where
adults and youths are in conflict or living in different
worlds, there is no one available from whom a youth can
learn proper values for law-abiding behaviour patterns in
order to live adequately with others under conditions of
constructive human interaction.

In the disorganized slum the most admired adult-role
symbol for the gang boy may be the drug pusher or the
local 'bookie'. This situation, combined with the effect of
the defective socialization process upon his personality
development, makes the local racketeer, vice merchant, or
hysterical gang leader an adequate role model for the
sociopathic gang youth. Cloward and Ohlin correctly point
out that in these neighbourhoods even such criminal adult
symbols are defective:

> Just as the unintegrated slum cannot mobilize legitimate re-
> sources for the young, neither can it provide them with access
> to stable criminal careers, for illegitimate learning and oppor-
> tunity structures do not develop. The disorganized slum, popu-
> lated in part by failures in the conventional world, also contains
> the outcasts of the criminal world. This is not to say that crime
> is nonexistent in such areas, but what crime there is tends to be
> individualistic, unorganized, petty, poorly paid, and unpro-
> tected. This is the haunt of the small-time thief, the grifter,
> the pimp, the jackroller, the unsophisticated 'con' man, the
> pick-pocket who is all thumbs, and others who cannnot

graduate beyond 'heisting' candy stores or 'busting' gas stations.[1]

An Addendum: The Suburban 'Disorganized Slum'

Although the factors described are highly prevalent in the *poor* disorganized slum, such a slum has no exclusive rights on gangs and deliquency. There is considerable evidence of a similar social malfunction and disorganization operative in the richer middle-class suburban area that has a similar structure. Such suburban areas may have greater economic resources and a small population; however, the problems of the disorganized urban area (that is, lack of cohesion, anonymity, and confused values) have increased here too. This, in part, may account for the fact that F.B.I. statistics in recent years reflect, for the first time, an increase in 'small-town' crime.

Old-line occupants of the first line of suburbia move farther out as new suburbanites escaping from city slums move in. The newly arrived 'middle-class' former city dweller who moves to suburbia in some cases is confronted with problems of prejudice, new values, new modes of life, a new economic form and other problems comparable in structure to those facing the newly arrived, formerly rural, lower-class city dweller. Part of the recent condition of higher delinquency rates and gang formations (often youth riots) may be explained by the same pattern of 'urbanizing' transition to the disorganized middle-class 'suburban slum'. The 'gangs' in such middle-class neighbourhoods may have different overt characteristics; however, the factors of social structure which produce them may be comparable to the described forces behind the violent gang.[2]

1. Richard A. Cloward and Lloyd E. Ohlin, *Delinquency and Opportunity: A Theory of Delinquent Gangs* (Glencoe, Illinois: The Free Press, 1960), p. 173.

2. Although violent gang leaders are generally from 'working-class groups', the gang-leader-power drive is felt by many disturbed youths. The middle-class gang leader may adopt more sophisticated 'symbols' of glory and form attuned to his higher social position and general level of educational attainment. A recent example occurred in Long Island where a youth attempted to carry out a gang-leader role by emulating the master violent

Despite some of the structural similarities of the extreme *poor* disorganized slum with the suburban disorganized neighbourhood, the suburban area does not apparently produce as much delinquency. Three factors in particular tend to explain the greater prevalence of the extreme violent gang in one area and not the other. One is the greater *intensity* of the described dislocations and onerous conditions in the poor slum (for example, this accounts for the higher rates of social and individual pathology found in the lower-class disorganized slum). Second, the 'suburban' area has more positive factors in its community that may neutralize or vitiate negative forces. (For example, greater legitimate opportunities for success and achievement, and so on.) Third, the pressure of social and economic discrimination is considerably greater on minority group populations inhabiting the poor disorganized slum.

COMMUNITY PREJUDICE AND THE VIOLENT GANG

A significant element of the disorganized slum that has its impact upon the violent gang is the twisting threads of prejudice and discrimination. It is not within the province of this discussion to present a full background of the

------

gang leader – Adolf Hitler. The following news article by Roy Metcalf and Richard Wilson, which described the youth's personal dynamics, has some parallel with the Balkan Egyptian Kings gang-leader syndromes, despite this boy's use of a more sophisticated symbolic leadership theme:

'A FLOP AT EVERYTHING – "FUEHRER" FIZZLES OUT

'All his life the trouble with George Leggett, who prefers to call himself George von Licter because the name "has a proud, regal and aristocratic tone", was his unshakeable conviction that he was indeed a superior person.

'George, now 20, whose short life already had been studded with failures, believed himself born to the mantle of leadership.

'Yet, there is little in either the physical or mental attainments of this kid-gang ringleader, now accused of planning a bank robbery to finance an Aryan-Nordic renaissance, to warrant his self-esteem.

'Despite his devotion to the ideal of the heroic superman, George is a sullen, sloppy-fat, blondish youth, certainly not Nazi stormtrooper material. And despite a high IQ, he quit or flunked out of every school he went to. He exercised his "call" to leadership by surrounding himself with younger boys, and would play the grand host at wild parties when his parents made occasional trips.' *New York Daily Mirror*, 18 January 1958.

emergence or the origins of this complicated problem in American society.[1] It does, however, surround many youths and aggravate the violent-gang problem in a variety of ways.

Prejudice first appears in the 'community' to force the family of the minority-group gang member into the disorganized slum. This results from both direct and indirect discriminatory causes. Indirectly this emanates from an economic blockade against minority groups that prevents their entrance into certain higher-paying occupational positions. Most of the newly arrived population are unskilled labour, and this too affects their economic and financial condition. This complex of factors places the family in a marginal economic position and almost forces them to live in the disorganized slum neighbourhood. Their 'decision' to live in this area is also partially accounted for by the 'breadwinner's' sporadic income. Because he is unable to pay a full month's rent in advance, the weekly rental in the rooming-house area is found to be more compatible with his financial condition. On the more direct discriminatory level, minority groups, particularly Negroes and Puerto Ricans, do not have equal access or are simply barred from living in certain neighbourhoods regardless of financial ability to pay their rent regularly.

Some groups react with 'hat in hand' and bowed head to social and economic discrimination, at least on the surface. Others become militant and direct their clear hostile reactions upon their antagonist. Powdermaker describes the possible range of reactions to discrimination. Although her discussion is essentially related to the case of the Negro slave vis-à-vis his white oppressor, the themes involved have general usefulness and apply to the current scene:

First, there is direct aggression against its true object. Since the whites had, and still have, superior power, and since Negroes are highly realistic, they rarely use this method on any

1. For a fuller analysis of the basic causes of prejudice, see especially Gordon Allport, *The Nature of Prejudice* (New York: Doubleday & Company, Inc., 1954).

large scale except in times of crisis, and then as a climax to a long series of more indirect aggressive behavior patterns. The knocking-down of a white overseer, the direct attack on other whites, has occurred, but only occasionally. One of the reasons advanced by many southern white planters for their preference for colored share croppers to white ones is that the former do not fight back like the latter.

A second method consists in substituting a colored object for the white object of aggression. This was, and still is, done very frequently. The high degree of intra-Negro quarreling, crime, and homicide, revealed by statistics and observation, can be directly correlated with the Negro's frustration in being unable to vent his hostility on the whites. The mechanism of the substitution of one object of aggression for another is well known to the scientist and to the layman. The substitution of Negro for white is encouraged by the culture pattern of white official and unofficial leniency toward intra-Negro crime. Courts, more particularly southern ones, are mild in their view of intra-Negro offenses, and the prevailing white attitude is one of indulgence toward those intra-Negro crimes which do not infringe on white privileges.

A third possibility is for the Negro to retreat to an 'ivory tower' and attempt to remain unaffected by the interracial situation. But this type of adjustment is very difficult and consequently a rare one.[1]

Victims of prejudice thus respond at different levels of reaction and with a variety of patterns. Some individuals may react with extreme hostility directed at their felt oppressor; others accept their lot and status of victim with 'hat in hand'. Some victims of prejudice displace their violent responses against themselves or members of their own group. This latter problem has been described by Kurt Lewin as 'self-hatred'. It is the condition in which the victim of discrimination begins to hate especially the member of his own group who fits the stereotype specified by the out-group.[2] In this process the members of minority

1. Hortense Powdermaker, 'The Channelling of Negro Aggression by the Cultural Process', in *Personality in Nature, Society, and Culture*, edited by Clyde Kluckhohn and Henry A. Murray (New York: Alfred Knopf, 1949), p. 477.

2. Kurt Lewin, *Resolving Social Conflicts* (New York: Harper & Brothers, 1948).

groups displace their aggression against other members of their own minority group instead of against the real object of their aggression, the discriminators.

Violent-gang activity often provides an outlet for the prejudice condition. 'They called me a Spick' or 'They called me a nigger' are 'rational' reasons given by gang boys for battling another gang, even though the very gang or individual they fight may be of the same ethnic background as they. Much of this type of self-hatred, prejudice, and discrimination is associated with action by the marginal populations who stand to lose most from the influx of the newly arrived. In East Harlem, for example, some older Negro and Puerto Rican residents tend heavily to prejudge and discriminate in this way against the newly arrived populations belonging to their ethnic category.

The intensity of 'felt' discrimination varies among different groups and people. For example, newly arrived Puerto Rican groups in New York City are often keenly aware of being American citizens and tend to have a high self-image and a great sense of personal honour about this status. This causes them to react more intensely against prejudice than other minority groups who do not have this proud self-concept. Thus for many Puerto Rican youths the violent gang serves (in part) as a medium for acting out their hostile responses (and those of their families) to prejudices they resent very strongly. There is some evidence that although this violent-gang pattern is overtly disapproved by the parents of violent-gang members, it may be encouraged by them on a covert level. Some victims of prejudice, who are at the same time parents, 'act' out their responses to the hurt of prejudice, using their children as targets for displaced aggression or using them as weapons for the aggression against the oppressors. (I have observed many cases of minority-group parents consciously and unconsciously provoking their children to 'get the bastards'.) All of these patterns of prejudice and reaction to prejudice pour gasoline on the fires of gang violence.

The Direct Prejudice of Gang Wars

The simplest, and perhaps oldest, form of gang rivalry was based on racial, religious, or ethnic lines of conflict. (As Asbury reported in *Gangs of New York*, Italian gangs fought Negro gangs in Harlem, Jewish gangs fought Irish gangs on the lower East Side, and so on.) These rivalries and battles were fairly clear-cut enterprises organized along religious, ethnic, or racial lines. So that on one clear level, gang violence may simply involve one or all of the same racial or religious gang doing battle with another.

This elemental or classical form of gang reaction to prejudice is described in the MacIver Report:

> Gangs draw their members from the immediate area, with the result that they generally represent the ethnic and racial composition of the neighborhood. Thus many gangs in New York City, like the neighborhood to which they belong, are dominated by a single ethnic or racial group, such as the Negro, Puerto Rican, Irish, or Italian, although it is not uncommon to have some mixing. There have been fights between gangs because of racial and ethnic animosities but differences in racial and ethnic backgrounds generally are not at the heart of gang strife. Rather, such tensions are usually symptoms of under-lying maladjustments from which gang fighting is another out-growth. The arrival of a new ethnic or racial group in an area is often the signal for unrest among the more unruly youth of the older groups. As a result, the boys of the new group are forced to take defensive measures and a cycle of gang warfare is touched off. This proved to be the case in the Lower East Side in 1953, when the movement of Puerto Ricans into the area resulted in gang warfare between them and the established Irish and Italian gangs. The defensive groups may then con-tinue to exist long after the original reason for their formation has been forgotten.[1]

This form is generally outmoded among violent gangs, although many *social gangs* still find it a basis for minor conflict. Violent gang prejudice is more intricate and complicated.

1. From Interim Report No. XIV, Juvenile Delinquency Evaluation Project of the City of New York, 1960.

The Prejudice Label

Most modern violent gangs are mixed groups. The Kings, Villains, and Balkans, for example, although formed predominantly of Negroes and Puerto Ricans, also had some Italian and Irish members as well as various other backgrounds. Despite this, members of the same gang will use bigoted labels against each other. A Negro may call a Puerto Rican a 'Spick', and he, in turn, may call his antagonist a 'black bastard'. But the sharp bite of prejudice is not usually intended except in a jocular fashion. The 'prejudice' tends to be an almost playful part of the general 'sounding' hostility. The bigotry label is simply tacked on partially because it is fashionable in the rationale of the larger society where such terms are more 'logical' items of antagonism. In the violent gang they are almost playful terms of affection and have a different meaning to the gang boy than they do in larger society.

Prejudice on the Surface – Aggression Below

Overt prejudice in the violent gang is often used as a cover-up for deeper personal problems. Some gang boys, like bigots in the larger society, use prejudice to work out aggressions related to personal problems. (The Nazi use of the Jews as a scapegoat is an extreme case of this type of dynamics.) For example, Duke, at the height of the Villain attack, presented a confused statement of his hostilities and problems. At the end of his statement he tacked on a comment that was almost irrelevant to his other problems:

No, I wouldn't have fought them if my grandfather hadn't died. I used to talk to him about the situation all the time. He always used to advise me and keep me cool-minded and tell me what the right thing to do was, and he never got excited. Then, when he died, you know I sort of went to pieces and I figured that I just had to get even for something. That was too much. I had nobody to turn to then. I couldn't talk to my father, so that's when I decided that the Villains would have to pay for what they done. . . . *Most of them were Puerto Ricans and Spanish*

*and I figured I was going to get even with them for dirtying up my
block. . . . Teach everyone a lesson once and for all.*

The element that makes his expressed hostility against
Puerto Ricans ludicrous is that half of his gang was Puerto
Rican. [handwritten: race a good excuse but no basis for it]

Gang Violence as a Reaction to a Persistently Felt Prejudice

As indicated, some individual victims of prejudice use the
gang vehicle of violence as a direct weapon for 'getting
even'. In some specific cases a youth will manifest paranoia
about prejudice. Although the Kings' individual rationales
for fighting the Jesters included territorial dispute and
rep, there was another theme for several King gang
members:

> They kept callin' me a Spick. They kept on sayin, 'You dirty
> Spick, get out of this block.' Every time I go in the pool, they
> said to me the same thing. I don't bother them, 'cause you know,
> I don't want to get into no trouble with them, but one day they
> beat me up. You know, there was about five of them, and they
> wouldn't leave me alone. They beat me up, and I had to take
> a chance to get the boys so we could beat them up.

This boy and several others carried the hurt and aggression of being victims of prejudice with them into all
gang battles. To them the gang was an opportunity to
retaliate against felt discrimination. The attack upon
Michael Farmer for these boys was clearly a racial issue,
even though for other Kings it was irrelevant: 'They
[the Jesters] called us Spicks and that goes real deep down
in me because I'm Spanish and I'm proud of it. I ain't
going to let nobody insult my race.'

The King gang member claimed to go to the gang fight
because the Jesters insulted his group:

> I never been prejudiced. I never had anything against any-
> body. I been growed up with coloured mostly in my life and
> Spanish. Half the club is always coloured the other is Spanish.
> . . . The Jesters come along and call our whole club Spicks and
> Niggers. It got me so mad I could shoot them all.

The structure of the gang thus reflects both sides of the prejudice coin. It enables youths, on the one hand, to use an understandable, 'socially acceptable' pattern – gang warfare – for acting out aggressions that are related to other hostilities and personal difficulties (for example, hostility towards parents, towards adults in general, and so on). On the other hand, the gang provides a vehicle through which some youths, who are almost paranoid about being 'victims of prejudice', can react to their constant feeling of being discriminated against.

Paradoxically, in many cases, this type of gang dynamic (fighting in response to felt prejudice) involves the 'discriminatory victim' fighting *alongside* and *against* representatives of the group he believes is discriminating against him. For example, there is the case of one Egyptian King who constantly described the Jesters as a 'white-Irish' group that 'picked on the Spanish'. This was why he wanted to 'get them'. At the killing the same boy struck down Farmer alongside, and with the aid of, a 'white-Irish' Egyptian King gang compatriot.

Twisted Forms of 'Gang Prejudice'

In New York City the Negro seems to have greatly improved his social status, and has become upwardly mobile. This is not necessarily true with the newly arrived Puerto Rican. The issue of who has higher status in the community, the Puerto Rican or the Negro, appears to be a problem to which currently there is no clear answer. The situation is further complicated by the fact that many individuals from Puerto Rican backgrounds are dark-skinned, many Negroes are light-skinned, and many 'whites' are dark-skinned. Some of the dynamics of this complex problem are revealed by Mills, Senior, and Goldsen:

> It is a confused situation. In some areas of Harlem, Negroes and Puerto Ricans, neither wishing to be identified with the other, are in frequent and bitter conflict. . . . On the other hand, it is reliably reported that some American Negroes in Harlem are attempting to learn Spanish!

When he comes to New York, the Puerto Rican migrant is either plunged into one of two worlds, or just exists between them. If he is white, he must adjust himself to the white culture of New York; if he is not white, he has no choice but to blend into the Negro community. The white migrant must take on the behavior and values of white America. The colored migrant finds that the world to which he must adapt himself is the Negroes' America.

For those in the intermediate racial classification – the indio or grifo – the position is more difficult. The Negro with 'good' features or with Negro features but light skin, hair, and eyes, in Puerto Rico was likely to have held a position somewhat above the darker Negro – a world somewhere between the colored and the white worlds.

Although no other community will accept him, the intermediately colored migrant is frequently unwilling to identify himself with the Negro community. . . . He has little motivation to make friends; the customs of America seem even stranger and more bewildering to him than to either the white or the clearly Negro migrant. He has a stronger feeling of not being accepted by the New York world. He is more sensitive to slights, more alert to discriminating experiences, although he feels them to have been directed against all Puerto Ricans. More than the others, he feels that Americans look down upon Puerto Ricans. In the same way, he becomes more quickly aware of the identity of other ethnic minorities within the city and he is more likely to take on prejudices against them. He finds that if he learns English, he is even more likely to lose the slight advantage he holds in New York over the American Negro – for somehow a non-American Negro receives privileged treatment in the New York community. For this reason he is less likely to know English well and he is more likely to use Spanish in public places so that he will be identified not as a Negro but as a Latin. Confronted by painful contradictions, he suffers all the difficulties of any newcomer, and, in addition, those of a racial problem for which he is relatively untrained.[1]

The question is not so much the self-identification 'Am I Puerto Rican or Negro?' but 'Will I be better off as a Puerto Rican or a Negro?' Which self-identification has

1. C. Wright Mills, Clarence Senior, and Rose Goldsen, *The Puerto Rican Journey* (New York: Harper & Brothers, 1950), pp. 132–4.

higher status? One of the 'inhabitants' makes the following extreme prediction about this complex condition:

... the Negroes and the Puerto Ricans will fight for New York. They will fight for the apartments, the jobs, for every new building that the white people move out of ... the Puerto Ricans will win the fight because they haven't learned how to lose or how to fight. The Puerto Ricans come like children to New York. The whole city is waiting ready-made. I think soon the street signs will be in Spanish.[1]

This complicated problem takes on some interesting patterns in the gang and is partially revealed by the following incident: a boy came into my office and remarked that he was quite puzzled. The previous evening an individual in his twenties, very dark-complexioned ('He was coloured'), had approached him and attempted to draft him into a gang. The individual trying to draft him into the gang told the boy, 'We want everyone around here to join our gang so we can clean out the niggers.' The boy being drafted was white, and the drafter was very dark-skinned and had a Spanish accent. The complexity of discrimination in the gang is evidenced here. The drafter, who was both Negro and Puerto Rican (depending on his self- or other definition), was trying to disassociate himself from his Negro background by intimating he was a Puerto Rican who hated Negroes. The gang in this case was his vehicle for getting out of a discriminatory 'box' in which society had placed him.

Another aspect of the complicated form prejudice takes is the response of the gang against their enemies – the out-group. In this case it is not a matter of skin colour, but a retaliation against an unfair majority group. An interesting kink in the problem is revealed by Coleman in an article on 'community disorganization':

A young mathematician from England was recently at the University of Chicago for a short period. When he was walking across the Midway, he was accosted by several Negro boys who demanded his wallet. He objected, one of

1. Horwitz, op. cit., p. 92.

them produced a knife, and they led him over toward bushes beside the walk. The ensuing conversation went something like this, according to his later account: One boy said, 'Come on, now, give us your wallet, or we'll have to get tough with you.' He replied, 'Look here, I don't want to give up my wallet to you. Besides, I've just arrived here from England, and I don't think this is the way to treat someone who's a visitor here.' The boys looked at one another, and then one said, 'Oh. We thought you were one of those white guys,' and they quickly went away.

To these Negro boys, 'white guys' had nothing to do with skin color per se, for the English mathematician was white. 'White guys' were their fellow community members, the whites from whom they felt alienated because there had been no processes to create common identity between them, only those creating hostility. The Englishman was not a 'white guy' against whom a reserve force of hostility had been built up.[1]

In short, gang membership and gang warfare in the disorganized slum do not function simply in the classical tradition of racial or ethnic gang *A* doing battle with racial or ethnic gang *B*. Not only the racial mixture of the gangs but also the individual member's social and psychological dynamics demand assessment if the forces at work in the disorganized slum that produce violent gangs are to be properly evaluated.

Concluding Note

The demise of a community into a modern disorganized slum produces bewildered youths with defective personality systems. They are exposed to confusing adult role models and value systems. The types of reference points available for self-definition in the more cohesive community are hazy or absent in the disorganized slum. In the real 'community' there were clearly others who knew, understood, and cared about youths; these 'others' expected, demanded, and received a conformity in behaviour. Youth

1. James Coleman, 'Community Disorganization', in *Contemporary Social Problems*, edited by Robert Merton and Robert Nisbet (New York: Harcourt, Brace & Company, 1961).

was socialized as a coherent personality even when the role models and values presented were deviant and the individual became a clearly defined delinquent or criminal.

The anonymity and conflict of the disorganized slum produces an asocialized individual, one who may not even be capable of adequate participation in organized deviance. For this type of *sociopathic youth* the violent gang functions as an adequate adjustment pattern in the sea of social confusion he confronts in the disorganized slum. A closer analysis reveals the interlocking nature of the *sociopathic personality* with the violent gang.

race? — used as vehicle as prejudice — emphasises sociopathic personality e.g. negro may pretend to be Peurto Rican + anti negro.

12. The Sociopathic Youth in the Violent Gang

The socio-cultural milieu of the disorganized slum is fertile ground for spawning a higher rate of deviant response than that found in more stable communities. Assuming that these forces help nurture the emergence of the violent gang as a deviant 'opportunity structure', the important question, as previously indicated, remains: why do certain youths living in this milieu become violent-gang members, while others work out different deviant adjustment patterns (for example, 'lone-wolf' theft, *social- or delinquent-*gang membership, drug addiction, psychosis). Stating this same issue in another way, violent gangs are essentially a product of the unstable slum; however, this fact alone does not explain why certain boys 'join' violent gangs and many others, with the same opportunity, do not. The explanation of this more explicit issue necessitates going beyond the socio-cultural influences into the social-psychological condition of the *individual violent-gang member*.

The working hypothesis that will guide the inquiry of this chapter may be stated as follows: the violent-gang structure recruits its participants from the more sociopathic youths living in the disorganized-slum community.[1] The youth with this type of personality structure

1. The element of chance also enters into the selection of the violent gang over another adjustment pattern. Other forms of emotionally disturbed expression, such as individual bizarre violence or small-group violence (e.g. stomp slayers), would take priority over the *violent-gang syndrome*, if the violent-gang structure was not as readily available. The chance factor in personality formation and expression is described by Kluckhohn and Murray:

'... there are things which "just happen" to people. Even casual contacts of brief duration ("accidental", – i.e., not foreordained by the cultural patterns for social interrelations) are often crucial, it seems, in determining whether a person's life will proceed along one or another of various possible paths. ... Chance events may not immediately and directly change the

is most adaptable to participation in the violent gang because of his particular need-disposition and lack of personal competence for participation in more demanding deviant or social groups.

DEFECTIVE SOCIALIZATION AND THE SOCIOPATH

The youth most susceptible to violent-gang membership emerges from a social milieu that trains him inadequately for assuming constructive social roles. In fact, the defective socialization process to which he is subjected in the disorganized slum fosters a lack of social 'feelings'. At hardly any point is he trained to have human feelings of compassion or responsibility for another. The youth with this type of sociopathic personality syndrome living in the disorganized-slum neighbourhood is most prone to participation in the violent gang.

Gough's description of the 'psychopathic' tends to reveal the type of personality most amenable to participation in the violent gang. He is 'the kind of person who seems insensitive to social demands, who refuses to or cannot cooperate, who is untrustworthy, impulsive, and improvident, who shows poor judgment and shallow emotionality, and who seems unable to appreciate the reactions of others to his behaviour'.[1]

Although various terms such as 'moral imbecility', 'constitutional inferiority', 'anethopathy', 'psycopath', and 'semantic dementia' have been applied to this personality type, the term *sociopath* is used in this discussion since it appropriately relates to the social-pathological condition that produces this personality type.

A basic and apparent personality defect of the sociopath is a lack of social conscience towards almost all others to whom he relates. This characteristic is most apparent in

1. Harrison G. Gough, 'A Sociological Theory of Psychopathy', *American Journal of Sociology* (March 1948), p. 360.

young man's personality, but may set in motion a chain of events which put him into situations that are decisive. . . .' *Personality in Nature, Society and Culture* (New York: Alfred Knopf, 1949), p. 43.

the violent-gang offenders' limited feelings of any real sympathy or post-assault regret for their victims. Thus a lack of empathy and guilt for their destructive actions is a dominant personality characteristic. Rabin succinctly describes the trait of defective 'social conscience' apparent in the sociopathic personality:

There are two major related aspects to this notion of defective conscience. ... The first aspect is represented in the inability ... to apply the moral standards of society to his behavior; he cheats, lies, steals, does not keep promises, and so on. He has not absorbed the 'thou shalts' and the 'thou shalt nots' of his society and cultural milieu. The second aspect is that of absence of guilt. Guilt is an important part of any well-developed conscience. When a normal person violates the moral code he feels guilty; he feels unhappy and blames himself for the transgression. ... Guilt is an unknown experience for the personality with no superego. There is none of this automatic self-punishment that goes along with the commission of immoral and unethical acts. The psychopath [sociopath] continues to behave irresponsibly, untruthfully, insincerely, and antisocially without a shred of shame, remorse, or guilt. He may sometimes express regret and remorse for the actions and crimes which he may have perpetrated; however, these are usually mere words, spoken for the effect, but not really and sincerely felt.[1]

The more adequate 'social self' is developed from a consistent pattern of interaction with another in a normative socialization process. The 'other' is usually a parent or an adequate adult-role model from whom the youth can learn social feelings of compassion and sympathy. Such 'others' necessary for adequate socialization are absent from the social environment of youths 'growing up' in the disorganized slum.[2]

1. Arthur Rabin, 'Psychopathic (Sociopathic) Personalities', in *Legal and Criminal Psychology*, edited by Hans Toch (New York: Holt, Rinehart & Winston, 1961), p. 278.

2. The notion of adequate self-emergence through constructive social interaction with others is grounded in the works of Charles Horton Cooley, and later developed by J. L. Moreno and G. H. Mead. As Mead developed the theme: 'The self arises in conduct when the individual becomes a social object in experience to himself. This takes place when the individual as-

Thus the sociopathic youth produced by the socialization process, characteristic of the disorganized slum, tends to be self-involved, exploitative, and disposed towards violent outbursts. This sociopathic type of individual lacks 'social ability' or the ability adequately to assess the role expectations of 'others'. *He is characteristically unable to experience the pain of the violence he may inflict on another, since he does not have the ability to identify or empathize with any others.* He is thus capable of committing spontaneous acts of 'senseless' violence without feeling concern or guilt. The classic sociopathic comment of the King who used the bread knife in the assault on Michael Farmer aptly describes this pattern of feeling: 'What was I thinking about when I did it? Man, are you crazy. I was thinking about whether to do it again!'

The Sociopathic Sex Pattern of the Gang

Unfeeling violence is one sociopathic gang pattern. Egocentric, exploitative heterosexual relations is another characteristic that serves further to illustrate the nature of the violent-gang member's sociopathic personality. To him sex is an itch that is scratched when the opportunity arises, without any compassion or identification with the impact on his 'sexual object'. Practically no emotional relatedness, except the physical or fantasy manipulation

---

sumes the attitude or uses the gesture which another individual would use and responds to it himself.' The child through socialization gradually becomes a social being. 'The self thus has its origin in communication and in taking the role of the other.' George H. Mead, *Mind, Self and Society* (University of Chicago Press, 1934).

In a similar appraisal, the self, according to Sullivan, is made up of 'reflected appraisals'. The child lacks equipment and experience necessary for a careful and unclouded evaluation of himself. The only guides he has are those of the significant adults or others who take care of him and treat him with compassion. The child thus experiences and appraises himself in terms of how parents and others close to him react. By empathy, facial expressions, gestures, words, deeds, they convey to him the attitudes they hold toward him, their regard or lack of feeling for him. This set of positive sympathetic responses needed for adequate self-growth are generally absent in the development of the youth who becomes a sociopathic violent-gang member. Harry Stack Sullivan, *Conceptions of Modern Psychiatry* (Washington, D.C.: The William Alanson White Psychiatric Foundation, 1947).

of another is apparent in the gang's 'sociopathic' form of sex activity.

The gang boys tend towards three extreme patterns of sexual behaviour: the 'gang bang', 'idolatrous' love, and an overt disdain for girls combined with homosexual overtones. Each pattern almost rules out the possibility of a warm empathic human relationship.

In the 'gang bang' pattern a promiscuous female is 'lined up', and often as many as fifteen or twenty boys will indulge themselves with her in some form of sexual act. The female 'sexual victim' is generally a mental defective or severely disturbed girl, sometimes violated by forceful rape. The sexual situation may occur on one occasion, or the acts may occur serially over several days.

In another pattern the gang youth romantically 'falls in love' and fantasizes a perfect female ideal. The allusion by another gang member that 'his girl' is prone to promiscuous relations produces an explosive response. The 'boy friend' attempts to maintain an illusion of virginity and perfection about his girl friend that is usually in conflict with the facts. Here again he relates, not in significant human interaction, but on what approaches an unfeeling fantasy level.

Another sociopathic mode of relating by violent-gang members entails disdain and exploitation of girls. In this pattern girls are viewed as objects to be manipulated or used for 'rep' making and ego gratification. The girl becomes a target for hostility and physical brutality, which when reported back to the gang confers prestige on the violator. 'Why waste your time with broads?' 'You can't trust them', 'I belted her a few times', are common expressions that reflect the gang's general opinion.

In the three cases cited, a warm, loving, human heterosexual relationship is a rarity. All patterns almost prohibit this type of affect. There may be some playful interaction around sexual intercourse; however, for the violent-gang boy a close, warm relationship with a female entailing mutual responsibility and empathy is rare.

Fear of responsibility and emotional isolation from females generates the gang as a kind of 'homosexual' community. Constant condemnation of other gang members as 'faggots' (homosexuals) or by saying 'he eats it' may be viewed as projections of felt internal homosexual problems. Most gang leaders, in particular, manifest homosexual attitudes in their ridicule, exploitation of females, and their closer feelings about members of their male peer group.

Along these lines there is evidence of homosexual experimentation among gang boys. This is not usually overtly carried out by gang members among themselves; however, a common pattern for them is to become the passive recipient of homosexual relations with definite homosexuals. The ritual which often recurs was expressed by one gang member as follows: 'After this queer bastard blew us [*laughs*], we beat the hell out of him – but good.' (In some cases the initially passive homosexual gang youth becomes an overt active homosexual. Frenchy of the Villains was a case in point.)

Contrary to the popular, yet erroneous, images created by *The West Side Story* and other glamorized 'fictional' versions of violent-gang activity, the sociopathic gang youth maintains a type of 'homosexual' relationship system in the gang that reflects his personality. The youth who tends towards a more compassionate female relationship is generally a more marginal violent-gang member. The most sociopathic core gang members will ridicule the youth who attempts to relate to a girl on a human level beyond a simple sexual 'trick' or as an object for exploitation.

The tendency to manipulate another for egocentric gratifications is an apparent trait of the sociopathic youth in his sexual activity. This pattern, however, is simply a more obvious extension of his exploitative approach for relating to all 'others'.

The Sociopathic Youth: Summary Note

The defective socialization process operative in the disorganized slum produces youths with limited social feelings, identity, and compassion for others. Such youths manifest sociopathic personalities that reflect some if not all of the following characteristics: (A) a defective social conscience marked by limited feelings of guilt for destructive acts against others, (B) limited feelings of compassion or empathy for others, (C) the acting out of behaviour dominated by egocentrism and self-seeking goals, (D) the manipulation of others in a way possible for immediate self-gratification (for example, sexual exploitative modes of behaviour) without any moral concern or responsibility.

The most sociopathic youths of the type described find that the violent gang provides for them a vehicle through which they can acquire and achieve gratifications consistent with their personality ability and needs.

Incapable of ego achievement through normal channels, the sociopathic youth selects or helps to construct in the violent-gang role patterns in which he is a 'successful' person. These various roles that provide 'competence' or 'success' in the gang have sociopathic implications and may be viewed as a striving for personal and 'social' success in a disturbed compensatory fashion.

The extent of the gang youth's sociopathic personality is a determinant of the level of participation and involvement of the individual in the violent gang. The less sociopathically disturbed youth is a 'marginal' member, whereas the more sociopathic youth tends to become the violent-gang leader. Such 'core' members are heavily – almost completely – committed to gang activity. They belong essentially because it is an easily accessible social structure in which they can operate with some level of acceptance and adequacy. The malleable nature of the violent gang makes it a useful vehicle of illusionary achievement for the defectively socialized youth.

THE SOCIOPATHIC YOUTH AND VIOLENT-GANG ACHIEVEMENT

Despite his deficient personality, the sociopathic youth gets caught up in the sweep of a culture dominated by the drive for success and achievement. Deprived of 'social ability', and generally blocked from achieving through normal channels, many sociopathic youths find the violent gang a most adequate device for successful self-gratification.

The Anomie Pattern of Gang Violence[1]

need for success

In American society all youths are provoked by the mass media to desire a great variety of cultural goals they can seldom obtain through legitimate means. They are induced by a high-powered propaganda system, which has no apparent conscience, to desire a variety of success objects without which they may feel frustrated.

Moreover, most youths are led to believe that a great many social statuses are available to all – when it is at the same time apparent that the facts of class, ethnicity, race, and other background factors sharply limit certain segments of the population in the achievement of social goals. The possibility and means for acquiring many of these highly valued social statuses and objectives are slight for a majority of American youths – in particular, those who come from a lower-class background or a minority group. Although the 'socially deprived' segment of the population is not fully blocked from means for achievement available to other segments, the 'degrees of availability' are not fully equal.

Not only do the background factors indicated block 'success', the status of youth itself tends to place young people in a minority position. For a youth, many material objects and cultural items adults take for granted are difficult to attain; yet his interest in achievement is encouraged at the same level of intensity as theirs, if not more sharply.

Given these varied forces, the more susceptible sociopathic youth is pushed harder into devious methods, outside the normal bounds of society, to achieve goals not

1. This cultural means-goals conception is derived from the theoretical formulations of Merton, Durkheim, Cloward and Ohlin. It is essentially a restatement of the theoretical theme of 'anomie' previously discussed in 'The Gang in Recent Sociological Theory' (Chapter 9).

attainable through socially prescribed patterns of behaviour. Such short-cutting of normal expectations for
behaviour to acquire culturally prescribed success goals
entails deviant patterns, often, but not necessarily, illegal.
Among the alternatives to him in his search for 'success'
are such institutionalized deviant patterns as illegal behaviour opportunities (theft, robbery, vice for profit), illusion and fantasy techniques (alcoholism, drug addiction),
and contemporary, thrill-seeking kicks based on assault
and violence.

Within this framework of anomic (means-end) social
forces, the better-adjusted youth trained in delinquent
values is more inclined towards direct, deviant behaviour
to attain status. Because he has greater personal resources
and self-organization, he tends towards participation in
the *delinquent gang*. In this deviant social system he may
steal or assault for profit in a somewhat more rational attempt at attaining success. A more bizarre and psychically
oriented route toward success is taken by the sociopathic
youth in the violent gang.[1]

The Violent Gang as a Means of Successful Self-gratification

A sociopathic youth can, through the proper use of violent-gang organization and its violence, become a 'successful leader' with status; avoid mundane, dull life, and
achieve notoriety. If only in caricature fashion, he can
become the 'success' so important in American society.
All these self-gratification possibilities are available to him
in the malleable, violent gang – which he helps to construct
and maintain as a vehicle for achievement. A brief closer
examination of each of these factors reveals the functional

1. The different choice of behaviour between the violent and the delinquent gang may be illustrated by an example of car theft. Delinquent-gang
members would plan the theft carefully, steal the car, sell it, or strip the
parts and sell them for profit. The violent gang, on the other hand, would
steal the car on the spur of the moment, for kicks, and drive it around 'to
show off as big-shots'. Ideally the violent-gang member is concerned with
ego gratification. The delinquent-gang member, on the other hand, acquires
a material gratification more normative to and rationally understood within
the context of the overall society.

nature of 'usefulness' of gang violence for the 'success-motivated' sociopathic youth who is blocked or *incapable* of utilizing normal social channels for achievement.

GANG STATUS. In the violent gang, a sociopathic youth with limited social ability can become a gang president, or war lord, control vast domains, and generally act out a powerful although fantasized success image. Gang boys can mutually expand the degree of their shared and highly valued success by reinforcing each other's fantasies of power. In discussing gang fantasies, the unwritten contractual agreement among gang boys is 'Don't call my bluff and I won't call yours; I'll support your gang-leader image if you'll support mine.' This lends prestige to all youths involved in the 'charade'.

This pattern of illusionary 'social contracts' is not original with or found exclusively in the gang. Individuals in other social spheres 'divide the world' among themselves in a deceptive way. In the violent gang, however, little if anything is required except an occasional act of violence to support the desired success image.

A 'SOCIAL NARCOTIC' AND 'FAME'. 'The exorbitant goal-inadequate means of achievement' dislocation in society provokes still another pattern of compensatory solution. The violent gang can serve as a 'social narcotic', a device enabling sociopathic youths to move into unreality and to avoid the anxieties of the normal social responsibilities which they feel ill-equipped to meet. In the violent gang the only requirement for entrance is, as indicated, a periodic ritual of violence to validate and confirm gang membership and status.

Gang violence or homicide is a readily available means for sociopathic youths to achieve a notoriety and fame impossible to attain in any other way (unless he commits suicide). Frayed press notices carried by the Kings and Balkans were repeatedly displayed as testimonials of such 'social achievement' and fame.

THE ROLE OF VIOLENCE. The selection of violence by the sociopathic youth in his adjustment process is not difficult to understand. Violent behaviour requires limited training, personal ability, or even physical strength. (As one gang boy stated: 'A knife or a gun makes you ten feet high.') Because violence is a demonstration of easily achieved power, it becomes the paramount value of the gang. In the violent gang it is a symbol of ability possessing a parallel importance with such lofty values as dedication, sincerity, and responsibility, the idealized symbols of the larger society. Moreover, violence requires characteristics gang boys have in quantity: limited social ability and training, considerable resentment and aggression, and a motivation to retaliate against others. It thus serves as a quick and sure means for upward social mobility within the violent gang and, to a limited extent, in the overall society.

In addition to the position of violence as a prestige symbol in the gang, the larger society covertly approves of, or is at least intrigued by, that which is depicted in literature, radio, television, the movies, and other mass media. Although on the surface most members of society condemn violence, on a covert level there is a tendency to aggrandize and give recognition to perpetrators of violence. The sociopathic personality who commits intense, sudden acts of violence is the 'hero' of many plays and stories portrayed in contemporary mass media. The incompetent sociopathic youth senses this condition, and this may also account in part for his selection of the violent hoodlum role – one he can adequately fulfil.

In a society that values success and notoriety, marginal youths may attempt to achieve it by any means. For the product of the disorganized slum, the sociopathic youth, violence in the gang is a reasonable and convenient means for acquiring notoriety and prestige – hallmarks of success in American society.

13. The Nature of Violent-gang Organization

The violent-gang member has been described as a sociopathic personality characterized by a limited social conscience, inability to identify with others, with a tendency to be egocentric and exploitative in his general relations with others. The next important issue to be assessed in the development of the original assumptions about violent gangs centres around the nature of the relationship system of the violent gang. This can best be illuminated by attempting to answer the question: what are the structure and function of relationships in the violent gang? The working hypothesis that attempts to deal with this issue may be roughly stated as follows: owing to the sociopathic defective social ability of its membership, violent-gang organization is characterized by limited group cohesion and different levels of commitment to the organization; and membership has a different meaning for each participant. Violent gangs tend to be only partially organized into a type of 'near group'. In order to appraise the nature of violent-gang structure, several important themes of its organization require closer attention and explanation. In particular, the meanings of *membership* and *leadership* reveal a great deal about the nature of violent-gang organization.

SOME SIGNIFICANT THEMES OF VIOLENT-GANG ORGANIZATION

The Nature of Gang 'Membership'

Sociopathic youths join violent gangs for a variety of individualized, personal reasons. In some respects each youth has his own special motive for violent-gang membership, and this can be related to the intensity of his gang

affiliation. The gang boy's degree of emotional involvement in the gang is indicated by his level of participation,
which may be either core or marginal. The more sociopathic youth tends to be a core member, and the less
pathological youth tends to be somewhat more marginal.
Unlike participation in more defined groups, the amorphous quality of violent-gang organization provides the
possibility for the sociopathic member to perceive the
gang, especially its size, in his own particular way and to
utilize it for adjusting a variety of individual problems.

CORE MEMBERS. The core category includes both the
leaders, who are at the centre of the gang's structure, and
the most dedicated and involved members. These central
members know each other in face-to-face relationships,
live in the same neighbourhood, hang around the same
corner, play together, fight among themselves, sound on each
other, worry together, and plan gang strategy for warfare.
The solidarity of the core members is much greater than
that of the outer ring of more marginal gang participants.
Gang membership is close to the core members' lifeline of
activity, and to them the gang constitutes their primary
world. Their ego strength, position in the world, and any
status or pleasure they enjoy are tied to gang activity.
Their turf and activities, particularly the gang's violence,
give meaning to their existence. The core gang member is
easy to identify by this tremendous degree of around-the-
clock involvement. This is not so with the more marginal
gang member.

MARGINAL MEMBERS. At the second level of overall
violent-gang membership (and emotional involvement) are
marginal members. Their participation in gang activities
takes several forms: Category I – the sociopathic youth
with immediate emotional problems; Category II – the
sociopathic violence-dominated youth who is seeking his
kicks through violence; and Category III – the 'mythical
member'.

Marginal Members: Category I. The marginal member who joins the violent gang to resolve his immediate emotional state and needs does not usually know most other gang members. His closest friends are not core gang members, not does he identify closely with the many real and imagined problems the gang consistently has with other gangs. This type of marginal member appears at gang-war discussions and battles at those times when he has a temporary need for violent behaviour that he believes may be satisfied through gang activity.

One such marginal member of the Egyptian Kings went along the night of the murder because 'I just had a fight with my old man and I was mad at everybody'. Another went along, as he put it, 'for old time's sake'. He never really 'belonged' to the Kings nor was he defined by himself or others as a gang member. To reiterate his reason for participation:

> I was walking uptown with a couple of friends and we ran into Magician [one of the Egyptian King gang leaders] and them there. They asked us if we wanted to go to a fight, and we said yes. When he asked me if I wanted to go to a fight, I couldn't say no. I mean, I could say no, but for old time's sake, I said yes.

Marginal Members: Category II. Other youths who may be included in the category of marginal gang membership are the sociopathic individuals almost *always* ready to fight with any available gang. They seek out violence or provoke it simply as they describe it: 'for kicks or action'. They are not necessarily members of any particular violent gang, yet are in some respects members of all. They join gangs because for them it is a convenient and easily accessible opportunity for violence. When the gang, as an instrument, is not appropriate they 'roll their own' form of violence (for example, the three stomp slayers who kicked a man to death for 'whistling a song we didn't like'). For example, in one typical pattern utilized by this type of gang boy, he will approach a stranger with the taunt 'What did you say about my mother?' An assault is then delivered upon the victim before he can respond to the question, which, of course, has no appropriate answer for preventing the attack. Some muggings (robbery combined with assault) are carried out by this type of gang member, not for money but for violent kicks. Such boys are 'members' of all gangs and at the same moment 'members' of none. If there is the possibility for violence, cloaked in the 'rationality' and 'legitimacy' of gang assault, they 'join'.

Marginal Members: Category III. A third category of marginal gang member may have no clear personal awareness of his membership. His essential 'membership qualification' is to be identified as such by a core member. On many occasions during tours of the upper West Side with core gang leaders, particularly at times of gang-war stress, practically every boy seen by the leaders was identified as a gang member. At every corner where there was a collection of boys hanging around (a common sight in New York) the leaders pointed out members. Such 'illusionary members' were identified essentially to satisfy the leaders' needs to 'possess' a large membership. The leaders were not consciously lying; the imagined membership was part of their fantasy world.

In summary, the marginal, second-level gang 'members' can be divided into three essential categories: gang 'people' who exist in actuality and 'join' to work out temporary violent needs; the continuous violence seekers; and gang 'people' who exist in the fantasies and distorted conceptions dreamed up by core members in their efforts to reassure themselves of strength and power.

Miscellaneous Gang 'Members'. Some gang-war participants (who become 'gang members' through identification by official agencies) defy categorization. The youth who arrives at the scene of a rumble simply out of curiosity and then gets arrested illustrates this type of gang 'member', one difficult to count and categorize.

The following more detailed case illustrates this miscellaneous category more specifically. A youth who had no affiliation in any way with either the Balkans, Scorpions, or Villains 'participated' in the June gang-war battle and was arrested at the scene as a gang member. According to his story, the evening of the fight he had nothing else to do, heard about the rumble, and decided that he would 'make the scene just to see what was happening'. On his way to the gang fight (at Grant's Tomb), he thought it might be a good idea to invite a few friends: 'Just to be safe – like, man, who knows what's shakin'?' This, of course, increased the final number of youths arriving at the scene of the gang fight, since there were many other boys who apparently did the same. He denied (and I had no reason to disbelieve him) 'belonging' to either of the gangs, and the same applied to his friends. His arrest at the scene of 'battle' was on two charges – disorderly conduct and possession of weapons.

I asked him: 'Why did you carry the knife and zip gun when you went to the gang fight if you did not belong to either of the gangs and intended to be, as you say, a peaceful observer?' His response was: 'Man, are you crazy? . . . I'm not going to a rumble without packin'.' He took along weapons for protection in the event he was attacked. The possibility of his being attacked in the somewhat confused situation involving hundreds of youths, who had no clear idea of what they were doing at the rumble, was paradoxically quite good. Therefore (within his framework of reasoning) he was correct in taking along weapons for self-protection.

This type of rationale characterizes much 'marginal' gang membership. The problem remains, however, that what may in fact be a confused situation involving miscellaneous youths with marginal membership and varied motives is too often defined by observers as a case of two highly mechanized and organized gang groups battling each other over territory. They project organization on to the gang and membership status on to a fellow curiosity seeker.

Another example of this difficult category of marginal membership is revealed by a different 'gang-war' incident.

A clearly psychologically disturbed youth (this boy had been in the Bellevue Hospital Psychiatric Ward on several occasions) manifested his emotional disorder by stabbing another boy in the neighbourhood. When arrested and questioned about committing the offence, he continually maintained that he had carried out his assault against the boy (who was definitely not a gang member) because 'We had to get even with the bastards.' He rationalized his individual act of assault by claiming to be a member of a gang getting even with a 'rival' gang, which was 'out to get him'. For this disturbed youth, membership in the malleable violent-gang organization became both his syndrome and rationale for violence.

It may be that such common psychotic syndromes as believing to be Napoleon, God, or Christ, and similar patterns so popular over the years, have been replaced on city streets by the rationale of gang membership (a rationale too often mistakenly accepted at 'face value' by gang workers and authorities). Not only is the gang a convenient excuse for violence, but, as previously indicated, some disturbed youths find this behaviour rewarded, nationally accepted, and aggrandized by many representatives of society. Public officials, such as police officers and social workers, in their interpretation of a violent incident, may thus help structure an individualistic act by one youth into a 'gang-war' explanation because it is to them and the gang youth himself a more logical reason for a difficult-to-define, senseless act. This error can result from a misconceived image of the violent gang and the complex meaning of membership.

There is some indication that the following typical 'gang incident' involving mistaken identity is a case in point:

TWO TEEN GANGSTERS HELD IN 'MISTAKE' SHOOTING

Two members of a shoot-first-and-ask-questions-later teen-age gang were arrested yesterday, charged with seriously wounding another youth with a shotgun.

The victim, police said, was not even a member of the rival

gang the assailants were hunting to avenge an attack two weeks ago on one of their members.

Juan Melendez, 19 – known as 'Angel' – of 40 Ave. D, and Samuel Carrion, 18 – known as 'Ace' – of 70 E. 99th St., were held on charges of felonious assault and Sullivan Law violation. A third youth known as 'The Fat Man' is still being hunted.

Their victim, Robert Castro, 19 of 636 E. Fifth St., is in serious condition in Bellevue Hospital with shotgun wounds in the back and elbow.

According to police, Castro and a friend, Abdul Zukur, 18, of 230 Clinton St., were walking on Madison St. at 12.10 A.M. yesterday after rehearsing with a singing group, when Melendez and the two others jumped them and began beating them.

'Are you Dragons?' one asked, and without waiting for an answer police said Melendez pulled the shotgun from under his coat and let go two blasts. One missed. The other hit Castro.

An hour later Patrolmen Lester Sloan and Solomon Meadero of the Clinton St. Station nabbed Melendez carrying a shotgun. They said he admitted seeking revenge for 'The Sportsmen' on a rival gang, 'The Dragons'.[1]

This type of gang incident is most apt to be an individual act of aggression, rationalized as gang revenge by 'Angel' and 'Ace', and erroneously accepted as a gang act by the police and public.

Some Varied Functions of Gang Membership

Violent-gang membership has an adaptable, chameleon characteristic. A youth can belong one day and quit the next without the necessity of telling anyone. It is often possible to take the gang boy's emotional temperature by asking him daily whether he is a Dragon or a King. It is somewhat comparable to asking him 'How do you feel today?'

This individualized emotional interpretation helps reveal the function of gang membership. Some boys say that the gang is organized for protection and that one role of a gang member is to fight – how, when, with whom, and for what reason he is to fight are seldom clear, and answers vary from member to member. One gang boy may define

1. *New York Daily Mirror,* 30 June 1959.

himself more specifically as a protector of the younger boys in the neighbourhood. Another defines his role in the gang as a response to prejudice: 'We're going to get all those guys who call us Spicks.' Still others say their participation in the gang was forced upon them against their will by a vaguely defined seducer. There appears to be no clear consensus of role expectation in violent-gang membership, and this conveniently enables each gang boy to project his own definition on to the meaning of his 'membership'.

Despite the different degrees of participation ('core' and 'marginal'), and the individualized interpretations of gang membership, a unifying bond among gang members is the belief that through gang membership they acquire prestige and status. It is also quite clear that the vagueness that surrounds the delineation of gang membership and organization enables the gang member to fulfil many varied needs. If qualifications for membership were more exact, most members, especially the more sociopathic leaders, would be unable to participate, for they lack the ability to assume the social responsibilities required for more structured normal organizations. As indicated, the acts of violence as 'rites of passage' for participation in this type of gang demand limited ability and training. The violent gang is thus a human collectivity where even the most socially deficient youth is able to play some membership role.

Some youths clinging to membership in this diffuse human organization sometimes employ violence simply to maintain a human affiliation. Many gang members act out violence as part of their emotional disturbance; however, most gang members use violence to enjoy 'a feeling of belonging' and keep their rep, both aspects of membership. The Kings expressed their varied needs for gang membership in their own fashion:

I didn't want to be different. I didn't want to be like . . . you know, different from the other guys. Like they hit him, I hit him. In other words, I didn't want to show myself as a punk.

It makes you feel like a big shot.

It make you feel like a big shot. You know, some guys think they're big shots and all that. They think, you know, they got the power to do everything they feel like doing. They say, like 'I wanna stab a guy', and then the other guy says 'Oh, I wouldn't dare do that.' You know, he thinks I'm acting like a big shot. That's the way he feels. He probably thinks in his mind, 'Oh, he probably won't do that.' Then, when we go to a fight, you know, he finds out what I do.

For selfishness

Momentarily I started to thinking about it inside; then I have my mind made up, I'm not going to be in no gang. Then I go on inside. Something comes up here come all my friends coming to me. Like I said before, I'm intelligent and so forth. They be coming to me – they talk to me about what they gonna do. Like, 'Man, we'll go out here and kill this guy.' I say 'Yeah.' They kept on talkin'. I said 'Man, I just gotta go with you.' Myself, I don't want to go, but when they start talkin' about what they gonna do, I say 'No, he isn't gonna take over my rep. I ain't gonna let him be known more than me.' And I go ahead just for selfishness.

For a build-up

If I would of got the knife, I would have stabbed him. That would have gave me more of a build-up. People would have respected me for what I've done and things like that. They would say 'There goes a cold killer.'

For some youths being a cold-killer 'member' of a gang is better than being a lone 'violent psycho'. The violent gang with its minimal demands and its grand alliances provides the sociopathic youth with some minimal 'sense of belonging'. He 'belongs' because it may be the only type of human organization whose demands are minimal enough for his sociopathic ability to participate. However different this 'belonging' may be compared to other groups, it is still a form of participation and, in its unique fashion, 'membership'.

sense of belonging

THE VIOLENT-GANG LEADER

According to Moreno, the leader is a function of the group, and the leadership pattern reveals something about the nature of the group being led.

Leadership is a function of group structure. The form it takes depends upon the constellation of the particular group. The power index of a leader depends upon the power indices of the individuals who are attracted to and influenced by him. Their indices are again expressed by the number of individuals who are attracted to and dominated by them. The power index of the leader is, however, also dependent upon the psychological communication networks to which his referents belong and the position which the networks themselves have within the entire collective within which his leadership is in operation.[1]

The core sociopath in the violent gang is generally the leader. Contrary to many widely held misconceptions that these leaders could become 'captains of industry if only their energies were redirected', the gang leader appears as a socially ineffectual youth incapable of transferring his leadership ability and functioning to more demanding social groups. The low-level expectations of the violent gang, with its minimal social requirements, is appropriate to the leader's ability. Given his undersocialized personality attributes, he could only be a leader of a violent gang.

The Gang Leader's 'Mask of Sanity'[2]

The violent-gang leader obsessively needs the gang, and provides it with its basic cohesive force. In a gang of some thirty boys there may be five or six core leaders who desperately rely on the gang to build and maintain their rep. They mould the gang's image and work to keep the 'members' involved in violent action. The enlistment of

1. J. L. Moreno, *Who Shall Survive?* (New York: Beacon House, 1952).
2. This expression is taken from Hervey Cleckley's classic volume *The Mask of Sanity*. In his discussion he makes the cogent point that many deviant persons, who appear normal on the surface, when stripped of their 'mask of sanity' reveal the psychopath beneath.

new members (by force), plotting, and talking about gang warfare fills most of the waking hours. The gang is central to their existence.

The gang leader's age, revealed as five to ten years older than that of gang members, provides a clue to his pathological nature. A twenty- or twenty-five-year-old person leading a group of fourteen- or fifteen-year-old youths in a fantasy world of power and violence would appear to have problems. (If he was dealing with concrete objectives such as stealing for personal gain, as in the *delinquent gang*, his leadership would have greater rationality.) In addition to the sociopathic personality emerging from the 'disorganized slum', gang leaders, in depth interviews, reveal the feeling that they are attempting to relive, at an older age, a 'powerful' role which they were unable to fulfil during youth. Gang leadership appears as an important fulfilment of the disturbed youth's childhood dreams of glory – a regressive effort to achieve now what he failed at earlier in life.

The gang leader deprived of his gang appears as a pathetic figure. Loco and Duke, after the demise of the Kings and Balkans, bore some resemblance to Coleridge's 'Ancient Mariner', mumbling stories about events and conditions no longer appropriate or relevant. The loss of their gang leaves the leader almost physically shaken – somewhat like a drug addict without a 'shot'.

Leading a violent gang is a more highly desirable pathological syndrome than many other patterns that are viewed with greater opprobrium. The person who is in a position to accept this 'face' for his pathology is not generally considered 'crazy'. Even more advantageous is the fact that he takes on a public role glorified by some popular 'American heroes' of the past, such as Capone and Dillinger.

Currently, a cloak of social immunity and even aggrandizement is provided for *pathological violence* of the Western heroes on TV. Interestingly, these 'modern' television heroes enacting brutal violence are found almost equally on both sides of the law. The 'good guy', sheriff, or lawman is as sociopathic and enjoys his violence as much as the Robin Hood type of outlaw. Within this media context, the violence role is justified and aggrandized by any flimsy pretext of a story line. The form of violence depicted is not really important as long as the violent hero is not clearly described as 'sick' or psychotic. (For example, it would be difficult to imagine a Western psychologist telling the 'Gunslinger' or Elliott Ness, 'You really are disinterested in law enforcement; you simply love to assault and torture criminals because you are a sick man.')

Although the current violent-gang leader appears to be at a considerable social distance from the 'Western violent hero', the underlying structure of his violence in the social scheme has some similarity. *He assumes a popular role socially supported, and his violent behaviour is often aggrandized rather than stigmatized with a pathological label.*

The notion of gang size as a symbol of power reveals another facet of the leader's pathological perceptions and needs. In the course of a one-hour interview, the gang leader may manipulate gang size, affiliations, and territory in accord with his cyclical emotions. In such interviews, gang membership will jump, according to the leader's estimate, from 100 to 4,000; alliances from five brother gangs to sixty; and territorial control from ten square blocks to jurisdiction over all the boroughs of New York City, New Jersey, and part of Philadelphia.

Gang leaders act out a standard pattern to demonstrate their ability to mobilize vast gang forces. An illustration of two gang leaders in a standard street-corner conference (attended by several silent constituents from each gang) reveals the meaning of this 'numbers game' to the gang leader. One leader will brag how he can muster 2,000 'people' from various boroughs to help him and his gang fight the other leader's gang. In turn, the other leader claims he can muster 3,000 'people'. Gang size increases at a ridiculous rate. Later, when the leaders were interviewed separately, both admitted lying. Yet in the moment of lying neither showed any strong indication to invalidate the other leader's story, since such a refutation might induce a challenge and invalidate his own story. Thus, there is an unspoken pact among violent-gang leaders to accept each other's story – a kind of mutual distortion society to bolster each leader's gang ego and rep. Their roles interlock in a grand illusion that helps to satiate their needs for power and status. (This process of mutual acceptance of fantasy is a common practice among some mental patients.)

Duke's Hitler-like five-year plan for expansion of the Balkan forces gives some further clues to the quality of mythical divisions and alliances so characteristic of the gang leader's fantasy world:

Each division must pay 50 cents a week dues per member and each and every club that we take over by war must pay $1.00 per person per week or they must supply us with fighting men in case we need them. For every club that joins willingly we will fight for them 100% and they pay only the dues that a member would pay and they will be given all advantages a member of our club could be given. . . . Cars will be bought for each division. . . .

The first clique that we are going to try to take over are the Villains. The second group will be the Braves. The third is what is left of the Scorpions, Rebels, Knights, Saxons, and Vultures and then the Dragons, and then we will move up to 150th Street and down to 105th Street from 8th Avenue to Riverside Drive. We will let the Harlem Syndicate alone for now, also the Anzacs, Saints, Rebels, Sea Hawks, Knights. Our aim is to take over all clubs in the 20th, 24th and 30th precinct [police], leaving alone only those listed. The plan is a five-year plan at which time we hope to have at least 500 people in each precinct.

Duke's grand-alliance fantasies pervaded all boroughs of New York. The exaggeration of gang networks throughout the city is of course not complete fantasy. It has some measure of rational explanation and is hinged to real social conditions. Since the families of gang boys are transient, a Dragon or Balkan moving to another neighbourhood may 'organize' another 'division'. He probably does not, but brags that he has when he visits his old neighbourhood. This gives the local gang leader further fuel for claiming more extended alliances. Thus, alliances or brother gangs are, essentially, psychological weapons that give the leader and his gang some feeling of security and a readily available threat he can use on adversaries, real or imagined. Moreover, attacking enemy gangs and syndicates, for example 'the invading Dragons', are usable 'concrete' enemies to be feared by paranoid youths who already manifest some feelings of being persecuted.

The fear of attack by a mass gang syndicate, which they cannot concretely identify, also gives the gang leader an enemy or problem that may serve as a convenient excuse for not facing immediate responsibilities of school, work, or duty to his family – responsibilities he is incapable of fulfilling adequately in any case. In his delusionary world he is involved with hordes of brother gangs, and too many 'important' dangers and problems exist for him to cope with the meaningless and mundane responsibilities of day-to-day life.

This institutionalized violent-gang leader pattern of 'drafting' reveals another dimension of the leader's 'social mask'. The drafting procedure is essentially a pattern of coercion. Getting another youth to 'join' or 'belong' to the gang becomes an end in itself rather than a means to an end. The process, which usually involves assault, coercion, or threatening violence upon another youth, under the guise of getting him to join, tends to satisfy many emotional needs of the leader. He is not truly concerned with acquiring another gang member, since the meaning of membership is at best vague; however, acting in this power role, forcing another youth to do something against his will becomes meaningful to his personal needs. The leader often implements initiation rites created on the spot for his personal gratification. These might include sadistic torture, cigarette burnings, a simple assault, or the practical act of extortion by collecting 'loot' in the form of 'club dues'.

In the process of 'drafting', the leader accomplishes

several goals at once. He asserts the strength and identity of 'his gang'; he achieves greater power by adding a new member (if only theoretically); he has a 'legitimate' opportunity for acting out violence and domination.

Despite the overt appearance of bravado displayed before his gang, the gang leader when alone expresses deep feelings of inadequacy. His senseless violence is often a quick, sudden effort at releasing himself from fear, in part as an effort continually to prove to himself and the boys around him that 'he isn't afraid and he isn't yellow.' The leader fears self-exposure: 'Jack, I'm scared – I'll admit it; you're always scared. The cops – your own boys – someone's liable to make you look like a punk. I can't stand to look like a punk so I keep fighting.'

A counterpoint to the fearful, disturbed gang leader is the less sociopathic youth from the same difficult neighbourhood, who has the resources to resist violent-gang coercion: 'Man, I don't need to always be beating up on people to prove I'm a big man. Loco and all those guys know I can take any of them. . . . When they sound on me and give me this drafting and bopping bullshit, I laugh in their face.'

Within some violent gangs such youths with adequate leadership potential for constructive activities exist, but they are generally marginal members. Often such a marginal-level gang member emerges as a leader when part of the gang membership able to do so shifts to and participates in some constructive activity (for example, a dance, baseball, and so on). They may also appear as leaders in deviant but demanding activities of the violent gang; the reigning leader remains the most violent core member.[1]

1. The gang social worker, attempting to redirect a gang into constructive activities, is more apt to deal with the marginal, less sociopathic leader than with the violent-gang leader, who is not so easily amenable to redirection into non-violent constructive activities. This situation, in part, explains why some youth workers perceive the gang leader as a more stable personality. The real leader of gang violence remains in the background, only to emerge when the gang bursts into violent activity.

The Violent-gang Model

One of the violent-gang leader's vital functions for gang membership is to serve as a symbol of idealized violence. Cast in his violent role, he is a shining example for core gang followers. The leader, in their view, has 'heart', and will pull a trigger, swing a bat, or wield a knife without any expression of fear or, most important, regret. As a prototype of the violent gang, the leader is thus an ideal model. Free-floating violence, pure and unencumbered by social restrictions, conscience, or regret, is the goal.

Beneath these fantasies of power, the leader has delusions of being persecuted. Rather than accept responsibility for his own feelings of extreme hostility, he projects the blame for his violent tendencies on to others, sometimes society in general, but primarily other gangs. The leader maintains an attitude of 'Let's get them before they get us.' Combined with the needs of other disturbed gang members, the result is mob action at a rumble. Such gang-war episodes, provoked by the leaders, produce a pattern of hysteria and group contagion characteristic of the leaders' personality. This 'disturbed-leader pattern', interaction with other susceptible youths, and an opportune situation provide the active ingredients for a 'senseless' violent-gang killing. The leader thus embodies in his sociopathic self the idealized attributes of violent-gang organization.

14. The Violent Gang as a Near Group

Normal groups are constellations of roles and norms defining prescribed ways in which members may interact effectively and harmoniously. The normal group may be viewed partially as a projected model for behaviour towards the accomplishment of the mutually agreed-upon goals of its members. A dominant characteristic of such a group is the fact that most members are in consensual agreement about the important norms and reciprocal expectations that regulate and determine each group member's behaviour. Thus an essential element in a normal group is that its members agree upon and are able to fulfil certain prescribed norms or standards of behaviour.

According to Cameron a group makes certain demands upon the individual, and the normative pattern of life the individual gives of himself to group demands. This the normal individual finds satisfying. On the daily level of group interaction, relevant others validate the individual's group participation at a minimal level of social expectation. However, 'under certain circumstances individuals with socially inadequate development fail progressively to maintain such a level, with the result that they become socially disarticulated and very often have to be set aside from the rest of their community to live under artificially simplified conditions'.[1] *The violent gang in this context serves as a 'simplified' withdrawal for the sociopathic youth from the more demanding community.*

The type of person who requires this forced or sometimes voluntary disassociation from the general community has sociopathic characteristics. As has been discussed, his essential limitation is his ineffectuality in taking the role

1. Norman Cameron, 'The Paranoid Pseudo-Community', in *American Journal of Sociology*, 49 (July 1943), pp. 32–8.

of another, except for egocentric purposes. He lacks a social conscience. In an oversimplified fashion this type of individual tends to become paranoid and have interchangeable delusions of persecution and excessive grandeur. These emotions result from an essentially correct assessment of his personal-social inability – an inability developed in a vacuum of effective socializing agents and processes. The paranoids' reactions of illusion and persecution are useful in fooling themselves that they are powerful and at the same time blaming their social inability upon a world that unfairly persecutes them. Both paranoid devices ('grandeur' and 'persecution') tend temporarily to take the pressure off of blaming their already battered ineffectual selves for their problem.

This delusional process is at first internal and on the personal thought level; however, in time it tends to become projected on to and involved with the surrounding community. According to Cameron:

> The paranoid person, because of poorly developed role-taking ability, which may have been derived from defective social learning in earlier life, faces his real or fancied slights and discriminations without adequate give-and-take in his communication with others and without competence in the social interpretation of motives and intentions.[1]

This type of person, whose role-taking skills are impaired, lacks the ability adequately to assess the 'other' in interaction. He begins to take everything the wrong way and, because of his social inabilities to think as others do, he becomes increasingly alienated and disassociated from the 'real world'. His delusional fantasies become hardened and he begins to see and experience things not consensually validated or similarly felt by others. As Cameron specifies, he 'becomes prejudiced with regard to his social environment'. His responses tend first to select reactions from his surroundings that fit into such an interpretation and then to reshape in retrospect things that seemed innocent enough when they occurred, in such a way that they sup-

1. Cameron, loc. it., p. 33.

port the trend of his suspicions. Partially because of his already incipient disturbance, and particularly if the individual is evolving in a defective socializing community (for example, the disorganized slum), he is unable to get relevant responses from others to counteract a developing reaction formation, which finally hardens into what Cameron has termed a 'paranoid pseudo-community':

As he begins attributing to others the attitudes which he has toward himself, he unintentionally organizes these others into a functional community, a group unified in their supposed reactions, attitudes, and plans with respect to him. He in this way organizes individuals, some of whom are actual persons and some only inferred or imagined, into a whole which satisfies for the time being his immediate need for explanation but which brings no reassurance with it and usually serves to increase his tensions. The community he forms not only fails to correspond to any organization shared by others but actually contradicts the consensus. More than this, the actions and attitudes ascribed by him to its personnel are not actually performed or maintained by them; they are united in no common undertaking against him. What he takes to be a functional community is only a pseudo-community created by his own unskilled attempts at interpretation, anticipation, and validation of social behavior.

This pseudo-community of attitude and intent which he succeeds in thus setting up organizes his own responses still further in the direction they have been going; and these responses in turn lead to greater and greater systematization of his surroundings. The pseudo-community grows until it seems to constitute so grave a threat to the individual's integrity or to his life that, often after clumsy attempts to get at the root of things directly, he bursts into defensive or vengeful activity. This brings out into the open a whole system of organized responses to a supposed functional community of detractors or persecutors which he has been rehearsing in private. The real community, which cannot share in his attitudes and reactions, counters with forcible restraint or retaliation.[1]

The fact of the real community's response and retaliation only serves to strengthen the individual's suspicions

1. Cameron, loc. cit., p. 35.

and distorted interpretations. He utilizes this as further evidence of the unfair discrimination to which he is being subjected. He comes out into the open with overt action against his supposed enemies and manages to bring down actual social retaliation upon himself. This new phase makes the paranoid pseudo-community more objective and real to him. 'The reactions of the real community in now uniting against him are precisely those which he has been anticipating on the basis of his delusional beliefs.'[1] The pseudo-community calcifies, becomes more articulate and real to the person caught in this whirlpool of processes. He begins after a while to live in 'it' almost to the exclusion of other social alternatives.

The processes through which an individual becomes enmeshed in a paranoid pseudo-community closely parallel the processes that 'hook' a sociopathic youth into the violent gang. The sociopathic youth 'growing up' in the disorganized slum has a personality syndrome that easily interlocks with the paranoid pseudo-community of the violent gang.

The Sequence of Events

Summarily the pseudo-community processes as they apply to the violent gang show the following sequential pattern of development:

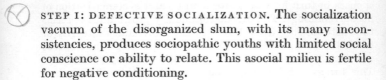

STEP I: DEFECTIVE SOCIALIZATION. The socialization vacuum of the disorganized slum, with its many inconsistencies, produces sociopathic youths with limited social conscience or ability to relate. This asocial milieu is fertile for negative conditioning.

STEP II: ALIENATION AND DISASSOCIATION. Owing to their sociopathic tendencies, these youths are further disconnected and alienated from the more consensually real and constructive community. Their negative self-feelings of 'difference', social ineffectiveness, and rejection become

1. Cameron, loc. cit.

reinforced and hardened by the disorganized and callous world to which they are exposed.

STEP III: PARANOID REACTIONS – DELUSIONS OF GRANDEUR AND PERSECUTION. Two paranoid patterns, delusions of grandeur and persecution, become articulated out of self-defence in reaction to the world around them. These patterns become functional in shifting the responsibility from themselves to others and take the pressure off an already weak and suffering self. Delusions of grandeur, 'gang leadership', 'control of large divisions', 'being part of a vast youth gang army', and a violent rep give the depressed youth some illusionary ego strength. Indications of being persecuted, 'enemy gangs', 'getting kicked out of school', and so on, are seized upon and enable the sociopathic youth to shift the responsibility from himself to 'society'. His prejudice towards the community hardens and he selectively perceives the outside world's behaviour to fit his emotional needs.

STEP IV: THE PSEUDO-COMMUNITY OF THE VIOLENT GANG. The violent gang of both reality and unreality becomes, for this type of youth, a convenient pseudo-community, one that is functional in at least temporarily alleviating his personal inadequacies and problems. The structure of the violent gang, with its flexibility of size, power roles, and delusionary possibilities, make it a most convenient and socially acceptable escape-hatch for the sociopathic youth.

The 'Legitimate' Quality of Violent-gang Structure

The worship of the 'hoodlum' as a 'hero' and the acceptance of violent-gang behaviour as normal by the larger society help to harden the gang's arteries. Most pathological behaviour is stigmatized and/or sympathized with – not so the violent gang. The general community response of intrigue, and in some fashion, covert aggrandizement, reinforce the violent gang as a most desirable, stigma-free pseudo-community for the sociopathic youth. The community's almost positive response to this pattern of pathology may be partially accounted for by a traditional American worship of aggressive, adventuresome, sociopathic heroes who 'go it alone', unencumbered by social restraints or conscience.[1]

Another possible speculation about the seeming public acceptance of the violent-gang syndrome may be related to an assumption that pathological behaviour is restricted only to individual behaviour; that is, the argument that if one individual commits a bizarre act he is considered disturbed; however, the same act committed in a group provides the individual actor with a degree of immunity from being considered pathological. The appraisal of collective behaviour patterns gives some clue to this element of group legitimization and sanction for bizarre and pathological group action. Lang and Lang make this point in a discussion of 'crowds'. They comment that certain aspects of a group situation help to make pathological acts and emotions acceptable:

... The principle that expressions of impulses and sentiments are validated by the social support they attract extends to collective expressions generally. The mere fact that an idea is held by a multitude of people tends to give it credence.

The feeling of being anonymous sets further limits to the sentiment of responsibility. The individual in the crowd or mass is often unrecognized; hence, there is a partial loss of critical self-control and the inhibitions it places on precipitate action. There is less incentive to adhere to normative standards when it appears to the individual that his behavior is not likely to provoke sanctions against him personally.

... each person sees himself acting as part of a larger collectivity which, by inference, shares his motives and sentiments

1. To some extent the competitive, successful, aggressive saleman, unencumbered by conscience, serves as a positive role model. Other models of sociopathic heroes include many mass-media leading men (i.e., Marlon Brando as 'The Wild One', George Raft as a 'hood', etc.). In the criminal tradition, John Dillinger, Al Capone, and currently Frank Costello have served as idealized figures for many youths. (Frank Costello when recently released from prison was mobbed by a crowd of autograph hunting hero-worshippers of all ages.)

and thereby sanctions the collective action. In this sense the crowd is an *excuse* for people all going crazy together.[1]

In the violent gang when all the boys 'go crazy' together their behaviour tends, at least in the public view, to have greater rationality. Gang '*legitimacy*' therefore partially derives from the fact that group behaviour, however irrational, is generally not considered truly bizarre. Although society may disapprove, the gang remains as a rational social group in the public mind. Thus, public agencies give recognition to the violent gang and try to redirect it as an entity. (In 'detached street gang worker' projects, for example, the violent gang is viewed as a legitimate, non-pathological entity suffering only from misguided activities that need to be redirected into 'constructive channels'.)

Another clue to the legitimation of gang violence as non-pathological behaviour may be its uncomfortable closeness to the behaviour of the overall society. The 'crazy machination' of the violent gang and its 'military structure' are bizarre replicas of current structures of international violence and warfare. Using the social context of the current international scenes as a 'normal' reference point, violent-gang machinations do not appear too pathological. Although many gang adjustments require closer examination, the violent gang interestingly caricatures many patterns of the upper world. The gang president (even if he doesn't really lead), drafting new soldiers (even if they are not really members), grand alliances (even if they do not fully co-operate), 'summit peace meetings' (even if they are only for propaganda and solve nothing) are all constructs that bear some resemblance to the international climate of violence.

The gang thus emerges as a desirable pseudo-community reaction for many sociopathic youths. Different degrees of 'membership' participation are a function of the individual's momentary emotional needs. The gang leader and the core gang member are more closely identified with the

1. Kurt Lang and Gladys Engel Lang, *Collective Dynamics* (New York: Thomas Y. Crowell Co., 1961), p. 35.

violent-gang paranoid pseudo-community than are more marginal members. Of considerable significance is the fact that the nature of the violent gang's pathological membership produces an unusual pattern of group structuring. Stated in reverse, group organization in the pathological pseudo-community has a quality and arrangement different from the structure usually found in normal groups.

The Near-group Conception

The organization of human collectives may be viewed on a continuum of organization factors. At one extreme, an organized, cohesive collection of persons interacting around shared functions and goals for some period of time form a normal group. At the other extreme of human organization a collection of individuals generally characterized by anonymity, spontaneous leadership, motivated and ruled by momentary emotion (for example, lynch mob, youth riots, people in panic, and so on), forms a mob or crowd. Although the term *mob* fits a youth riot and *group* fits a cohesive delinquent gang, neither the conception of *group* nor that of *mob* seems especially appropriate in describing violent-gang structure. (See Diagram I, 'Collective Structures', as a guide to this discussion.)

Diagram 1 **Collective Structures**

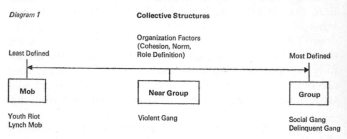

'Groups' that emerge midway on an organized–unorganized continuum are distorted in one or the other direction by most perceivers. It appears as if there is a psychological (autistic) need to consolidate one's view of the world. Violent-gang organization, therefore, despite considerable evidence to the contrary, is often mistakenly perceived by observers as a cohesive group. And in some youth riots no organization is seen despite the fact that in most cases a degree of organization exists.

Because no existing 'group conceptions' seem suitable for describing the violent gang, the following formulation is constructed to delineate its organization correctly. *This sociological category will be referred to as a* NEAR GROUP. The *near group* stands midway on the mob–group (organized–unorganized) continuum. It is differentiated from other collectivities that are temporarily midway because it has some degree of *permanence* or *homeostasis* as a *near group*. A cohesive group may be partially disorganized for a period of time but it is in a state of 'becoming' either organized or disorganized. The violent gang as a *near group*, however, consistently maintains its partial state of organization. (Diagram I illustrates the location of these relevant collective structures and makes reference to such organizational elements as cohesion, norm, and role definition.)

The violent gang as an ideal-type *near-group* structure includes most of the following characteristics:

1. Participants in the *near-group* violent gang are generally sociopathic personalities. The most sociopathic are core participants or leaders, and the less sociopathic are more marginal members.

2. The *near-group* gang to these individuals is a compensatory paranoid pseudo-community, and serves as a more socially desirable adjustment pattern than other pathological syndromes available in the community.

3. Individualized roles are defined to fit emotional needs of the participant.

4. The definition of membership is diffuse, and varies for each participant.

5. Behaviour is essentially emotion-motivated within loosely defined boundaries.

6. Group cohesiveness decreases as one moves from the centre of the collectivity to the periphery.

7. Limited responsibility and social ability are required for membership or belonging.

8. Leadership is self-appointed and sociopathic.

9. There is a limited consensus among participants in the collectivity as to its functions or goals.

10. There is a shifting and personalized stratification system.

11. Membership is in flux.

12. Fantasy membership is included in the size of the collective.

13. There is a limited consensus of normative expectations for behaviour.

14. Norms and behaviour patterns are often in conflict with the inclusive social system's prescriptions.

15. Interaction within the collectivity and towards the outer community is hostile and aggressive, with spontaneous bursts of violence to achieve impulsively felt goals.

A CAPSULE VIEW OF THE OVERALL VIOLENT-GANG PROBLEM

The conception and sequence of violent-gang development in the entire analysis is presented in Diagram II. The following comments are offered as a guide to its appraisal.

1. *Causal Factors.* Each of the varied socio-cultural factors stated has a different degree of impact upon youths growing up in the disorganized slum. The social structure of the neighbourhood produces and reinforces the different types of individual and gang adjustment pattern indicated.

2. *Emergent Personality Types.* The concern here is not with personal psychological characteristics but with the degree and kind of *socialization* that occurs and its effect on each individual youth.

(A) *The sociopathic youth* who is relatively *unsocialized* or socialized in a distorted fashion will find the *near-group violent gang* and/or disturbed *individual adjustments* most compatible with his personality formation.

(B) The youth trained into delinquent patterns, the *socialized delinquent*, is *differentially socialized*. His

Diagram 2

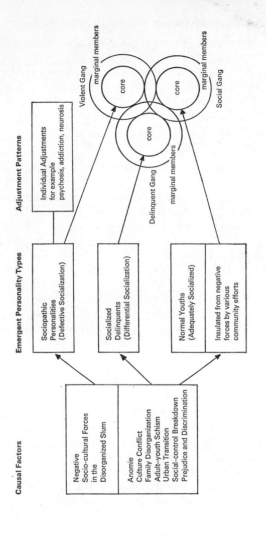

Causal Factors

Negative
Socio-cultural Forces
in the
Disorganized Slum

Anomie
Culture Conflict
Family Disorganization
Adult–youth Schism
Urban Transition
Social-control Breakdown
Prejudice and Discrimination

Emergent Personality Types

Sociopathic
Personalities
(Defective Socialization)

Socialized
Delinquents
(Differential Socialization)

Normal Youths
(Adequately Socialized)

Insulated from negative
forces by various
community efforts

Adjustment Patterns

Individual Adjustments
for example
psychosis, addiction, neurosis

Violent Gang

marginal members

core

core

marginal members

Social Gang

Delinquent Gang

core

marginal members

personality type is most adaptable to the *delinquent gang* adjustment.

(C) The 'normal' youth finds a maximum satisfaction and personal expression in the socially approved activities supported by the values and norms of the larger society. He is most likely to find the *social gang* personally compatible.

3. *Adjustment Patterns.* Various adjustment patterns emerge out of the socio-cultural factors described, and become 'calcified' by the personal-need satisfaction they provide for participants. Through a process of 'cultural transmission' they develop and exist as institutionalized and available social structures. A compatibility exists between the individual youth's personality type and each adjustment pattern.

4. *Core-Marginal Member Gang Participation.* The *core* members of each gang are basic to its organization, and the gang pattern is in turn vital to them. They are ideal-type role models in their gang. The more *marginal* members, depending on personal and momentary conditions, are prone to participation in other gang types. For example, the marginal violent-gang member may, under certain conditions, shift his adjustment patterns to the *delinquent* or *social* gang. The same possibility exists for other gang members to shift their allegiance to another adjustment pattern under certain motivating conditions. *Marginal members* may become *core members* of their gang if they find this direction compatible with their shifting personal needs. Thus, as indicated, the individual and the adjustment pattern generally make a satisfactory fit. For the sociopathic youth, the structure of the violent gang serves as a most amenable and appropriate adjustment pattern.

Programmes for Gang Control:
Evaluation and Recommendation

15. Coping with the Problem

*Obviously best to try to get
at roots by broad social changes
but if not poss. treat
within its present [?]*

The Levels of Attack

Whatever specific factors determine the emergence of a
specific violent gang at a particular time and place, there
is little reason to question the observation that the *existence* of violent gangs as *recurrent social phenomena in many
places* must ultimately be related to deeper, more general
disruptions in the social fabric itself. If this consideration
is relevant to a thorough assessment of the problem, it
must be equally relevant to the issue of a thoroughly
effective attack upon it. Since the roots go deep, we cannot
expect the problem to disappear without recourse to
remedies that go to the roots. All of which is to make the
commonplace observation that a society that fails to find
remedies for its own disorganization and for its own institutionalized inequities is likely to continue to suffer from
their consequences – those of violent gangs among them.

Nothing in this perhaps over-repeated observation provides a valid argument for inaction. What is implied, however, is a working discrimination between the necessary
strategy for broad social change and the practical tactics
of local control.[1] If we cannot 'immediately' eradicate the
roots, there may well be something immediate and effective we can do about the branches and tendrils as they
emerge in the social soil of our particular communities.
Accordingly, the central emphasis of this discussion will
be upon the treatment and control of the violent gang in
its emergent form.

---

1. On the broader societal front, governmental and private programmes
aimed at reducing social and economic inequalities, equalizing opportunities, facilitating the integration of new populations – each of these would
work to ameliorate the background conditions that foster the gang problem.

Reaching the Violent Gang

Community gang-prevention projects are usually sub-divisions of larger delinquency-control programmes. The only type of preventive project expressly designed for the violent gang is the 'detached worker' method. In this approach a professional, usually a social worker, is assigned to a particular gang. The essential avowed goal of the youth worker is to redirect the gangs from destructive behaviour patterns into 'constructive' activities.

The most highly developed detached-worker programme, which has served as a model for gang control in large urban areas nationally, is the approach designed and utilized by the New York City Youth Board. In the Youth Board manual, *Reaching the Unreached*, the board's diagnosis of the gang problem and principles for work with gangs are stated as follows:

1 – Participation in a street gang or club, like participation in any natural group, is a part of the growing-up process of adolescence. Such primary group associations possess potentialities for positive growth and development. Through such a group, the individual can gain security and develop positive ways of living with other individuals. Within the structure of his group the individual can develop such characteristics as loyalty, leadership and community responsibility.

2 – Some street clubs or gangs, as a result of more fundamental factors such as family disorganization, economic insecurity, racial and religious discrimination, poor housing, lack of recreational and educational facilities, emotional maladjustments of their leaders and members, etc., have developed patterns of anti-social behavior, the most widely known of which is street fighting. This type of teen-age gang warfare over the past decade has produced an annual toll of innumerable injuries and several deaths.

3 – While the protection of the community at times necessitates the use of repressive measures in dealing with the anti-social street clubs or gangs, these methods do not bring about basic changes in attitudes or behavior.

4 – Street club members can be reached and will respond to sympathy, acceptance, affection and understanding when

approached by adults who possess those characteristics and reach out to them on their own level.

5 – The positive relationship that is developed between an adult worker and a street club can serve as a catalytic agent for modifying anti-social attitudes and behavior. This relationship can also be used to help the individual member meet his needs in some more positive way. . . .

6 – To be effective detached work must be coordinated, unified and applied on a saturation basis.

7 – Because of the close relationship that is necessary for workers to develop with club members, and because of such factors as group loyalty, distrust and fear of other clubs, it is imperative that detached workers be assigned to only one street club.[1]

On the basis of these assumptions, the Youth Board established seven goals for work with street gangs:

1. Reduction of anti-social behavior, particularly street fighting: 2. Friendly relationships with other street gangs: 3. Increased democratic participation within the gangs: 4. Broadened social horizons: 5. Responsibility for self-direction: 6. Improved personal and social adjustment of the individual: 7. Improved community relations.

Issues Involved in Detached Gang Work

Reaching the gang through detached youth workers, utilizing the above-stated principles and goals, often entails pitfalls not specified in policy or in the manuals. Foremost among these potential problems is the possibility of inaccurately diagnosing gang structure. Distinctly different treatment methods are required for treating the *social*, the *delinquent*, and the *violent gang*. The blurring of these differentiations produces ineffectual approaches, even with a sincere and dedicated worker.

With reference to the violent gang in particular, the fact that differential levels of involvement (core and different marginal categories) and participation dictate different treatment prescriptions is of crucial significance.[2] The

1. *Reaching the Unreached: Fundamental Aspects of the Program of the New York City Youth Board* (New York City Youth Board, 1952), pp. 107–8.   2. See Chapter 14.

marginal gang member can generally be reached through the more conventional methods of recreation, providing a job, some counselling, and so on, whereas the core violent-gang leader and participants require a differential approach.[1]

The diagnostic assumption that working through the violent-gang leader will redirect the gang provides another problem. Often working through the leader of a violent gang solidifies its structure. Official sanction of the socio-pathic leader by a worker may give status to an individual who was formerly considered a 'character' by most of the marginal gang participants.

Merely gaining access to violent-gang participants is frequently mistaken for acceptance and rapport. Contrary to popular belief, getting in touch with the gang is not difficult for a detached worker. However, the meaning given to the relationship by gang members varies and is of major significance. If the gang worker appears as a 'mark' to most members, a 'do-gooder' who doesn't know the score, they will simply use him for money, cigarettes, or whatever favours they can obtain. The negative nature of this situation is not simply the gang worker being duped, but his incorrect assumption of success. Many gang workers, rather than resocializing gang members, become themselves affected negatively by the gang. They may rationalize their personal motives towards 'adventuresome' gang behaviour as necessary to maintain their relationship. In fact, this behaviour is not necessary. Becoming themselves a 'gang member' neutralizes their impact as an adequate adult role model. The negative nature of the gang worker's mistaken assumptions is revealed by the following verbatim statement of a detached gang worker in *Reaching the Unreached*:

Shortly afterward I got another break. One afternoon the boys were hanging around and a 'crap' game started. I decided it would be strategic for me to participate so that I might

1. A new approach to the core gang member will be developed in the latter part of this chapter.

get closer to them. During the course of the game one of the fellows turned to me and said, 'Say, man, you're supposed to be out here to change us and it seems like we're making you like us instead.' *Actually there was real significance in his words because the boys were beginning to understand that I accepted them as they were and in turn their acceptance of me was growing.* [Emphasis added.][1]

When the detached gang worker is duped by the gang or misinterprets the meaning of a situation, he is reinforcing rather than modifying illegal behaviour. In his capacity as gang worker he is, in effect, a carrier of the values and norms of the larger society. Initially the gang member resists the intrusion into the subculture he has created (to act out his problems). The gang will attempt to get what it can without changing and then seduce the detached worker into becoming part of the gang. The gang worker should be aware of the negative implication of compromising the relevant norms of the larger society in order to gain false acceptance and superficial approval. When he does this he is fairly quickly eliminated as a force for changing the gang since they begin to view him as a mark or sucker susceptible to manipulation. This defeats the objectives the worker is attempting to achieve.

The gang worker requires a realistic image of gang structure, or he is likely to be duped by the illusory conceptions of the gang described by its members. The worker's acceptance of the fantastic stories created by core gang participants produces a reinforcement of undesirable gang mythology.

The validity of such anti-social patterns as gang warfare, territory, and peace meetings should be challenged and discouraged rather than accepted and in some cases aggrandized and given legitimacy. The enlightened detached gang worker can operate effectively through the use of ridicule, disbelief, and criticism. As an example, the employment of this approach with the Balkans in the Dragon invasion had the ultimate effect of minimizing the possibility of a mass rumble and scattering the gang. In

1. New York City Youth Board, op. cit., pp. 113–14.

contrast, giving status to gang leaders by calling various peace meetings for negotiation, in effect 'legitimizing' the violent gang and its organization, increases its status and definition. Recognition helps to produce rather than deter potential violent eruptions.

In the word-battle of 'sounding', standard procedure for any gang, the worker is inevitably tested. He is presented with wild stories of gang activity, some believed and some not believed by the gang participants themselves. If he 'buys' their story he becomes a dupe who loses his potential for positive influence. On the other hand, if the worker pushes the 'gang stories' of divisions and warfare to their illogical conclusion by sensitive caricaturing, he makes treatment progress. First he achieves stature with the boys as an adult person who can't be 'conned' or manipulated. This the gang boys respect. Secondly, he turns the gang and its members back upon self-evaluation and assessment. This process causes them to begin to look at themselves and their gang as it exists in reality.

A Case in Point

Four marginal gang boys enter my office obviously nervous beneath but attempting to give a 'cool' appearance:

FIRST GANG BOY: Well, that's it – we'll whip it on tonight at seven and then the whole city will rumble. I mean we're not going to sit still for that bullshit. The Dragons are through once and for all.

L.Y.: Now really what is all this bullshit anyway? Wait a minute, I have to make a call. [I make an inconsequential phone call, emphasizing my disinterest in the mass rumble that is supposed to engulf the city. I then turn to the boys with a look of disgust.] Now what's all this rumble stuff about?

GANG BOY: Well, they're suppose to whip it on tonight. Duke says . . .

L.Y.: Wait a minute now. Duke told you this? [*In disbelief*] He told you this and you believe him?

GANG BOY: Well, yeah – he and Pete met with Loco from the uptown Dragons, and he says that –

L.Y. [*interrupting*]: Just a minute. You mean to tell me those nuts Duke, Loco, and Pete cook up some nonsense about a rumble and you guys jump right into the fire. [*In disbelief*] How stupid can you get?

SECOND GANG BOY: I told them it was a lot of crap and –

L.Y.: Don't tell *them*. Why didn't you tell Duke – right there? Besides, you guys don't really have anyone to fight for you anyway. [I refer back at length to a previous meeting with twelve of the 'gang' where they finally agreed they were the only twelve they could count on in a fight.]

THIRD GANG BOY: Well, Duke and Jerry say our ten divisions can –

FOURTH GANG BOY [*interrupts*]: Oh, man, you guys still dig all that bullshit. [*Turns to me.*] I didn't believe none of it – but they all got excited.

L.Y.: Maybe one of these days you guys will wise up. Let's talk about something important. Are you all set up for the game at the Columbia gym Sunday?

At the time I drop the gang-war subject, but proceed to pick it up later with the police and another social agency in order to check it out further. If I had become involved and called a peace meeting with relevant gang leaders, I would have poured gasoline on the fire by possibly reinforcing, joining, and helping develop a possible gang rumble. What occurred as a result of my not being drawn in was to destroy the potential support of many *marginals* for a rumble, discredit the gang leader's fantasy, cause the youths to examine some of the mythology of their near-group structure, and change over to a positive subject. Another main goal in this type of ridiculing approach is to have the marginals confront the fantasy of the gang and gang-war plans on their own at the source – the leader. In some cases they effectively mimic the worker's sarcastic and caustic comments with the provocative gang leader, vitiating the leader's negative impact towards violence. Castrating his fantasy through sarcasm and ridicule helps to minimize his negative effect, rather than support and reinforce the gang leader's potential impact.

The 'conned' detached worker tends unwittingly to reward what is in fact sociopathic behaviour. The misguided worker not only legitimizes the gang and its core but also provides them with a type of 'social director'. In this role he aids the violent-gang leader in his nefarious activities by providing attractive activities, dances, athletic events and so on, for marginal members.

He may become incorporated into and part of the gang's structure. Having a gang worker attached to one's gang becomes a status symbol of being a real 'down', 'bad', or tough gang. As one violent-gang leader expressed it: 'We're a real down club. We got a president, a war counsellor, and a Youth Board man.'

The incorrectly oriented detached worker may indirectly help to produce and articulate violent-gang culture. *New York City, which has the most highly developed and intensive detached-worker programme also has the most highly refined and defined violent-gang structures and problem.*

Some Guidelines for the More Effective Use of the Detached-worker Approach

Reaching the gang in its own milieu through the detached gang worker is a significant approach to the violent-gang problem. However, several issues require revision and redefinition if this approach is to modify rather than solidify or reinforce violent-gang structure and behaviour. On the basis of the near-group conception of violent-gang organization and other factors that have emerged in the analysis, the following guidelines are suggested for a more effective approach to the violent-gang problem.

(A) It is necessary for the detached gang worker to be trained to diagnose accurately several types of gang structure. Different approaches are required for the *social*, *delinquent*, and *violent* gangs.

(B) The accurate diagnosis of the violent gang reveals different degrees of participation and involvement. Marginal members may be worked with through more conventional treatment approaches; core violent-gang participants and leaders require a different and more intense form of treatment.

(C) A violent gang can be further integrated by working through the leaders. The detached gang worker should avoid giving the leader credence since this may reinforce violent gang structure. Providing the sociopathic leader with 'official' status and activity opportunities for his gang tends to defeat rather than achieve sound corrective goals.

(D) The detached gang worker, as an official representative of the more inclusive society, must avoid sanctioning or participating in deviance to gain what will turn out to be a false acceptance and rapport. He should serve as an adequate law-abiding adult role model. In this way he may become a bridge or vehicle for bringing the larger society's constructive values and norms to the gang.

Violent gangs should not be worked with in any official community programme as a 'legitimate' social structure. Giving credence to the violent gang by providing it with an official representative of society is giving tacit authorization to pathology and violence. For example, peace meetings that involve gang leaders and paid representatives of city government implicitly provide an illegal, pathological enterprise with official support.

These conclusions are not based upon moral or legal considerations, but upon the nature of gang organization. A pathological entity, such as the violent gang, cannot be treated as a unit. The type of detached-worker policies and the programme that have been employed appear to solidify and legitimize the violent gang, reinforcing its pathological behaviour rather than modifying its anti-social activity.

Rather than 'redirecting' and implicitly reinforcing the violent gang as an institutionalized and legitimized pattern of illegal behaviour, the focus should be upon *eliminating* it as an entity. This goal may be worked towards by a combination of modified detached gang work, police action, incarceration, group therapy, and a new 'milieu therapy' approach to sociopathic behaviour. Utilizing these approaches the violent gang may be dismembered, its participants resocialized and legally reconnected into the inclusive society.

TREATMENT OF THE MARGINAL GANG MEMBER
'Stripping the Artichoke'

The detached worker must keep in mind that his ultimate goal is not the 'redirection of the gang into constructive activities' but its eventual dismemberment. Within the framework of this goal an effort will be made to extricate the marginal participant from the violent gang and provide the means for his closer association and integration into the legal society.

The first step entails establishing contact with the gang as it exists. Contact is best established by a direct approach in which the worker specifies his role and plan for helping gang members participate in constructive social activities. This procedure is not so difficult as it may at first appear. Currently most gang members have some concept of street-gang workers and what they are attempting to accomplish. In the first phase the worker would be a provider of favours: cigarettes, trips, and possible recreational events. Rather than concentrating upon the more recalcitrant disturbed leader and core members, the worker should attempt to establish a close relationship with the more easily reached marginal members. They will generally respond more readily to the constructive activity programme he attempts to provide.

Utilizing these principles and methods, the worker should consciously act upon the gang and dismember it as if he were stripping an artichoke. The marginal members, once they become hooked into more constructive enterprises, will find less energy and time for violent-gang activity. The constructive activities utilized should be viewed less for their intrinsic value and more for their usefulness as a 'gimmick' or means of extricating marginals from participation in the violent gang and involving them in activity within the inclusive society. Several types of projects especially lend themselves as means towards this objective.

Adult–youth Associations

It was proved on Morningside Heights that marginal gang youths can be involved in meaningful adult–youth associations. The problem of the adult–youth schism was attacked by producing natural relationships around recreation, project planning, and other activities that brought adults and youths together in constructive interaction.

The use of citizen-volunteers who willingly gave of their time was essential to the A-Y-A operation. The usual approach of using citizens to help a social agency was reversed in A-Y-A. The social agency and its professional staff attempted to help and support the adult to relate 'naturally' with neighbourhood youths.

Many boys growing up in the A-Y-A programme tend to turn around at a later age and become adults (surrogate fathers) to other neighbourhood youths. The emphasis in the A-Y-A approach is to build it into the natural weave of the community so that whether the professional agency continues or not, something positive is at work in a somewhat changed neighbourhood.

The A-Y-A type of project can be successful in peeling off the more easily reached marginal gang youth and involving him in a meaningful relationship with an adult, thus helping to resolve the neighbourhood adult–youth schism. The detached gang worker can serve as the bridge and co-ordinator for making this possible. The activities *per se* are not the primary issue; adult–youth interaction is the core of the approach.

Recreation as an A-Y-A Approach

Recreation is a good gimmick for involving neighbourhood adults and marginal gang youths in constructive activities. In the process of planning, a natural interaction takes place that is difficult to duplicate. Emphasis should be placed on some degree of organized league activity rather than on random play. The organizational procedures required for finding a gym or field for the league, developing rules, age limits, team-size quotas, scheduling, and so on, involves adults and youths in a natural and productive interaction.

In developing an athletic league care must be taken not to make the gang structure more cohesive. In using the league idea, efforts should be made to have the teams form around athletic ability rather than around affiliation. A good league will reshuffle the neighbourhood's gang structure and thus minimize violent-gang activity. Marginal gang members begin to revolve around a social athletic club rather than around their destructive gang.

Building the recreational activity into the social fabric of the neighbourhood is basic. Emphasis should be placed on maximizing the involvement of local adult volunteers; utilizing neighbourhood facilities, for example, gymnasiums, meeting rooms, halls, and so on; gaining local citizen monetary and moral support. The effort should be made so that whether the basic organizing social agent, the detached worker, continues on the project or not, there is sufficient community involvement to keep the adult–youth activity in motion on its own strength.

Prefabricated or overly prestructured recreation programmes, prepared in advance by adults or professionals, into which youths are moved in an assembly-line fashion are of limited help towards involving the youth and resocializing him adequately. However, developing recreation activities in which the youths take some role in defining what they want, what they get, and how they get it, combined with the assistance of interested adult volunteers, produces activities that become part of their natural milieu.

The Gang Committee

An A-Y-A type of community organization has many positive side effects. One such effect is the development of a closer working relationship between social agencies and professionals operating in the same area. Agencies, gang workers, gang members, police youth officers, and local citizens may at first interact around a specific project, such as an athletic league. This may later lead to co-operation in other areas of mutual interest.

On Morningside Heights the A-Y-A project resulted in spearheading a co-operative effort of social agencies and gang workers that became known as the West Side Gang Committee. The committee met periodically and concentrated upon exchanging information and knowledge about gang organization in the area. In addition to compiling data on gang patterns, the more than thirty members of the committee discussed effective programming for gang control and dealing with such special problems as drug addiction. All the meetings were attended by local police, and this fostered a more effective relationship between the social agencies involved and the police. The committee developed a statement that summarized its goals and objectives:

Gang Information
Information (both rumored and factual) about the size, organization, and so on, of gangs and delinquent groups is interchanged among the members of the Committee. This interaction is carried on through such means as questionnaires, discussion at meetings, and phone calls.

Gang-Work Techniques and Methods
The Committee attempts to discuss and continually develop more effective techniques and methods for detecting, preventing, dealing with and eliminating gang and related individual problems. These methods would include group discussion with gang members, methods for working out social agency–police–youth relationships and dealing with gang-narcotics problems.

Pressure Group
The Committee will take action in making known on a citywide basis its considered opinion on issues related to gang and youth problems. This will include such issues as city-agency appropriations, social-agencies approaches, or police action.

Community Education
The Committee will disseminate information and educate the public on gang problems and issues which are of relevance.

Research and Experimentation
The Committee will carry on limited-range surveys, research

and experimentation in order to aid the group to more effectively carry out its objectives. The Committee will make recommendations to universities, the City or other organizations about needed research.

Community Centres

Community centres have evolved in large urban areas in an effort to restore a sense of community to the anonymous urban condition. Youth programmes operating within the framework of a centre can involve the marginal gang youth if they are not overorganized. Highly developed programmes in which a youth has no planning role do not even involve the marginal, much less the core gang member.

In order to be maximally effective a centre's youth project should reach out to utilize facilities and citizen volunteer resources available in the community. This type of non-building-centred project is most apt to ensnare marginal gang youths in its programme, provide worthwhile activities, and constructively build a bridge between them and the larger society.

Job Opportunities

Vital to the success of a programme that would involve marginal gang members is a concerted effort to provide job opportunities for youth.[1] Two aspects of the problem are of significance: training for work and acquiring employment possibilities a difficult youth can fulfil. Since most gang youths are school dropouts with much time on their hands, employment is required if the youth is to adjust adequately to a role in the legal society.

Therapy: Group and Individual

If only by the fact of their limited participation in the violent gang, most marginal youths have personal difficulties. Their drives to participate in the violent gang may range from a momentary situational 'push' to a deep-

1. Federal Government is currently involved in planning and developing a programme in this area within the framework of the President's Committee on Delinquency and Youth Crime and the Secretary of Labor's Office.

seated emotional need. Generally, the marginal's emotional difficulty is not as severe as, or different in character from, that of the core gang participant. After adequate individual diagnosis a youth may be induced to co-operate with the therapeutic help he requires.

In the therapeutic situation the asocial or anti-social gang youth requires a therapist who can communicate in terms understandable to the youth. The therapist operating with gang youths requires special training in the cultural and emotional traits of his client. The 'square' remote therapist is practically useless for meaningful therapeutic interaction with a gang youth. The charisma of titles is irrelevant to a gang boy; he can only respond to the therapist as a human being who understands him and his milieu sufficiently to interact in a meaningful fashion.

For this reason and others group methods are superior to an individual approach. To cite a few advantages:

1. The therapist can be aided by co-operative youths within the group whom he can enlist to provide a bridge of communications between himself and more difficult, less communicative youths.

2. Gang youth in a group are more apt to detect and dissect each other's problems. Essentially multiple 'therapists' are involved in the group if the group therapist effectively exploits the situation.

3. The therapist encounters his clients in a more natural milieu in group therapy than in the artificial situation of a one-to-one relationship. Most gang members find it uncomfortable to talk to anyone alone, especially an adult.

4. Group interaction will bring to the surface more underlying problems than the individual situation produces. The 'all in the same boat' condition of gang members can help focus and resolve many mutually existent problems.

The process of involving marginal gang members in a therapeutic situation necessitates flexibility. Time arrangements and expectations of participation need to be adapted to the group rather than rigidly imposed upon it.

Relations with Law Enforcement Agencies

Specially trained youth police working closely with social agencies and detached gang workers are essential to any plan for controlling gangs. Their training should entail a comprehension of gang structure, behaviour, causal factors, and agency tie-in policy. These criteria must be met if the objectives for an adequate police and social agency gang-control programme is to function effectively. Information about specific gang structuring and identification of cores and marginals should be mutually shared information. (This can be handled through a 'gang committee'.)

Close co-operation among the social agency, the police, and the court facilitates the dismantling of the gang. After peeling off the marginal youths, those more easily reached by the projects described, the core gang member can then be dealt with readily by more intensive devices.

In summary, the various conventional methods described, A-Y-A, recreation, community centres, group therapy, should all be co-ordinated with adequate law enforcement to peel off the marginal, more easily reached violent-gang participant. At the same time the readily identifiable core-gang participants and leaders require a more intensified and novel approach to treatment, because they are generally not reached by the described conventional methods.

TREATING THE CORE GANG MEMBER

A review of the core violent-gang member's personality characteristics reveals a disassociated, hostile, status-involved youth who has a limited social conscience or concern for others. Most people are for him enemies to be manipulated, used, or assaulted, depending on the given situation. His gang associates are partners in violence or crime, but not *friends* in the sense of a shared relationship to which he will give of himself. He has no concern for others since he lacks the empathic ability to identify with them. Consequently, acts that are ego-gratifying or rep-making dominate his behaviour.

Exhortations or sermons pointing out the 'immorality' of his behaviour are meaningless. Standard forms of therapy directed at producing insights are also ineffectual, since the sociopath has no interest in changing himself. He is not concerned with modifying his instrumental behaviour because it produces the kicks and ego-gratification he seeks.

Any plan of treatment that hopes to succeed must take into account the described nature of the sociopath's relationship ability. He acts as he does because his sociopathic complex is functional within his peculiar milieu – the disorganized slum. In order for change to occur, both the youth's personality and his milieu must receive an intense form of shock treatment and change.

Institutional custody, even in the 'new reformatory' using methods involving group psychotherapy and other advanced forms of treatment, do not seem to engage or treat the core sociopath. The artificial nature and form of the inmate community usually supports and reinforces rather than modifies sociopathic behaviour. In fact it helps to nurture it further, for in order to survive in 'the prison' the sociopathic mode of adjustment is most functional.[1] If any change is to be produced in the asocialized core gang youth, an intensive form of treatment involving a live-in situation, with almost a twenty-four-hour-a-day manipulation of their environment in a mode different from the usual custodial condition, seems indicated.

The Anti-criminal Society: A Projected Plan for Treating Core Gang Members

The potential of an anti-criminal society for modifying difficult offenders was forecast by Donald R. Cressey in a classic article published in 1954 in the *American Journal of Sociology*.[2] His projection of the need for this treatment

1. See Richard Korn and Lloyd McCorkle, *Criminology and Penology* (New York: Henry Holt, 1958).
2. Donald R. Cressey, 'Changing Criminals: The Application of the

approach was based upon Sutherland's causal theory of
criminal 'differential association'. Cressey logically specu-
lated that 'if the behavior of an individual is an intrinsic
part of the groups to which he belongs, attempts to change
the behavior must be directed at groups'.[1]

Cressey utilizing 'differential association' theory as a
diagnostic base projected the necessity for an anti-criminal
society to modify deviant behaviour.

The differential association theory of criminal behavior
presents implications for diagnosis and treatment consistent
with the group-relations principle for changing behavior and
could be advantageously utilized in correctional work. According to it, persons become criminals principally because they
have been relatively isolated from groups whose behavior
patterns (including attitudes, motives, and rationalizations) are
anticriminal, or because their residence, employment, social
position, native capacities or something else has brought them
into relatively frequent association with the behavior patterns
of criminal groups. A diagnosis of criminality based on this
theory would be directed at analysis of the criminal's attitudes, motives, and rationalizations regarding criminality and
would recognise that those characteristics depend upon
the groups to which the criminal belongs. Then, if criminals
are to be changed, either they must become members of
anticriminal groups, or their present pro-criminal group relations must be changed.[2]

Cressey's future projection emerged almost as if by plan
in a spontaneous fashion. Interestingly, by coincidence,
the first anti-criminal social system Cressey predicted
developed in proximity to his base of academic operation
at the University of California at Los Angeles.

Theory of Differential Association ', *American Journal of Sociology* (September 1954), pp. 116–20.

1. Cressey, loc. cit., p. 117.

2. Cressey, loc. cit. This theme had its historical roots in a classic mono-
graph on criminal regrouping by J. L. Moreno first published in 1932 and
reissued as *The First Book on Group Psychotherapy* (New York: Beacon
House, 1957).

S.S. Hang Tough

Early in August 1959, homeowners along the stylish Pacific Ocean beaches in Santa Monica, Calif., were dismayed to get a new set of neighbors; a bedraggled platoon of half a hundred men and women, who moved into a run-down, three-story, red brick building that once was a National Guard armory. White and black, young and middle-aged, criminals and innocents, artists and loafers, the unlikely assortment shared one trait: they were narcotics addicts determined to kick their habit for good.

Scrounging lumber, paint and old furniture, the troupe converted the top floor of the armory into a barracks-style men's dormitory. They turned the second floor into offices, kitchen, dining hall and living room, and the main floor into women's sleeping quarters. Over the doors in the living room they hung their emblem: a life preserver with the words '*S.S. Hang Tough*,' slang for 'Don't give up.' . . .

Such was the formal dedication of Synanon House, a self-run haphazardly financed experiment in human reclamation whose success has been hailed by Dr. Donald Cressey, University of California at Los Angeles sociologist, as 'the most significant attempt to keep addicts off drugs that has ever been made.' The technique was patterned roughly after the group-therapy methods of Alcoholics Anonymous. Dr. Cressey describes the psychology: 'A group in which Criminal A joins with some noncriminals to change Criminal B is probably most effective in changing Criminal A.'

In the often brutally frank personal exchanges, the addicts slowly reveal themselves . . . and through daily contact with similarly beset persons are reinforced in their determination to quit narcotics permanently. Says the founder of Synanon House, 48-year-old Charles E. Dederich, a potbellied Irishman who was once an alcoholic but never a drug addict: 'It is something that works.'

The Synanon curriculum is divided into three stages. During the first phase, the emotionally shaken, physically weak addict gradually adjusts to his new surroundings. . . . During the second stage, the ex-addict works at a regular job on the outside, contributing part of his wages to the group, continues to live at the house. . . . In its final stage, Synanon sends its member out into society.[1]

1. *Time*, 7 April 1961, Vol. LXXVII, No. 15.

THE BROTHER IN THE TOMBS

EGYPTIAN KING: My father wants me to be better than my other brother. That's why every time he comes to me and say 'You see, you gonna be like your brother. The one that's in the Tombs [Prison]. If you keep on doing wrong, you gonna be like him.' He kept on telling me that, so I said 'Well, if he wants me to be like him, I'm gonna be like him.'

The potential of Synanon for treating core gang members in its anti-criminal society occurred to me as a result of meeting and learning the case history of Frankie, one of the successful residents of this unique organization. From a series of intensive discussions with him, I learned that he had formerly been a violent-gang leader on the upper West Side of New York. When his gang-violence days came to an end ('I got too old for that b.s.'), he turned to 'pimping, pushing, and shooting drugs'. Frankie and I became good friends in the process of discussing these matters and 'our' old neighbourhood on the West Side.

Frankie first came to my attention in an unusual fashion. The founder and director of Synanon, Charles Dederich, while listening to some tapes I was playing of the Egyptian King killing, detected a voice that sounded familiar. Dederich upon hearing one King comment, 'I kicked him in the head; it was the least I could do', remarked, 'That sounds like Frankie.' I later confirmed the fact that Frankie was this particular Egyptian King gang member's older brother. An intensive series of interviews revealed that Frankie's early case history and violent-gang pattern parallelled his younger brother's. As a result of his community life experience at Synanon, Frankie was, at the time, free and clear of drugs and violence for over two years.

SYNANON'S DYNAMICS: A CASE STUDY. 'Frankie would never use a knife – unless he had to. Mostly with his fists he would beat a guy down and try to kill him right there. They pulled him off this big guy one time – he wouldn't stop punching him in the face.' This was the casual observation made by Frankie's former 'crime partner', the girl friend with whom he had lived for five years in New York. (She too is a resident of Synanon.)

Frankie's first reaction to Synanon was confusing. 'The first thing they hit me with flipped me. This tough-looking cat says to me "There are two things you can't do here, shoot drugs or fight".' Frankie told me, scratching his head, 'I was all mixed up – these were the only two things I knew how to do.'

Frankie went to California, at the insistence of his parents, to try a new way of life. He accepted the plane ticket they gave him, but in California he tried to continue his old way of life. In Los Angeles he had difficulty getting a good drug connexion and stealing enough money to supply his habit. He became increasingly depressed, heard about Synanon, and decided to try it out. His thought was 'to get cleaned up a little' and either get organized for a new onslaught on Los Angeles or steal enough to return to New York and his old criminal pattern. Something happened at Synanon to make Frankie stay 'clean' for two years and later assume the administrative role of 'co-ordinator'.[1]

The Synanon environment was interesting and exciting for Frankie. There were, in the gang boys' jargon, lots of 'hip' people: Jimmy the Greek, who at forty-four had been an addict for twenty years and a criminal and con man for over thirty; Jimmy M., thirty-six, an old con who had done eight years in the Jackson, Michigan, prison, been involved in the riots there, and now ran the kitchen at Synanon. Frankie's first job at Synanon was in the kitchen, scouring pots, pans, and mopping floors. Jimmy M. could not be conned or manipulated out of position like the therapist Frankie had encountered at the Rikers Island Prison in New York. Jimmy M., of course, knew the score, and to him Frankie with his talk of all his exploits was a 'young punk' who could give him no trouble. 'I've met kids like this all my life – in and out of the joint.'

1. The co-ordinator works an eight-hour shift, answering phones, catering to visitors, and generally handling the House's business as it emerges. It requires some ingenuity and administrative ability.

When Frankie wanted to fight Jimmy over a disagreement about work, Jimmy laughed and told him if he wanted to fight he would be thrown out of Synanon. The situation was confusing to Frankie. In the 'joint' (prison) if he got in trouble confinement became increasingly severe, down to the 'hole' (solitary confinement). At Bellevue Hospital (psychiatric ward), where Frankie had also been, it was a straitjacket. What made Frankie behave in order to stay at Synanon, with its open door?

The 'geographic cure' was part of the positive impact. The fact that Frankie moved from New York to Los Angeles was a significant force initially in keeping him at Synanon. As he stated it: 'At times I felt like splitting [leaving]; then I thought, It will be hard to make it back to New York. I didn't know Los Angeles and I was afraid to make it out there, 'cause I didn't know the people. Synanon was better than anything else I could do – at the time.'

Also, Synanon House was on the beach, and the meals were good. In the evening many ex-addict top musicians would play 'cool' jazz. Also there were, according to Frankie, 'broads to dance with and get to know'. And – highly important in this anti-addiction, anti-delinquency society – there were others who understood him, had made the same 'scenes', and intuitively knew his problems and how to handle him. He respected people he could not con. He belonged, and was one of them.

At Synanon, Frankie could make a rep without getting punished or locked up. In prison, the highest he could achieve in terms of the values of 'his people' was to become 'King' of the sociopathic inmate system, acquire a stash of cigarettes, and obtain some unsatisfactory homosexual favours. In the 'inmate system' of Synanon he could achieve any role he was 'big enough of a man' to acquire, and this carried the highest approval of his fellows. He could actually become a director of this organization, which was now in the national spotlight. Articles on Synanon had been published in national magazines like *Time*, *Life*, and *The Nation*, and were appearing daily in the Press. For the first time in his life, Frankie was receiving status for being clean and non-delinquent.

Of course, when he first arrived at Synanon he attempted to gain a rep by conniving and making deals. He was laughed at, ridiculed, and given a 'haircut' (a verbal dressing down) by other old-time con men of the organization. He was accused of 'shucking and sliding' (not performing adequately). The old-time Synanonists were adamant about keeping the organization, which had literally saved their lives, operating smoothly.

Frankie found that rep was acquired in this social system (unlike ones he had known) by truth, honesty, and industry. The values of his other life required a complete reversal if he was to get a rep at Synanon. These values were not goals *per se* that someone moralized about in a meaningless vacuum; they were means to the end of acquiring prestige in this tough social system with which he now intensely identified.

In the small-*s* synanons, three nights a week Frankie participated in a form of leaderless group psychotherapy. In these synanons truth was brutally demanded. Any system of rationalizations about past or current experience was demolished by the group. There was an intensive search for self-identity. In the process the individual attempted to learn what goes on beneath the surface of his thoughts. For Frankie this was the first time in his life that he discovered others had some idea about what he was thinking underneath. Though he had had individual and group therapy in prison, there he could 'con' the therapist; and, most important, 'I said what I thought they wanted to hear so I could hit the street sooner.' Frankie now began to get some comprehension of what others thought in a social situation. The fact of identifying with the thoughts and feelings of another human being becomes a significant reality.

At first Frankie began to be empathic in his usual pattern of sociopathic self-centred manipulation. However, a new force was introduced into the situation: he began to care about what happened to others at Synanon. At first this was selfish. Synanon was for him a good, an interesting way of life. He had identified with the synanon system. If any synanon member failed, Frankie too was diminished, and failed. In Cressey's words, which Frankie learned to quote, since after all Professor Cressey was a friend of his, 'When I help another guy, it helps me personally.'

In the status system Frankie's rise to the role of co-ordinator was not quick or easy. He moved from the 'dish-pan' to serving food at the kitchen counter. After several months he was allowed to work outside on a pick-up truck that acquired food and other donations. With two other individuals who worked with him on the truck the decision was made one day that 'one shot wouldn't hurt'. One individual knew a 'connexion' on the route. They went to his home. All they could get were some pills. When they arrived back at Synanon, their slightly 'loaded' appearance immediately became apparent to the group: 'They spotted us right away.' They were hauled into the main office and ordered to tell all ('cop out') or get out of the building. A general meeting was called and they were forced to reveal everything before the entire group. Frankie was back at work on the dishpan that evening.

Such 'slips' often come out in the synanon. In a sense, in addition to other forces of growth from the synanon, these sessions serve as a form of 'first-aid' therapy. If anyone reveals a minor 'slip', the personal wound is examined and cleaned up by the group before a serious act of misbehaviour occurs. (The synanon situation has some of the characteristics of an underground organiza-tion operating during wartime. If any member slips it may entail the destruction of the entire organization.)

The norms of Synanon society are the reverse of those of the delinquent world. On one occasion Frankie was with two other members of Synanon on a walk into town. One individual suggested buying a bottle of wine. (No drinking is permitted by Synanonists.) The other two (including Frankie) smashed the idea. However, no one revealed the incident until two days later in a synanon. The group jumped harder on Frankie and the other individual who did not reveal the 'slip' than on the transgressor who had suggested the wine. Frankie and the other 'witness' were expected to report such 'slips' immediately, since the group's life depended on keeping each other 'straight'. For the first time in his life Frankie was censured for 'not squealing'. The maxim 'Thou shalt not squeal', basic to the existence of the usual underworld criminal culture, was reversed at Synanon, and just as ferociously sanctioned. An individual could get kicked out of Synanon for *not* being a stoolie.

The role of no physical violence was at first extremely difficult for Frankie to grasp and believe, as his usual response to a difficult situation had been to leap over verbal means of communication fists-first into assault. As a result of the synanons and other new patterns of interaction, Frankie's social ability to communicate increasingly minimized his assaultive impulse. Although at first he was restrained from committing violence by the fear of ostracism, he later had no need to use violence because he now had some ability to interact effectively. He could express himself with a new form of communication on a non-violent verbal level.

On occasion Frankie would 'slip' and have the motivation for assault, but the system had taken hold. In one synanon session I heard him say 'I was so fuckin' mad yesterday, I wished I was back in Rikers (prison). I really wanted to hit that bastard Jimmy in the mouth.'

Before Synanon, Frankie had seldom voluntarily and legitimately worked in his life. Other than gang-fighting, pimping, armed robbery, pushing heroin, and some work in prison, he had seldom acted in any role resembling formal work. His theme had been 'Work is for squares'. He learned how to work at Synanon automatically as a side effect of his desire to rise in the status system. As a side effect of the work process, he also learned the startling fact that 'talking to someone in the right way made them do more things than belting them'.

As a consequence of living in the Synanon social system Frankie developed an increasing residue of social learning and ability. His sociopathic pattern of relating withered away because it was no longer functional for him within his new way of life. Synanon developed his empathic ability, produced an attachment to different, more socially acceptable values, and reconnected him adequately to the larger society within which Synanon functioned as a valid organization.

PRINCIPAL FORCES AT WORK IN THE SYNANON SOCIAL SYSTEM

Involvement. Initially, Synanon society is able to involve and control the sociopathic youth. This is accomplished by providing an interesting social setting comprising associates who understand him and will not be taken in by his manipulative behaviour.

An Achievable Status System. Within the context of this system the youth can (perhaps for the first time) see a realistic possibility for legitimate achievement and prestige. Synanon provides a rational and attainable opportunity structure for the success-oriented youth.

New Social Role. Synanon creates a new social role, which can be temporarily occupied in the process of social growth and development. This new role is a legitimate one supported by the ex-offender's own community as well as by the inclusive society.

Social Growth. In the process of acquiring legitimate social status in Synanon the youth necessarily, as a side effect, develops the ability to relate, communicate, and work with others. The values of truth, honesty, and industry become necessary means to the goal of achievement. After a sufficient amount of practice and time, the youth socialized in this way develops a real capability for behaving adequately with reference to these values.

Social Control. The control of deviance is a by-product of the youth's status-seeking. Conformity to the norms is necessary in order to achieve. Anomie, the dislocation of goals and means, becomes a minimal condition. The norms are valid and are adhered to within this social system because the means are available for attainment of the goal.

Another form of control is embodied in the threat of ostracism, which becomes a binding force. After becoming initially involved in Synanon and stripped of his street code of life, the youth does not at the time feel adequate for participation in the larger society. After a sufficient residue of Synanon social living has been acquired, the individual no longer fears banishment; at the same time he is then better prepared for life on the outside. He no longer fears ostracism, and may remain voluntarily because he feels Synanon is a valid way of life for him. In Synanon at a later stage of development he acquires a valid social role that enables him as a 'co-ordinator' or a 'director' to help other individuals who can benefit from Synanon treatment.

Other forms of immediate social control include ridicule and the synanon session. The individual is required to tell the truth in the synanon. This also regulates his behaviour. Real-life transgressions are often prevented by the knowledge that the individual's deviance will automatically and necessarily be brought to the attention of his community within the synanon session. He is living within a community where others will know about and are concerned with his behaviour.

Empathy and Self-identity. The constant self-assessment required in the individual's daily life and in the synanon sessions fosters self-identity and empathy. The individual's self-estimation is under constant assessment and attack by others who are sensitive and concerned about him, since he is significant to their own existence. The process provides the opportunity for the individual almost literally 'to see himself as others do'. He is also compelled as part of this process to develop the ability to identify with and understand others. A side consequence of these processes is the development of self-growth, social ability, communicative powers, and empathic ability. The sociopathic behaviour pattern is reversed and corrected.

CONTROLLING THE VIOLENT-GANG PROBLEM:
CONCLUDING REMARKS

Basic to the control of the violent-gang problem is a shift of social attitude from legitimizing, indirectly institutionalizing, and regularizing violent-gang behaviour to perceiving it as a pathological entity requiring elimination. Once this has been accomplished, and after an accurate diagnosis of its structure as a near group, the various social methods described can be implemented.

Peeling off marginals and reconnecting them to constructive social facilities solves half the problem. The core sociopathic youths, after being properly identified, need to be arrested, temporarily incarcerated, and involuntarily forced into a community like the Synanon system which has the potential for involving them with, and adequately socializing them into, the inclusive society. It may be necessary to use the power of the law in court to force them into Synanon. The core gang youth when forced to select between the reformatory and Synanon is likely to pick Synanon. There is a precedent for this type of forced choice in the probation situation. Most youths when given the alternatives quickly select probation over incarceration. In a similar fashion Synanon, once it becomes established and known, will be a more desirable selection for a youth in court than the usual custodial institution.

Although emphasis has been placed here upon resolving the emergent problem of the violent gang and its sociopathic participants, the basic societal roots of the problem should not be minimized. At bottom the violent-gang problem arises in a social system that has a multitude of complex socio-cultural dislocations. In addition to providing realistic projects for modifying the emergent symptom, violent-gang organization, the base of this social problem needs to be affected by large-scale programmes directed at ameliorating more fundamental forces of social disorganization in society. Both points of attack are required to solve the violent-gang problem.

Index

More about Penguins and Pelicans

If you have enjoyed reading this book you may wish to know that *Penguin Book News* appears every month. It is an attractively illustrated magazine containing a complete list of books published by Penguins and still in print, together with details of the month's new books. A specimen copy will be sent free on request.

Penguin Book News is obtainable from most bookshops; but you may prefer to become a regular subscriber at 3s. for twelve issues. Just write to Dept EP, Penguin Books Ltd, Harmondsworth, Middlesex, enclosing a cheque or postal order, and you will be put on the mailing list.

Note: *Penguin Book News* is not available in the U.S.A., Canada or Australia